CASES AND MATERIALS ON FEDERAL CONSTITUTIONAL LAW

Volume I
Introduction to Interpretive Methods & Introduction to the Federal Judicial Power

Modular Casebook Series

CASES AND MATERIALS ON FEDERAL CONSTITUTIONAL LAW

Volume I

Introduction to Interpretive Methods &
Introduction to the Federal Judicial Power

Thomas H. Odom

 LexisNexis·

VOLUME I ISBN: 978-1-4224-2205-2

Odom, Thomas H.
Introduction to interpretive methods & introduction to the federal judicial power / Thomas H. Odom.
p. cm. -- (Cases and materials on federal constitutional law ; v. 1)
Includes index.
ISBN 978-1-4224-2205-2 (soft cover)
1. Courts--United States. I. Title.
KF8718.O36 2008
347.73'1--dc22   2008036946

NOTE TO USERS

To ensure that you are using the latest materials available in this area, please be sure to periodically check the LexisNexis Law School web site for downloadable updates and supplements at www.lexisnexis.com/lawschool.

Editorial Offices
744 Broad Street, Newark, NJ 07102 (973) 820-2000
201 Mission St., San Francisco, CA 94105-1831 (415) 908-3200
www.lexisnexis.com

MATTHEW◆BENDER

(2008–Pub.3261)

INTRODUCTION TO THE MODULAR CASEBOOK SERIES

By now you have realized that the course materials assigned by your instructor have a very different form than "traditional" casebooks. The *Modular Casebook Series* is intentionally designed to break the mold. Course materials consist of one or more separate volumes selected from among a larger and growing set of volumes. Each of those volumes is only about 225 to 250 pages in length so that an instructor may "mix and match" a suitable number of volumes for a course of varying length and focus. Each volume is designed to serve an instructional purpose rather than as a treatise. As a result, the volumes are published in soft cover. Publication of the separate volumes in soft cover also permits course materials to be revised more easily so that they will incorporate recent developments. Moreover, by purchasing only the assigned volumes for a given course students are likely to recognize significant savings over the cost of a traditional casebook.

Traditional casebooks are often massive tomes, sometimes exceeding 1000 or even 1500 pages. Traditional casebooks are lengthy because they attempt to cover the entire breadth of material that might be useful to an instructor for a two-semester course of five or six credits. Even with six credits, different instructors may choose which portions of a traditional casebook do not fit within the time available. As a consequence, traditional casebooks may include a range of materials that would leave hundreds of pages unexplored in any particular six-credit class. For a student in a three or four credit course, such a book is hardly an efficient means for delivering the needed materials. Students purchase much more book than they need, at great expense. And students carry large, heavy books for months at a time.

Traditional casebooks are usually hard cover publications. It seems as though they are constructed so as to last as a reference work throughout decades of practice. In fact, as the presence of annual supplements to most casebooks makes clear, many casebooks are obsolete very shortly after publication. Treatises and hornbooks are designed to serve as reference works; casebooks serve a different purpose. Once again, the traditional format of casebooks seems to impose significant added costs on students without much reason.

The form of traditional casebooks increases the probability that the contents will become obsolete shortly after publication. The publication of lengthy texts in hardcover produces substantial delay between the time the author completes the final draft and the time the book reaches the hands of students. In addition, the broader scope of material addressed in a 1,000 or 1,500 page text means that portions of the text are more likely to be superceded by later developments than any particular narrowly-tailored volume in the *Modular Casebook Series*. Because individual volumes in the Modular Casebook Series may be revised without requiring revision of other volumes, the materials for any particular course will be less likely to require supplementation.

We hope you enjoy this innovative approach to course materials.

Dedication

For MIG: Friend, mentor, and outstanding role model.

Acknowledgments

I would like to thank Dickinson School of Law and Pennsylvania State University for their financial support. I am indebted to my students whose daily interaction with me and the materials provide the impetus for constant improvement.

The hard work of numerous research assistants is reflected in this collection, notably: Michael Lynch, Justin Pickens, Chris VanLandingham, and Brian McMorrow.

Without the loving support of Janet, this project would not have been completed.

All remaining errors and omissions are my own.

Preface to the First Edition

Technological improvements permit the compilation of resources in a manner unthinkable when I was a law student. Materials that permit further examination of assigned reading can be delivered in a cost-effective manner and in a format more likely to be useful in practice than reams of photocopies. The associated DVD-ROM contains full, searchable text of several of the most important resources for interpreting the Constitution, lowering the wall between doctrinal courses and research courses.

With regard to assigned reading, there is no good reason to burden students with stacks of hand-outs or expensive annual supplements. Publication through the *Modular Casebook Series* virtually ensures that even very recent developments may be incorporated prior to publication. Moreover, if important cases are decided after publication of the latest edition of the volume, they will be included on the DVD-ROM. Cases and materials that shed additional light on matter in the hard copy casebook are also included.

I welcome comments from readers so that I may make further improvements in the next edition of this publication.

THO

TECHNICAL NOTE FROM THE EDITOR

The cases and other materials excerpted in this volume have been edited in an effort to enhance readability. Case citation forms have been revised to include the year of decision and reference to the volume number of the United States Reports. Many citations to secondary sources have been expanded to include the full names of authors or editors, and to reference the date of publication. Citations of multiple cases for a single proposition have been shortened in many places to reference only one or two prominent authorities.

In some places archaic language or spelling has been revised.

Headings were added to some of the longer decisions to permit ease of reference to various parts of the opinion. Such headings may also assist the reader in identifying a transition from one point to another.

None of these changes were intended to substantively alter the original materials.

With the exception of one or two cases per Volume, cases have been edited to a length suitable for reading as a single assignment. In order to achieve that result, many interesting but tangential points have been omitted. The length of some opinions also hindered the inclusion of excerpts from concurring or dissenting opinions. Where such opinions have been omitted, it is noted in the text. These omissions are not intended to present a biased view of the doctrine under review. In most instances, a subsequent case will present significant points raised by the omitted concurring and dissenting opinions. Any remaining unintentional bias is solely the responsibility of the editor.

THO

TABLE OF CONTENTS

TABLE OF CONTENTS

TABLE OF CONTENTS

CHAPTER 1

INTRODUCTION TO THE BASIC TEXTS AND FORMS OF CONSTITUTIONAL INTERPRETATION

This chapter introduces the United States Constitution as ratified in 1789, the first ten Amendments thereto, ratified in 1791 and commonly called the Bill of Rights, and the subsequent Amendments adopted thereafter. In addition, this Chapter includes the Articles of Confederation which preceded, and were superceded by, the Constitution.

This chapter also introduces three of the traditional forms of interpretation employed by lawyers. What distinguishes this course from one likely to be offered in the study of political science is the emphasis on forms of legal analysis, rather than policy-based arguments. Although additional bases for interpretation will be introduced in subsequent chapters, the material presented here invites attention to (1) the broad *structure* of government established by the Constitution, (2) the *historical setting* from which the Constitution emerged, and (3) the *text* of the Constitution itself. That order refers only to the order in which the three forms are introduced in this chapter; it does not imply relative superiority of forms of interpretation.

As the doctrinal focus of Volume 1 is on the structure of the government established by the Constitution and the powers held thereunder by its various branches, many extremely important subjects must await more specialized courses addressing certain individual rights and particular provisions of the First Amendment. The scope of constitutional law doctrine is extremely broad and permeates a substantial portion of the curriculum. For example, in *Civil Procedure*, students likely encountered the Due Process Clause in the study of personal jurisdiction, the Seventh Amendment in the determination when matters must be tried by a jury, and the Full Faith and Credit Clause in examining the bases for certain preclusion doctrines. Similarly, students are more likely to study the Takings Clause in a course on *Property*. In a course on *Criminal Procedure*, much of the focus is on the provisions of the Fourth Amendment, Fifth Amendment, and Sixth Amendment. This course addresses foundational matters not likely to be covered in any depth in any other course.

Exercise 1 (Structure):

Read the Constitution of 1789 and the Bill of Rights. In advance of class, write a brief description (50 to 100 words) of the governmental *structure* established by the Constitution. Although some subsequent Amendments modify the structure, focus, for now, on the original structure.

Do not simply outline the Constitution. Consider the major features of the government established by the Constitution rather than the structure of the document itself.

Please bring an extra copy of your description to class.

The Constitution of the United States

We the People of the United States, in Order to form a more perfect Union, establish Justice, insure domestic Tranquility, provide for the common defence, promote the general Welfare, and secure the Blessings of Liberty to ourselves and our Posterity, do ordain and establish this Constitution for the United States of America.

Article I

Section 1.   All legislative Powers herein granted shall be vested in a Congress of the United States, which shall consist of a Senate and House of Representatives.

Section 2.   The House of Representatives shall be composed of Members chosen every second Year by the People of the several States, and the Electors in each State shall have the Qualifications requisite for Electors of the most numerous Branch of the State Legislature.

No person shall be a Representative who shall not have attained to the Age of twenty five Years, and been seven Years a Citizen of the United States, and who shall not, when elected, be an Inhabitant of that State in which he shall be chosen.

Representatives and direct Taxes shall be apportioned among the several States which may be included within this Union, according to their respective Numbers, which shall be determined by adding to the whole Number of free Persons, including those bound to Service for a Term of Years, and excluding Indians not taxed, three fifths of all other Persons. The actual Enumeration shall be made within three Years after the first Meeting of the Congress of the United States, and within every subsequent Term of ten Years, in such Manner as they shall by Law direct. The Number of Representatives shall not exceed one for every thirty Thousand, but each State shall have at Least one Representative; and until such enumeration shall be made, the State of New Hampshire shall be entitled to chuse three, Massachusetts eight, Rhode-Island and Providence Plantations one, Connecticut five, New-York six, New Jersey four, Pennsylvania eight, Delaware one, Maryland six, Virginia ten, North Carolina five, South Carolina five, and Georgia three.

When vacancies happen in the Representation from any State, the Executive Authority thereof shall issue Writs of Election to fill such Vacancies.

The House of Representatives shall chuse their Speaker and other Officers; and shall have the sole Power of Impeachment.

Section 3.   The Senate of the United States shall be composed of two Senators from each State, chosen by the Legislature thereof, for six Years; and each Senator shall have one Vote.

Immediately after they shall be assembled in Consequence of the first Election, they shall be divided as equally as may be into three Classes. The Seats of the Senators of the first Class shall be vacated at the Expiration of the second Year, of the second Class at the Expiration of the fourth Year, and of the third Class at the Expiration of the sixth Year, so that one third may be chosen every second Year; and if Vacancies happen by Resignation, or otherwise, during the Recess of the Legislature of any State, the Executive thereof may make temporary Appointments until the next Meeting of the Legislature, which shall then fill such Vacancies.

No Person shall be a Senator who shall not have attained to the Age of thirty Years, and been nine Years a Citizen of the United States, and who shall not, when elected, be an Inhabitant of that State for which he shall be chosen.

The Vice President of the United States shall be President of the Senate, but shall have no Vote, unless they be equally divided.

The Senate shall chuse their other Officers, and also a President pro tempore, in the Absence of the Vice President, or when he shall exercise the Office of President of the United States.

The Senate shall have the sole Power to try all Impeachments. When sitting for that Purpose, they shall be on Oath or Affirmation. When the President of the United States is tried, the Chief Justice shall preside: and no Person shall be convicted without the Concurrence of two thirds of the Members present.

Judgment in Cases of Impeachment shall not extend further than to removal from Office, and disqualification to hold and enjoy any Office of honor, Trust or Profit under the United States: but the Party convicted shall nevertheless be liable and subject to Indictment, Trial, Judgment and Punishment, according to Law.

Section 4.   The Times, Places and Manner of holding Elections for Senators and Representatives, shall be prescribed in each State by the Legislature thereof; but the Congress may at any time by Law make or alter such Regulations, except as to the Places of chusing Senators.

The Congress shall assemble at least once in every Year, and such Meeting shall be on the first Monday in December, unless they shall by Law appoint a different Day.

Section 5.   Each House shall be the Judge of the Elections, Returns and Qualifications of its own Members, and a Majority of each shall constitute a Quorum to do Business; but a smaller Number may adjourn from day to day, and may be authorized to compel the Attendance of absent Members, in such Manner, and under such Penalties as each House may provide.

Each House may determine the Rules of its Proceedings, punish its Members for disorderly Behaviour, and, with the Concurrence of two thirds, expel a Member.

Each House shall keep a Journal of its Proceedings, and from time to time publish the same, excepting such Parts as may in their Judgment require Secrecy; and the Yeas and Nays of the Members of either House on any question shall, at the Desire of one fifth of those Present, be entered on the Journal.

Section 6.   The Senators and Representatives shall receive a Compensation for their Services, to be ascertained by Law, and paid out of the Treasury of the United States. They shall in all Cases, except Treason, Felony and Breach of the Peace, be privileged from Arrest during their Attendance at the Session of their respective Houses, and in going to and returning from the same; and for any Speech or Debate in either House, they shall not be questioned in any other Place.

No Senator or Representative shall, during the Time for which he was elected, be appointed to any civil Office under the Authority of the United States, which shall have been created, or the Emoluments whereof shall have been encreased during such time; and no Person holding any Office under the United States, shall be a Member of either House during his Continuance in Office.

Section 7.   All Bills for raising Revenue shall originate in the House of Representatives; but the Senate may propose or concur with Amendments as on other Bills.

Every Bill which shall have passed the House of Representatives and the Senate, shall, before it become a Law, be presented to the President of the United States; If he approve he shall sign it, but if not he shall return it, with his Objections to that House in which it shall have originated, who shall enter the Objections at large on their Journal, and proceed to reconsider it. If after such Reconsideration two thirds of that House shall agree to pass the Bill, it shall be sent, together with the Objections, to the other House, by which it shall likewise be reconsidered, and if approved by two thirds of that House, it shall become a Law. But in all such Cases the Votes of both Houses shall be determined by yeas and Nays, and the Names of the Persons voting for and against the Bill shall be entered on the Journal of each House respectively. If any Bill shall not be returned by the President within ten days (Sundays excepted) after it shall have been presented to him, the Same shall be a Law, in like Manner as if he had signed it, unless the Congress by their Adjournment prevent its Return in which Case it shall not be a Law.

Every Order, Resolution, or Vote to which the Concurrence of the Senate and House of Representatives may be necessary (except on a question of Adjournment) shall be presented to the President of the United States; and before the Same shall take Effect, shall be approved by him, or being disapproved by him, shall be repassed by two thirds of the Senate and House of Representatives, according to the Rules and Limitations prescribed in the Case of a Bill.

Section 8. The Congress shall have Power To lay and collect Taxes, Duties, Imposts and Excises, to pay the Debts and provide for the common Defence and general Welfare of the United States; but all Duties, Imposts and Excises shall be uniform throughout the United States;

To borrow Money on the credit of the United States;

To regulate Commerce with foreign Nations, and among the several States, and with the Indian Tribes;

To establish an uniform Rule of Naturalization, and uniform Laws on the subject of Bankruptcies throughout the United States;

To coin Money, regulate the Value thereof, and foreign Coin, and fix the Standard of Weights and Measures;

To provide for the Punishment of counterfeiting the Securities and current Coin of the United States;

To establish Post Offices and post Roads;

To promote the Progress of Science and useful Arts, by securing for limited Times to Authors and Inventors the exclusive Right to their respective Writings and Discoveries;

To constitute Tribunals inferior to the supreme Court;

To define and punish Piracies and Felonies committed on the high Seas, and Offences against the Law of Nations;

To declare War, grant Letters of Marque and Reprisal, and make Rules concerning Captures on Land and Water;

To raise and support Armies, but no Appropriation of Money to that Use shall be for a longer Term than two Years;

To provide and maintain a Navy;

To make Rules for the Government and Regulation of the land and naval Forces;

To provide for calling forth the Militia to execute the Laws of the Union, suppress Insurrections and repel Invasions;

To provide for organizing, arming, and disciplining, the Militia, and for governing such Part of them as may be employed in the Service of the United States, reserving to the States respectively, the Appointment of the Officers, and the Authority of training the Militia according to the discipline prescribed by Congress;

To exercise exclusive Legislation in all Cases whatsoever, over such District (not exceeding ten Miles square) as may, by Cession of particular States, and the Acceptance of Congress, become the Seat of the Government of the United States, and to exercise like Authority over all Places purchased by the Consent of the Legislature of the State in which the Same shall be, for the Erection of Forts, Magazines, Arsenals, dock-Yards, and other needful Buildings; — And

To make all Laws which shall be necessary and proper for carrying into Execution the foregoing Powers, and all other Powers vested by this Constitution in the Government of the United States, or in any Department or Officer thereof.

Section 9. The Migration or Importation of such Persons as any of the States now existing shall think proper to admit, shall not be prohibited by the Congress prior to the Year one thousand eight hundred and eight, but a Tax or duty may be imposed on such Importation, not exceeding ten dollars for each Person.

The Privilege of the Writ of Habeas Corpus shall not be suspended, unless when in Cases of Rebellion or Invasion the public Safety may require it.

No Bill of Attainder or ex post facto Law shall be passed.

No Capitation, or other direct, Tax shall be laid, unless in Proportion to the Census or Enumeration herein before directed to be taken.

No Tax or Duty shall be laid on Articles exported from any State.

No Preference shall be given by any Regulation of Commerce or Revenue to the Ports of one State over those of another; nor shall Vessels bound to, or from, one State, be obliged to enter, clear, or pay Duties in another.

No Money shall be drawn from the Treasury, but in Consequence of Appropriations made by Law; and a regular Statement and Account of the Receipts and Expenditures of all public Money shall be published from time to time.

No Title of Nobility shall be granted by the United States: And no Person holding any Office of Profit or Trust under them, shall, without the Consent of the Congress, accept of any present, Emolument, Office, or Title, of any kind whatever, from any King, Prince, or foreign State.

Section 10. No State shall enter into any Treaty, Alliance, or Confederation; grant Letters of Marque and Reprisal; coin Money; emit Bills of Credit; make any Thing but gold and silver Coin a Tender in Payment of Debts; pass any Bill of Attainder, ex post facto Law, or Law impairing the Obligation of Contracts, or grant any Title of Nobility.

No State shall, without the Consent of the Congress, lay any Imposts or Duties on Imports or Exports, except what may be absolutely necessary for executing it's inspection Laws: and the net Produce of all Duties and Imposts, laid by any State on Imports or Exports, shall be for the Use of the Treasury of the United States; and all such Laws shall be subject to the Revision and Controul of the Congress.

No State shall, without the Consent of Congress, lay any Duty of Tonnage, keep Troops, or Ships of War in time of Peace, enter into any Agreement or Compact with another State, or with a foreign Power, or engage in War, unless actually invaded, or in such imminent Danger as will not admit of delay.

Article II

Section 1. The executive Power shall be vested in a President of the United States of America. He shall hold his Office during the Term of four Years, and, together with the Vice President, chosen for the same Term, be elected as follows

Each State shall appoint, in such Manner as the Legislature thereof may direct, a Number of Electors, equal to the whole Number of Senators and Representatives to which the State may be entitled in the Congress: but no Senator or Representative, or Person holding an Office of Trust or Profit under the United States, shall be appointed an Elector.

The Electors shall meet in their respective States, and vote by Ballot for two Persons, of whom one at least shall not be an Inhabitant of the same State with themselves. And they shall make a List of all the Persons voted for, and of the Number of Votes for each; which List they shall sign and certify, and transmit sealed to the Seat of the Government of the United States, directed to the President of the Senate. The President of the Senate shall, in the Presence of the Senate and House of Representatives, open all the Certificates, and the Votes shall then be counted. The Person having the greatest Number of Votes shall be the President, if such Number be a Majority of the whole Number of Electors appointed; and if there be more than one who have such Majority, and have an equal Number of Votes, then the House of Representatives shall immediately chuse by Ballot one of them for President; and if no Person have a Majority, then from the five highest on the List the said House shall in like Manner chuse the President. But in chusing the President, the Votes shall be taken by States, the Representation from each State having one Vote; A quorum for this Purpose shall consist of a Member or Members from two thirds of the States, and a Majority of all the States shall be necessary to a Choice. In every Case, after the Choice of the President, the Person having the greatest Number of Votes of the Electors shall be the Vice President. But if there should remain two or more who have equal Votes, the Senate shall chuse from them by Ballot the Vice President.

The Congress may determine the Time of chusing the Electors, and the Day on which they shall give their Votes; which Day shall be the same throughout the United States.

No Person except a natural born Citizen, or a Citizen of the United States, at the time of the Adoption of this Constitution, shall be eligible to the Office of President; neither shall any Person be eligible to that Office who shall not have attained to the Age of thirty five Years, and been fourteen Years a Resident within the United States.

In the Case of the Removal of the President from Office, or of his Death, Resignation, or Inability to discharge the Powers and Duties of the said Office, the Same shall devolve on the Vice President, and the Congress may by Law provide for the Case of Removal, Death, Resignation or Inability, both of the President and Vice President, declaring what Officer shall then act as President, and such Officer shall act accordingly, until the Disability be removed, or a President shall be elected.

The President shall, at stated Times, receive for his Services, a Compensation, which shall neither be encreased nor diminished during the Period for which he shall have been elected, and he shall not receive within that Period any other Emolument from the United States, or any of them.

Before he enter on the Execution of his Office, he shall take the following Oath or Affirmation: — "I do solemnly swear (or affirm) that I will faithfully execute the Office of the President of the United States, and will to the best of my Ability, preserve, protect and defend the Constitution of the United States."

Section 2.   The President shall be the Commander in Chief of the Army and Navy of the United States, and of the Militia of the several States, when called into the actual service of the United States; he may require the Opinion, in writing, of the principal Officer in each of the executive Departments, upon any Subject relating to the Duties of their respective Offices, and he shall have Power to grant Reprieves and Pardons for Offenses against the United States, except in Cases of Impeachment.

He shall have Power, by and with the Advice and Consent of the Senate, to make Treaties, provided two thirds of the Senators present concur; and he shall nominate, and by and with the Advice and Consent of the Senate, shall appoint Ambassadors, other public Ministers and Consuls, Judges of the supreme Court, and all other Officers of the United States, whose Appointments are not herein otherwise provided for, and which shall be established by Law but the Congress may by Law vest the Appointment of such inferior Officers, as they think proper, in the President alone, in the Courts of Law, or in the Heads of Departments.

The President shall have Power to fill up all Vacancies that may happen during the Recess of the Senate, by granting Commissions which shall expire at the End of their next Session.

Section 3. He shall from time to time give to the Congress Information of the State of the Union, and recommend to their Consideration such Measures as he shall judge necessary and expedient; he may, on extraordinary Occasions, convene both Houses, or either of them, and in Case of Disagreement between them, with Respect to the Time of Adjournment, he may adjourn them to such Time as he shall think proper; he shall receive Ambassadors and other public Ministers; he shall take Care that the Laws be faithfully executed, and shall Commission all the Officers of the United States.

Section 4. The President, Vice President and all civil Officers of the United States, shall be removed from Office on Impeachment for, and Conviction of, Treason, Bribery, or other high Crimes and Misdemeanors.

Article III

Section 1. The judicial Power of the United States, shall be vested in one supreme Court, and in such inferior Courts as the Congress may from time to time ordain and establish. The Judges, both of the supreme and inferior Courts, shall hold their Offices during good Behaviour, and shall, at stated Times, receive for their Services, a Compensation, which shall not be diminished during their Continuance in Office.

Section 2. The judicial Power shall extend to all Cases, in Law and Equity, arising under this Constitution, the Laws of the United States, and Treaties made, or which shall be made, under their Authority; — to all Cases affecting Ambassadors, other public Ministers and Consuls; — to all Cases of admiralty and maritime Jurisdiction; — to Controversies to which the United States shall be a Party; — to Controversies between two or more States; — between a State and Citizens of another State; — between Citizens of different States; — between Citizens of the same State claiming Lands under Grants of different States, and between a State, or the Citizens thereof, and foreign States, Citizens or Subjects.

In all cases affecting Ambassadors, other public Ministers and Consuls, and those in which a State shall be a Party, the supreme Court shall have original Jurisdiction. In all the other Cases before mentioned, the supreme Court shall have appellate Jurisdiction, both as to Law and Fact, with such Exceptions, and under such Regulations as the Congress shall make.

The Trial of all Crimes, except in Cases of Impeachment, shall be by Jury; and such Trial shall be held in the State where the said Crimes shall have been committed; but when not committed within any State, the Trial shall be at such Place or Places as the Congress may by Law have directed.

Section 3. Treason against the United States, shall consist only in levying War against them, or in adhering to their Enemies, giving them Aid or Comfort. No Person shall be convicted of Treason unless on the Testimony of two Witnesses to the same overt Act, or on Confession in open Court.

The Congress shall have Power to declare the Punishment of Treason, but no Attainder of Treason shall work Corruption of Blood, or Forfeiture except during the Life of the Person attainted.

Article IV

Section 1. Full Faith and Credit shall be given in each State to the public Acts, Records, and judicial Proceedings of every other State. And the Congress may by general Laws prescribe the Manner in which such Acts, Records and Proceedings shall be proved, and the Effect thereof.

Section 2. The Citizens of each State shall be entitled to all Privileges and Immunities of Citizens in the several States.

A Person charged in any State with Treason, Felony, or other Crime, who shall flee from Justice, and be found in another State, shall on Demand of the executive Authority of the State from which he fled, be delivered up, to be removed to the State having Jurisdiction of the Crime.

No Person held to Service or Labour in one State, under the Laws thereof, escaping into another, shall, in Consequence of any Law or Regulation therein, be discharged from such Service or Labour, but shall be delivered up on Claim of the Party to whom such Service or Labour may be due.

Section 3. New States may be admitted by the Congress into this Union; but no new State shall be formed or erected within the Jurisdiction of any other State; nor any State be formed by the Junction of two or more States, or Parts of States, without the Consent of the Legislatures of the States concerned as well as of the Congress.

The Congress shall have Power to dispose of and make all needful Rules and Regulations respecting the Territory or other Property belonging to the United States; and nothing in this Constitution shall be so construed to Prejudice any Claims of the United States, or of any particular State.

Section 4. The United States shall guarantee to every State in this Union a Republican Form of Government, and shall protect each of them against Invasion; and on Application of the Legislature, or of the Executive (when the Legislature cannot be convened) against domestic Violence.

Article V

The Congress, whenever two thirds of both Houses shall deem it necessary, shall propose Amendments to this Constitution, or, on the Application of the Legislatures of two thirds of the several States, shall call a Convention for proposing Amendments, which, in either Case, shall be valid to all Intents and Purposes, as Part of this Constitution, when ratified by the Legislatures of three fourths of the several States, or by Conventions in three fourths thereof, as the one or the other Mode of Ratification may be proposed by the Congress; provided that no Amendment which may be made prior to the Year One thousand eight hundred and eight shall in any Manner affect the first and fourth Clauses in the Ninth Section of the first Article; and that no State, without its Consent, shall be deprived of it's equal Suffrage in the Senate.

Article VI

All Debts contracted and Engagements entered into, before the adoption of this Constitution, shall be as valid against the United States under this Constitution, as under the Confederation.

This Constitution, and the Laws of the United States which shall be made in Pursuance thereof; and all Treaties made, or which shall be made, under the Authority of the United States, shall be the supreme Law of the Land; and the

Judges in every State shall be bound thereby, any Thing in the Constitution or Laws of any State to the Contrary notwithstanding.

The Senators and Representatives before mentioned, and the members of the several State Legislatures, and all executive and judicial Officers, both of the United States and of the several States, shall be bound by Oath or Affirmation, to support this Constitution; but no religious Test shall ever be required as a Qualification to any Office or public Trust under the United States.

Article VII

The Ratification of the Conventions of nine States, shall be sufficient for the Establishment of this Constitution between the States so ratifying the Same.

Go. Washington — Presidt.
And deputy from Virginia

New Hampshire
John Langdon
Nicholas Gilman

New Jersey
Wil: Livingston
David Brearley
Wm. Paterson
Jona: Dayton

Massachusetts
Nathaniel Gorham
Rufus King
Connecticut
Wm. Saml. Johnson
Roger Sherman
New York
Alexander Hamilton

Pennsylvania
B Franklin
Thomas Mifflin
Robt. Morris
Geo. Clymer
Thos. Fitzsimons
Jared Ingersoll
James Wilson
Gouv Morris

Delaware
Geo: Read
Cunning Bedford jun
John Dickinson
Richard Bassett
Jaco: Broom

North Carolina
Wm: Blount
Richd. Dobbs Spaight.
Hu Williamson

Maryland
James McHenry
Dan of St. Thos. Jenifer
Danl. Carroll

South Carolina
J. Rutledge
Charles Cotesworth Pinckney
Pierce Butler.

Virginia
John Blair —
James Madison Jr.

Georgia
William Few
Abr Baldwin

The Bill of Rights
(1791)

Amendment I

Congress shall make no law respecting an establishment of religion, or prohibiting the free exercise thereof; or abridging the freedom of speech, or of the press; or the right of the people peaceably to assemble, and to petition the government for a redress of grievances.

Amendment II

A well regulated militia, being necessary to the security of a free state, the right of the people to keep and bear arms, shall not be infringed.

Amendment III

No soldier shall, in time of peace be quartered in any house, without the consent of the owner, nor in time of war, but in a manner to be prescribed by law.

Amendment IV

The right of the people to be secure in their persons, houses, papers, and effects, against unreasonable searches and seizures, shall not be violated, and no warrants shall issue, but upon probable cause, supported by oath or affirmation, and particularly describing the place to be searched, and the persons or things to be seized.

Amendment V

No person shall be held to answer for a capital, or otherwise infamous crime, unless on a presentment or indictment of a grand jury, except in cases arising in the land or naval forces, or in the militia, when in actual service in time of war or public danger; nor shall any person be subject for the same offense to be twice put in jeopardy of life or limb; nor shall be compelled in any criminal case to be a witness against himself, nor be deprived of life, liberty, or property, without due process of law; nor shall private property be taken for public use, without just compensation.

Amendment VI

In all criminal prosecutions, the accused shall enjoy the right to a speedy and public trial, by an impartial jury of the state and district wherein the crime shall have been committed, which district shall have been previously ascertained by law, and to be informed of the nature and cause of the accusation; to be confronted with the witnesses against him; to have compulsory process for obtaining witnesses in his favor, and to have the assistance of counsel for his defense.

Amendment VII

In suits at common law, where the value in controversy shall exceed twenty dollars, the right of trial by jury shall be preserved, and no fact tried by a jury, shall be otherwise reexamined in any court of the United States, then according to the rules of the common law.

Amendment VIII

Excessive bail shall not be required, nor excessive fines imposed, nor cruel and unusual punishments inflicted.

Amendment IX

The enumeration in the Constitution, of certain rights, shall not be construed to deny or disparage others retained by the people.

Amendment X

The powers not delegated to the United States by the Constitution, nor prohibited by it to the states, are reserved to the states respectively, or to the people.

Later Amendments

Amendment XI

(1798)

The judicial power of the United States shall not be construed to extend to any suit in law or equity, commenced or prosecuted against one of the United States by Citizens of another State, or by Citizens or Subjects of any Foreign State.

Amendment XII

(1804)

The Electors shall meet in their respective states and vote by ballot for President and Vice-President, one of whom, at least, shall not be an inhabitant of the same state with themselves; they shall name in their ballots the person voted for as President, and in distinct ballots the person voted for as Vice-President, and they shall make distinct lists of all persons voted for as President, and of all persons voted for as Vice-President, and of the number of votes for each, which lists they shall sign and certify, and transmit sealed to the seat of the government of the United States, directed to the President of the Senate; — The President of the Senate shall, in the presence of the Senate and House of Representatives, open all the certificates and the votes shall then be counted; — the person having the greatest number of votes for President, shall be the President, if such number be a majority of the whole number of Electors appointed; and if no person have such majority, then from the persons having the highest numbers not exceeding three on the list of those voted for as President, the House of Representatives shall choose immediately, by ballot, the President. But in choosing the President, the votes shall be taken by states, the representation from each state having one vote; a quorum for this purpose shall consist of a member or members from two-thirds of the states, and a majority of all the states shall be necessary to a choice. And if the House of Representatives shall not choose a President whenever the right of choice shall devolve upon them, before the fourth day of March next following, then the Vice-President shall act as President, as in the case of the death or other constitutional disability of the President. The person having the greatest number of votes as Vice-President, shall be the Vice-President, if such number be a majority of the whole number of Electors appointed, and if no person have a majority, then from the two highest numbers on the list, the Senate shall choose the Vice-President; a quorum for the purpose shall consist of two-thirds of the whole number of Senators, and a majority of the whole number shall be necessary to a choice. But no person constitutionally ineligible to the office of President shall be eligible to that of Vice-President of the United States.

Amendment XIII

(1865)

Section 1. Neither slavery nor involuntary servitude, except as a punishment for crime whereof the party shall have been duly convicted, shall exist within the United States, or any place subject to their jurisdiction.

Section 2. Congress shall have power to enforce this article by appropriate legislation.

Amendment XIV

(1868)

Section 1. All persons born or naturalized in the United States, and subject to the jurisdiction thereof, are citizens of the United States and of the State wherein they reside. No State shall make or enforce any law which shall abridge the privileges or immunities of citizens of the United States; nor shall any State deprive any person of life, liberty, or property, without due process of law; nor deny to any person within its jurisdiction the equal protection of the laws.

Section 2. Representatives shall be apportioned among the several States according to their respective numbers, counting the whole number of persons in each State, excluding Indians not taxed. But when the right to vote at any election for the choice of electors for President and Vice President of the United States, Representatives in Congress, the Executive and Judicial officers of a State, or the members of the Legislature thereof, is denied to any of the male inhabitants of such State, being twenty-one years of age, and citizens of the United States, or in any way abridged, except for participation in rebellion, or other crime, the basis of representation therein shall be reduced in the proportion which the number of such male citizens shall bear to the whole number of male citizens twenty-one years of age in such State.

Section 3. No person shall be a Senator or Representative in Congress, or elector of President and Vice President, or hold any office, civil or military, under the United States, or under any State, who, having previously taken an oath, as a member of Congress, or as an officer of the United States, or as a member of any State legislature, or as an executive or judicial officer of any State, to support the Constitution of the United States, shall have engaged in insurrection or rebellion against the same, or given aid or comfort to the enemies thereof. But Congress may by a vote of two-thirds of each House, remove such disability.

Section 4. The validity of the public debt of the United States, authorized by law, including debts incurred for payment of pensions and bounties for services in suppressing insurrection or rebellion, shall not be questioned. But neither the United States nor any State shall assume or pay any debt or obligation incurred in aid of insurrection or rebellion against the United States, or any claim for the loss or emancipation of any slave; but all such debts, obligations and claims shall be held illegal and void.

Section 5. The Congress shall have power to enforce, by appropriate legislation, the provisions of this article.

Amendment XV

(1870)

Section 1. The right of citizens of the United States to vote shall not be denied or abridged by the United States or by any State on account of race, color, or previous condition of servitude.

Section 2.   The Congress shall have power to enforce this article by appropriate legislation.

Amendment XVI

(1913)

The Congress shall have power to lay and collect taxes on incomes, from whatever source derived, without apportionment among the several States, and without regard to any census or enumeration.

Amendment XVII

(1913)

The Senate of the United States shall be composed of two Senators from each State, elected by the people thereof, for six years; and each Senator shall have one vote. The electors in each State shall have the qualifications requisite for electors of the most numerous branch of the State legislature.

When vacancies happen in the representation of any State in the Senate, the executive authority of such State shall issue writs of election to fill such vacancies: *Provided,* That the legislature of any State may empower the executive thereof to make temporary appointments until the people fill the vacancies by election as the legislature may direct.

This amendment shall not be so construed as to effect the election or term of any Senator chosen before it becomes valid as part of the Constitution.

Amendment XVIII

(1919)

Section 1.   After one year from the ratification of this article the manufacture, sale, or transportation of intoxicating liquors within, the importation thereof into, or the exportation thereof from the United States and all territory subject to the jurisdiction thereof for beverage purposes is hereby prohibited.

Section 2.   The Congress and the several States shall have concurrent power to enforce this article by appropriate legislation.

Section 3.   This article shall be inoperative unless it shall have been ratified as an amendment to the Constitution by the legislatures of the several States, as provided in the Constitution, within seven years from the date of the submission hereof to the States by the Congress.

Amendment XIX

(1920)

The right of citizens of the United States to vote shall not be denied or abridged by the United States or by any State on account of sex.

Congress shall have power to enforce this article by appropriate legislation.

Amendment XX

(1933)

Section 1.   The terms of the President and Vice President shall end at noon on the 20th day of January, and the terms of Senators and Representatives at noon on the 3d day of January, of the years in which such terms would have ended if this article had not been ratified; and the terms of their successors shall then begin.

Section 2. The Congress shall assemble at least once in every year, and such meeting shall begin at noon on the 3d day of January, unless they shall by law appoint a different day.

Section 3. If, at the time fixed for the beginning of the term of the President, the President elect shall have died, the Vice President elect shall become President. If a President shall not have been chosen before the time fixed for the beginning of his term, or if the President elect shall have failed to qualify, then the Vice President elect shall act as President until a President shall have qualified; and the Congress may by law provide for the case wherein neither a President elect nor a Vice President elect shall have qualified, declaring who shall then act as President, or the manner in which one who is to act shall be selected, and such person shall act accordingly until a President or Vice President shall have qualified.

Section 4. The Congress may by law provide for the case of the death of any of the persons from whom the House of Representatives may choose a President whenever the right of choice shall have devolved upon them, and for the case of the death of any of the persons from whom the Senate may choose a Vice President whenever the right of choice shall have devolved upon them.

Section 5. Sections 1 and 2 shall take effect on the 15th day of October following the ratification of this article.

Section 6. This article shall be inoperative unless it shall have been ratified as an amendment to the Constitution by the legislatures of three-fourths of the several States within seven years from the date of its submission.

Amendment XXI

(1933)

Section 1. The eighteenth article of amendment to the Constitution of the United States is hereby repealed.

Section 2. The transportation or importation into any State, territory, or possession of the United States for delivery or use therein of intoxicating liquors, in violation of the laws thereof, is hereby prohibited.

Section 3. This article shall be inoperative unless it shall have been ratified as an amendment to the Constitution by conventions in the several States, as provided in the Constitution, within seven years from the date of the submission hereof to the States by the Congress.

Amendment XXII

(1951)

Section 1. No person shall be elected to the office of the President more than twice, and no person who has held the office of President, or acted as President, for more than two years of a term to which some other person was elected President shall be elected to the office of the President more than once. But this article shall not apply to any person holding the office of President when this article was proposed by the Congress, and shall not prevent any person who may be holding the office of President, or acting as President, during the term within which this article becomes operative from holding the office of President or acting as President during the remainder of such term.

Section 2. This article shall be inoperative unless it shall have been ratified as an amendment to the Constitution by the legislatures of three-fourths of the several States within seven years from the date of its submission to the States by the Congress.

Amendment XXIII
(1961)

Section 1. The District constituting the seat of government of the United States shall appoint in such manner as the Congress may direct:

A number of electors of President and Vice President equal to the whole number of Senators and Representatives in Congress to which the District would be entitled if it were a State, but in no event more than the least populous State; they shall be in addition to those appointed by the States, but they shall be considered, for the purposes of the election of the President and Vice President, to be electors appointed by a State; and they shall meet in the District and perform such duties as provided by the twelfth article of amendment.

Section 2. The Congress shall have power to enforce this article by appropriate legislation.

Amendment XXIV
(1964)

Section 1. The right of citizens of the United States to vote in any primary or other election for President or Vice President, for electors for President or Vice President, or for Senator or Representative in Congress, shall not be denied or abridged by the United States or any State by reason of failure to pay any poll tax or other tax.

Section 2. The Congress shall have the power to enforce this article by appropriate legislation.

Amendment XXV
(1967)

Section 1. In case of the removal of the President from office or his death or resignation, the Vice President shall become President.

Section 2. Whenever there is a vacancy in the office of the Vice President, the President shall nominate a Vice President who shall take office upon confirmation by a majority vote of both Houses of Congress.

Section 3. Whenever the President transmits to the President pro tempore of the Senate and the Speaker of the House of Representatives his written declaration that he is unable to discharge the powers and duties of his office, and until he transmits to them a written declaration to the contrary, such powers and duties shall be discharged by the Vice President as Acting President.

Section 4. Whenever the Vice President and a majority of either the principal officers of the executive departments or such other body as Congress may by law provide, transmit to the President pro tempore of the Senate and the Speaker of the House of Representatives their written declaration that the President is unable to discharge the powers and duties of his office, the Vice President shall immediately assume the powers and duties of the office as Acting President.

Thereafter, when the President transmits to the President pro tempore of the Senate and the Speaker of the House of Representatives his written declaration that no inability exists, he shall resume the powers and duties of his office unless the Vice President and a majority of either the principal officers of the executive department or of such other body as Congress may by law provide, transmit within four days to the President pro tempore of the Senate and the Speaker of the House of Representatives their written declaration that the President is unable to discharge the powers and duties of his office. Thereupon Congress shall decide the issue, assembling within forty-eight hours for that purpose if not in session. If the Congress, within twenty-one days after receipt of the latter written declaration, or, if Congress is not in session, within twenty-one days after Congress is required to assemble, determine by two-thirds vote of both Houses that the President is unable to discharge the powers and duties of his office, the Vice President shall continue to discharge the same as Acting President; otherwise, the President shall resume the powers and duties of his office.

Amendment XXVI
(1971)

Section 1.   The right of citizens of the United States, who are 18 years of age or older, to vote, shall not be denied or abridged by the United States or any State on account of age.

Section 2.   The Congress shall have the power to enforce this article by appropriate legislation.

Amendment XXVII
(1992)

No law varying the compensation for the services of the Senators and Representatives shall take effect until an election of Representatives shall have intervened.

AN INTRODUCTION TO THE
CONCEPT OF "SOVEREIGNTY"

The influential political philosopher Jean Bodin first published his *Six livres de la republique* in 1576.[1] He defined sovereignty as the highest legal and political authority in any form of government. His views were understood by the English to establish the "characteristic of sovereignty that it is not only supreme, but single and undivided: there can be but one sovereign."[2] In England and the other European monarchies of his day, sovereignty was understood to reside in the monarch or "sovereign," tending toward absolute monarchy.

In England, the Glorious Revolution of 1688 was viewed as transferring sovereignty from the Crown to Parliament.[3] Any pretense of absolute monarchy ended as the Crown was thereafter "sovereign" only in conjunction with the Houses of Lords and Commons. Although John Locke authored a defense of the Glorious Revolution and its resulting theory of sovereignty,[4] Sir William Blackstone rejected such theory and summarized the prevailing view in the 1760s and 1770s:

> [A]s the power of making laws constitutes the supreme authority, so wherever the supreme authority in any state resides, it is the right of that authority to make laws; that is, in the words of our definition *to prescribe the rule of civil action.* . . . It can therefore be no otherwise produced than by a *political* union; by the consent of all persons to submit their own private wills to the will of one man, or of one or more assemblies of men, to whom the supreme authority is entrusted: and this will of that one man, or assemblage of men, is in different states, according to their different constitutions, understood to be *law.*[5]

Blackstone explained that the ultimate lawmaking power resided in Parliament collectively, rather than in the Crown.

> These are the constituent parts of a parliament, the king, the lords spiritual and temporal, and the commons. Parts, of which each is so necessary, that the consent of all three is required to make any new law that shall bind the subject. Whatever is enacted for law by one, or by two only, of the three is no statute; and to it no regard is due, unless in matters relating to their own privileges.[6]

And Blackstone made clear that the authority of Parliament was absolute.

> The power and jurisdiction of parliament, says Sir Edward Coke, is so transcendent and absolute, that it cannot be confined, either for causes or persons, within any bounds. . . . It hath sovereign and uncontrollable

---

[1] A modern translation of the pertinent portion of this treatise on public law and policy has been published as BODIN ON SOVEREIGNTY: FOUR CHAPTERS FROM THE *SIX BOOKS OF THE COMMONWEALTH* (Julian H. Franklin ed. 1992).

[2] C.H. MCILWAIN, CONSTITUTIONALISM AND THE CHANGING WORLD 26–27 (1939).

[3] For a recent, popular account of the Glorious Revolution, see MICHAEL BARONE, OUR FIRST REVOLUTION: THE REMARKABLE BRITISH UPHEAVAL THAT INSPIRED AMERICA'S FOUNDING FATHERS (2007).

[4] *See* JOHN LOCKE, TWO TREATISES OF GOVERNMENT (1698).

[5] 1 WILLIAM BLACKSTONE, COMMENTARIES ON THE LAWS OF ENGLAND 52 (1765). Blackstone opined that Locke was mistaken to consider sovereignty to reside in the people simply because a revolution could change the form of government. In those rare instances, there is "at once an entire dissolution of the bands of government" involving "anarchy." *Id.* For Blackstone, "sovereignty" was the ultimate source of authority *within* a constitutional structure rather than upon its dissolution. *Id.* at 157.

[6] *Id.* at 155.

authority in making, confirming, enlarging, restraining, abrogating, repealing, reviving, and expounding of laws, concerning matters of all possible
denominations, ecclesiastical, or temporal, civil, military, maritime, or
criminal: this being the place where that absolute despotic power, which
must in all governments reside somewhere, is entrusted by the constitution
of these kingdoms. . . . It can, in short, do every thing that is not naturally
impossible; and therefore some have not scrupled to call its power, by a
figure rather too bold, the omnipotence of parliament. True it is, that what
they do, no authority upon earth can undo.[7]

The concept of Parliament as the sovereign posed a serious theoretical challenge
to the American colonists who protested the legality of the Stamp Act and other
measures. In 1774, James Wilson published the argument that although the colonies
shared the same King as England, they were entitled to their own legislative
assemblies.[8] He relied upon the existing relationship with Ireland, which had its
own legislature in which the King participated as he did with the English
Parliament.[9] Wilson explained: "Allegiance to the king and obedience to the
parliament are founded on very different principles. The former is founded on
protection; the latter, on representation."[10] These early protests attacked the
overreaching of Parliament, not abuses by the King. And the position adopted by
the colonists recognized the question was one of absolutes: either Parliament had
power to legislate for the colonies on all matters or none at all, as sovereignty was
simply not divisible.[11]

Resolving the difficult problem of locating where the indivisible, ultimate
authority resided was a recurring challenge throughout the crisis leading to the
American Revolution, the framing of state constitutions, the adoption of the Articles
of Confederation, and the drafting and ratification of the U.S. Constitution.[12] In
modern writing, the term sovereignty may be more misleading than helpful.
Nonetheless, every form of government recognizes the underlying concept.

---

[7] *Id.* at 156.

[8] James Wilson, *Considerations on the Nature and Extent of the Legislative Authority of the British
Parliament* (1774), *in* 1 COLLECTED WORKS OF JAMES WILSON 3 (Kermit L. Hall & Mark David Hall eds.
2007).

[9] *See id.* at 18–20. Prior to the Act of Union of 1707, Scotland also had its own parliament while
sharing the same King as England.

[10] *Id.* at 20. Bernard Bailyn attributes the efforts of Wilson and other colonial theorists to their
"[a]cknowledging the impossibility of convincing the authorities in England that Parliament's sovereignty might be divisible." BERNARD BAILYN, THE IDEOLOGICAL ORIGINS OF THE AMERICAN REVOLUTION 224
(1967).

[11] *See, e.g.,* Alexander Hamilton, *A Full Vindication of the Measures of Congress* (1774), *in*
ALEXANDER HAMILTON: WRITINGS 12 (Joanne B. Freeman ed. 1961) ("How ridiculous then it is to affirm,
that we are quarreling for the trifling sum of three pence a pound on tea; when it is evidently the
principle against which we contend.").

[12] *See* GORDON S. WOOD, THE CREATION OF THE AMERICAN REPUBLIC, 1776–1787, at 345 (1998) (noting that
the concept of sovereignty "was the single most important abstraction of politics in the entire
Revolutionary era"); BERNARD BAILYN, *supra* note 10, at 198 (asserting that "sovereignty" was the one
"absolutely critical" issue and that "in the last analysis it was over this issue that the Revolution was
fought").

Exercise 2 (Historical Setting):

To the extent that the structure (or even particular provisions) of the U.S. Constitution are not clear from a cursory review of the text, it may be helpful to compare the Constitution to its historical antecedents. To the extent certain features of English government were identified as causes of the American Revolution, it might seem odd to read ambiguous provisions of the Constitution to produce the same result. And, to the extent the Constitution was framed to correct perceived problems with government under the Articles of Confederation, a comparison of the structure thought to be flawed may give insights to the meaning of the Constitution. (The DVD-ROM also has the text of selected States constitutions.)

Read the Declaration of Independence and the Articles of Confederation and re-read the Constitution. Compare the structure of the governments established by these documents. Consider the following questions in determining whether the historical context sheds additional light upon the structure of government established by the Constitution.

(1) What entities formed the Articles of Confederation? How, if at all, does that differ from the entities that formed the U.S. Constitution?

(2) Where does "sovereignty" reside under the Articles of Confederation? How, if at all, does that differ under the U.S. Constitution?

(3) Did the Articles of Confederation permit a State to secede? How, if at all, does the U.S. Constitution differ on that matter?

(4) Did the Articles of Confederation permit additional states to join the confederation? How, if at all, does the U.S. Constitution differ on that matter?

(5) What branches of the central government are created and/or authorized by the Articles of Confederation? How, if at all, does the U.S. Constitution differ on that matter?

(6) What process for revision and/or amendment was specified by the Articles of Confederation? How, if at all, does the U.S. Constitution differ on that matter?

(7) Under the Articles of Confederation, which matters are placed within the exclusive control of the central government, which matters are placed within the exclusive control of the several States, and which matters are reserved for the people? How, if at all, does the U.S. Constitution differ in that allocation? How, if at all, does the Bill of Rights change the allocation in the U.S. Constitution of 1789?

(8) What objections to exercises of the judicial power were specified in the Declaration of Independence? How, if at all, does the U.S. Constitution address those objections?

(9) Identify the objections presented with respect to the executive's interference with the legislative power. How, if at all, are those objections addressed in the U.S. Constitution?

THE DECLARATION OF INDEPENDENCE

[I]   When in the Course of human Events, it becomes necessary for one People to dissolve the Political Bonds which have connected them with another, and to assume among the Powers of the Earth, the separate and equal Station to which the Laws of Nature's God entitle them, a decent Respect to the Opinions of Mankind requires that they should declare the causes which impel them to the Separation.

[II]   WE hold these Truths to be self-evident, that all Men are created equal, that they are endowed by their Creator with certain unalienable Rights, that among these are Life, Liberty, and the Pursuit of Happiness — That to secure these Rights, Governments are instituted among Men, deriving their just Powers from the Consent of the Governed, that whenever any Form of Government becomes destructive of these Ends, it is the Right of the People to alter or to abolish it, and to institute new Government, laying its Foundation on such Principles, and organizing its Powers in such Form, as to them shall seem most likely to effect their Safety and Happiness. Prudence, indeed, will dictate that Governments long established should not be changed for light and transient Causes; and accordingly all Experience hath shewn, that Mankind are more disposed to suffer, while Evils are sufferable, than to right themselves by abolishing the Forms to which they are accustomed. But when a long Train of Abuses and Usurpations, pursuing invariably the same Object, evinces a Design to reduce them under absolute Despotism, it is their Right, it is their Duty, to throw off such Government, and to provide new Guards for their future Security. Such has been the patient Sufferance of these Colonies; and such is now the Necessity which constrains them to alter their former Systems of Government. The History of the present King of Great-Britain is a History of repeated Injuries and Usurpations, all having in direct Object the Establishment of an absolute Tyranny over these States. To prove this, let Facts be submitted to a candid World.

[A]   HE has refused his Assent to Laws, the most wholesome and necessary for the public Good.

HE has forbidden his Governors to pass Laws of immediate and pressing Importance, unless suspended in their Operation till his Assent should be obtained; and when so suspended, he has utterly neglected to attend to them.

HE has refused to pass other Laws for the Accommodation of large Districts of People, unless those People would relinquish the Right of Representation in the Legislature, a Right inestimable to them, and formidable to Tyrants only.

[B]   HE has called together Legislative Bodies at Places unusual, uncomfortable, and distant from the Depository of their public Records, for the sole Purpose of fatiguing them into Compliance with his Measures.

HE has dissolved Representative Houses repeatedly, for opposing with manly Firmness his Invasions on the Rights of the People.

HE has refused for a long Time, after such Dissolutions, to cause others to be elected; whereby the Legislative Powers, incapable of Annihilation, have returned to the People at large for their exercise; the State remaining in the mean time exposed to all the Dangers of Invasion from without, and Convulsions within.

[C]   HE has endeavoured to prevent the Population of these States; for that Purpose obstructing the Laws for Naturalization of Foreigners; refusing to pass others to encourage their Migrations hither, and raising the Conditions of new Appropriations of Lands.

[D]   HE has obstructed the Administration of Justice, by refusing his Assent to laws for establishing Judiciary Powers.

He has made Judges dependent on his Will alone, for the Tenure of their Offices, and the Amount and Payment of their Salaries.

[E]   He has erected a Multitude of new Offices, and sent hither Swarms of Officers to harass our People, and eat out their Substance.

[F]   He has kept among us, in Times of Peace, Standing Armies, without the consent of our Legislatures.

He has affected to render the Military independent of and superior to the Civil Power.

[G]   He has combined with others to subject us to a Jurisdiction foreign to our Constitution, and unacknowledged by our Laws; giving his Assent to their Acts of pretended Legislation:

[1]   For quartering large Bodies of Armed Troops among us;

[2]   For protecting them, by a mock Trial, from Punishment for any Murders which they should commit on the Inhabitants of these States;

[3]   For cutting off our Trade with all Parts of the World;

[4]   For imposing Taxes on us without our Consent;

[5]   For depriving us, in many Cases, of the Benefits of Trial by Jury;

[6]   For transporting us beyond Seas to be tried for pretended Offences;

[7]   For abolishing the free System of English Laws in a neighbouring Province, establishing therein an arbitrary Government, and enlarging its Boundaries, so as to render it at once an Example and fit Instrument for introducing the same absolute Rule into these Colonies;

[8]   For taking away our Charters, abolishing our most valuable Laws, and altering fundamentally the Forms of our Governments;

[9]   For suspending our own Legislatures, and declaring themselves invested with Power to legislate for us in all Cases whatsoever.

[H]   He has abdicated Government here, by declaring us out of his Protection and waging War against us.

He has plundered our Seas, ravaged our Coasts, burnt our Towns, and destroyed the Lives of our People.

He is, at this time, transporting large Armies of foreign Mercenaries to compleat the Works of Death, Desolation, and Tyranny, already begun with circumstances of Cruelty and Perfidy, scarcely paralleled in the most barbarous Ages, and totally unworthy the Head of a civilized Nation.

[I]   He has constrained our fellow Citizens taken Captive on the high Seas to bear Arms against their Country, to become the Executioners of their Friends and Brethern, or to fall themselves by their Hands.

He has excited domestic Insurrections amongst us, and has endeavoured to bring on the Inhabitants of our Frontiers, the merciless Indian Savages, whose known Rules of Warfare, is an undistinguished Destruction, of all Ages, Sexes and Conditions.

[J]   In every stage of these Oppressions we have Petitioned for Redress in the most humble Terms: Our repeated Petitions have been answered only by repeated Injury. A Prince, whose Character is thus marked by every act which may define a Tyrant, is unfit to be the Ruler of a free People.

[III]   Nor have we been wanting in Attention to our British Brethren. We have warned them from Time to Time of Attempts by their Legislature to extend an unwarrantable Jurisdiction over us. We have reminded them of the Circumstances of Emigration and Settlement here. We have appealed to their native Justice and Magnanimity, and we have conjured them by the Ties of our common Kindred to disavow these Usurpations, which, would inevitably interrupt our Connections and Correspondence. They too have been deaf to the Voice of Justice and of Consanguinity. We must, therefore, acquiesce in the Necessity, which denounces our Separation, and hold them, as we hold the rest of Mankind, Enemies in War, in Peace, Friends.

[IV]   **We, therefore,** the Representatives of the **United States of America**, in General Congress, Assembled, appealing to the Supreme Judge of the World for the Rectitude of our Intentions, do, in the Name, and by Authority of the good People of these Colonies, solemnly Publish and Declare, That these United Colonies are, and of Right ought to be, **Free and Independent States**; that they are absolved from all Allegiance to the British Crown, and that all political Connection between them and the State of Great-Britain, is and ought to be totally dissolved; and that as Free and Independent States, they have full Power to levy War, conclude Peace, contract Alliances, establish Commerce, and do all other Acts and Things which Independent States may of right do. — And for the support of this Declaration, with a firm Reliance on the Protection of divine Providence, we mutually pledge to each other our Lives, our Fortunes, and our sacred Honor.

[Signatures Omitted]

THE ARTICLES OF CONFEDERATION

Whereas the Delegates of the United States of America in Congress assembled did on the fifteenth day of November in the Year of our Lord One Thousand Seven Hundred and Seventyseven, and in the Second Year of the Independence of America agree to certain articles of Confederation and perpetual Union between the States of New-hampshire, Massachusetts-bay, Rhodeisland and Providence Plantations, Connecticut, New York, New Jersey, Pennsylvania, Delaware, Maryland, Virginia, North-Carolina, South-Carolina and Georgia in the Words following, viz.

Articles of Confederation and perpetual Union between the states of New-hampshire, Massachusetts-bay, Rhodeisland and Providence Plantations, Connecticut, New-York, New-Jersey, Pennsylvania, Delaware, Maryland, Virginia, North Carolina, South Carolina and Georgia.

I.   The stile of this confederacy shall be "The United States of America".

II.   Each State retains its sovereignty, freedom, and independence, and every power, jurisdiction, and right, which is not by this confederation expressly delegated to the United States, in Congress assembled.

III.   The said States hereby severally enter into a firm league of friendship with each other, for their common defense, the security of their liberties, and their mutual and general welfare, binding themselves to assist each other, against all force offered to, or attacks made upon them, or any of them, on account of religion, sovereignty, trade, or any other pretense whatever.

IV.   The better to secure and perpetuate mutual friendship and intercourse among the people of the different States in this Union, the free inhabitants of each of these States, paupers, vagabonds, and fugitives from justice excepted, shall be entitled to all privileges and immunities of free citizens in the several States; and the people of each State shall free ingress and regress to and from any other State, and shall enjoy therein all the privileges of trade and commerce, subject to the same duties, impositions, and restrictions as the inhabitants thereof respectively, provided that such restrictions shall not extend so far as to prevent the removal of property imported into any State, to any other State, of which the owner is an inhabitant; provided also that no imposition, duties or restriction shall be laid by any State, on the property of the United States, or either of them.

If any person guilty of, or charged with, treason, felony, or other high misdemeanor in any State, shall flee from justice, and be found in any of the United States, he shall, upon demand of the Governor or Executive power of the State from which he fled, be delivered up and removed to the State having jurisdiction of his offense.

Full faith and credit shall be given in each of these States to the records, acts, and judicial proceedings of the courts and magistrates of every other State.

V.   For the most convenient management of the general interests of the United States, delegates shall be annually appointed in such manner as the legislatures of each State shall direct, to meet in Congress on the first Monday in November, in every year, with a power reserved to each State to recall its delegates, or any of them, at any time within the year, and to send others in their stead for the remainder of the year.

No State shall be represented in Congress by less than two, nor more than seven members; and no person shall be capable of being a delegate for more than three years in any term of six years; nor shall any person, being a delegate, be capable of holding any office under the United States, for which he, or another for his benefit, receives any salary, fees or emolument of any kind.

Each State shall maintain its own delegates in a meeting of the States, and while they act as members of the committee of the States.

In determining questions in the United States in Congress assembled, each State shall have one vote.

Freedom of Speech and debate in Congress shall not be impeached or questioned in any court or place out of Congress, and the members of Congress shall be protected in their persons from arrests or imprisonments, during the time of their going to and from, and attendance on Congress, except for treason, felony, or breach of the peace.

VI.   No State without the consent of the United States in Congress assembled, shall send any embassy to, or receive any embassy from, or enter into any conference, agreement, alliance or treaty with any king, prince or state, nor shall any person holding any office of profit or trust under the United States, or any of them, accept any present, emolument, office or title of any kind whatever from any king, prince or foreign state; nor shall the United States in Congress assembled, or any of them, grant any title of nobility.

No two or more States shall enter into any treaty, confederation or alliance whatever between them, without the consent of the United States in Congress assembled, specifying accurately the purposes for which the same is to be entered into, and how long it shall continue.

No State shall lay any imposts or duties, which may interfere with any stipulations in treaties, entered into by the United States in Congress assembled, with any king, prince or state, in pursuance of any treaties already proposed by Congress, to the courts of France and Spain.

No vessel of war shall be kept up in time of peace by any State, except such number only, as shall be deemed necessary by the United States in Congress assembled, for the defense of such State, or its trade; nor shall any body of forces be kept up by any State in time of peace, except such number only, as in the judgement of the United States in Congress assembled, shall be deemed requisite to garrison the forts necessary for the defense of such State; but every State shall always keep up a well-regulated and disciplined militia, sufficiently armed and accoutered, and shall provide and constantly have ready for use, in public stores, a due number of field pieces and tents, and a proper quantity of arms, ammunition and camp equipage.

No State shall engage in any war without the consent of the United States in Congress assembled, unless such State be actually invaded by enemies, or shall have received certain advice of a resolution being formed by some nation of Indians to invade such State, and the danger is so imminent as not to admit of a delay, till the United States in Congress assembled can be consulted; nor shall any State grant commissions to any ships or vessels of war, nor letters of marque or reprisal, except it be after a declaration of war by the United States in Congress assembled, and then only against the kingdom or state and subjects thereof, against which war has been so declared, and under such regulations as shall be established by the United States in Congress assembled, unless such State be infested by pirates, in which case vessels of war may be fitted out for that occasion, and kept so long as the danger shall continue, or until the United States in Congress assembled shall determine otherwise.

VII.   When land-forces are raised by any State for the common defense, all officers of or under the rank of colonel, shall be appointed by the Legislature of each State respectively by whom such forces shall be raised, or in such manner as such State shall direct, and all vacancies shall be filled up by the State which first made the appointment.

VIII.   All charges of war, and all other expenses that shall be incurred for the common defense or general welfare, and allowed by the United States in Congress assembled, shall be defrayed out of a common treasury, which shall be supplied by the several States in proportion to the value of all land within each State, granted or surveyed for any person, as such land and the buildings and improvements thereon shall be estimated according to such mode as the United States in Congress assembled, shall from time to time direct and appoint.

The taxes for paying that proportion shall be laid and levied by the authority and direction of the Legislatures of the several States within the time agreed upon by the United States in Congress assembled.

IX.   The United States in Congress assembled, shall have the sole and exclusive right and power of determining on peace and war, except in the cases mentioned in the sixth article — of sending and receiving ambassadors — entering into treaties and alliances, provided that no treaty of commerce shall be made whereby the legislative power of the respective States shall be restrained from imposing such imposts and duties on foreigners, as their own people are subjected to, or from prohibiting the exportation or importation of any species of goods or commodities whatsoever — of establishing rules for deciding in all cases, what captures on land or water shall be legal, and in what manner prizes taken by land or naval forces in the service of the United States shall be divided or appropriated — of granting letters of marque and reprisal in times of peace — appointing courts for the trial of piracies and felonies committed on the high seas and establishing courts for receiving and determining finally appeals in all cases of captures, provided that no member of Congress shall be appointed a judge of any of the said courts.

The United States in Congress assembled shall also be the last resort on appeal in all disputes and differences now subsisting or that hereafter may arise between two or more States concerning boundary, jurisdiction or any other causes whatever; which authority shall always be exercised in the manner following. Whenever the legislative or executive authority or lawful agent of any State in controversy with another shall present a petition to Congress, stating the matter in question and praying for a hearing, notice thereof shall be given by order of Congress to the legislative or executive authority of the other State in controversy, and a day assigned for the appearance of the parties by their lawful agents, who shall then be directed to appoint by joint consent, commissioners or judges to constitute a court for hearing and determining the matter in question: but if they cannot agree, Congress shall name three persons out of each of the United States, and from the list of such persons each party shall alternately strike out one, the petitioners beginning, until the number shall be reduced to thirteen; and from that number not less than seven, nor more than nine names as Congress shall direct, shall in the presence of Congress be drawn out by lot, and the persons whose names shall be so drawn or any five of them, shall be commissioners or judges, to hear and finally determine the controversy, so always as a major part of the judges who shall hear the cause shall agree in the determination: and if either party shall neglect to attend at the day appointed, without showing reasons, which Congress shall judge sufficient, or being present shall refuse to strike, the Congress shall proceed to nominate three persons out of each State, and the Secretary of Congress shall strike in behalf of such party absent or refusing; and the judgement and sentence of the court to be appointed, in the manner before prescribed, shall be final and conclusive; and if any of the parties shall refuse to submit to the authority of such court, or to appear or defend their claim or cause, the court shall nevertheless proceed to pronounce sentence, or judgement, which shall in like manner be final and decisive, the judgement or sentence and other proceedings being in either case transmitted to Congress, and lodged among the acts of Congress for the security of the parties concerned: provided that every commissioner, before he sits in judgement, shall take an oath to be administered by one of the judges of the supreme or superior court of the State, where the cause shall be tried, "well and truly to hear and determine the matter in question, according to the best of his judgement, without favor, affection or hope of reward": provided also, that no State shall be deprived of territory for the benefit of the United States.

All controversies concerning the private right of soil claimed under different grants of two or more States, whose jurisdictions as they may respect such lands, and the States which passed such grants are adjusted, the said grants or either of them being at the same time claimed to have originated antecedent to such settlement of jurisdiction, shall on the petition of either party to the Congress of the United States, be finally determined as near as may be in the same manner as is before prescribed for deciding disputes respecting territorial jurisdiction between different States.

The United States in Congress assembled shall also have the sole and exclusive right and power of regulating the alloy and value of coin struck by their own authority, or by that of the respective States — fixing the standards of weights and measures throughout the United States — regulating the trade and managing all affairs with the Indians, not members of any of the States, provided that the legislative right of any State within its own limits be not infringed or violated — establishing or regulating post-offices from one State to another, throughout all the United States, and exacting such postage on the papers passing through the same as may be requisite to defray the expenses of said office — appointing all officers of the land forces, in the service of the United States, excepting regimental officers — appointing all the officers of the naval forces, and commissioning all officers whatever in the service of the United States — making rules for the government and regulation of the said land and naval forces, and directing their operations.

The United States in Congress assembled shall have authority to appoint a committee, to sit in the recess of Congress, to be denominated "a Committee of the States", and to consist of one delegate from each State; and to appoint such other committees and civil officers as may be necessary for managing the general affairs of the United States under their direction — to appoint one of their number to preside, provided that no person be allowed to serve in the office of president more than one year in any term of three years; to ascertain the necessary sums of money to be raised for the service of the United States, and to appropriate and apply the same for defraying the public expenses — to borrow money, or emit bills on the credit of the United States, transmitting every half year to the respective States an account of the sums of money so borrowed or emitted — to build and equip a navy — to agree upon the number of land forces, and to make requisitions from each State for its quota, in proportion to the number of white inhabitants in such State; which requisition shall be binding, and thereupon the Legislature of each State shall appoint the regimental officers, raise the men and clothe, arm and equip them in a solid-like manner, at the expense of the United States; and the officers and men so clothed, armed and equipped shall march to the place appointed, and within the time agreed on by the United States in Congress assembled: but if the United States in Congress assembled shall, on consideration of circumstances judge proper that any State should not raise men, or should raise a smaller number of men than the quota thereof, such extra number shall be raised, officered, clothed, armed and equipped in the same manner as the quota of each State, unless the legislature of such State shall judge that extra number cannot be safely spread out in the same, in which case they shall raise, officer, clothe, arm and equip as many of such extra number as they judge can be safely spared. And the officers and men so clothed, armed, and equipped, shall march to the place appointed, and within the time agreed on by the United States in Congress assembled.

The United States in Congress assembled shall never engage in a war, nor grant letters of marque or reprisal in time of peace, nor enter into any treaties or alliances, nor coin money, nor regulate the value thereof, nor ascertain the sums and expenses necessary for the defense and welfare of the United States, or any of them, nor emit bills, nor borrow money on the credit of the United States, nor appropriate money, nor agree upon the number of vessels of war, to be built or purchased, or the number of land or sea forces to be raised, nor appoint a commander in chief of the army or navy, unless nine States assent to the same: nor shall a question on any other point, except for adjourning from day to day be determined, unless by the votes of the majority of the United States in Congress assembled.

The Congress of the United States shall have power to adjourn to any time within the year, and to any place within the United States, so that no period of adjournment be for a longer duration than the space of six months, and shall publish the journal of their proceedings monthly, except such parts thereof relating to treaties, alliances or military operations, as in their judgement require secrecy; and the yeas and nays of the delegates of each State on any question shall be entered on the journal, when it is desired by any delegates of a State, or any of them, at his or their request shall be furnished with a transcript of the said journal, except such parts as are above excepted, to lay before the Legislatures of the several States.

X. The committee of the States, or any nine of them, shall be authorized to execute, in the recess of Congress, such of the powers of Congress as the United States in Congress assembled, by the consent of the nine States, shall from time to time think expedient to vest them with; provided that no power be delegated to the said committee, for the exercise of which, by the articles of confederation, the voice of nine States in the Congress of the United States assembled be requisite.

XI. Canada acceding to this confederation, and adjoining in the measures of the United States, shall be admitted into, and entitled to all the advantages of this Union; but no other colony shall be admitted into the same, unless such admission be agreed to by nine States.

XII. All bills of credit emitted, monies borrowed, and debts contracted by, or under the authority of Congress, before the assembling of the United States, in pursuance of the present confederation, shall be deemed and considered as a charge against the United States, for payment and satisfaction whereof the said United States, and the public faith are hereby solemnly pledged.

XIII. Every State shall abide by the determination of the United States in Congress assembled, on all questions which by this confederation are submitted to them. And the articles of this confederation shall be inviolably observed by every State, and the Union shall be perpetual; nor shall any alteration at any time hereafter be made in any of them; unless such alteration be agreed to in a Congress of the United States, and be afterwards confirmed by the Legislatures of every State.

And whereas it hath pleased the Great Governor of the world to incline the hearts of the Legislatures we respectively represent in Congress, to approve of, and to authorize us to ratify the said articles of confederation and perpetual union. Know ye that we the undersigned delegates, by virtue of the power and authority to us given for that purpose, do by these presents, in the name and in behalf of our respective constituents, fully and entirely ratify and confirm each and every of the said articles of confederation and perpetual union, and all and singular the matters and things therein contained: And we do further solemnly plight and engage the faith of our constituents, that they shall abide by the determinations of the United States in Congress assembled, on all questions, which by the said confederation are submitted to them. And that the articles thereof shall be inviolably observed by the States we respectively represent, and that the Union shall be perpetual.

In Witness whereof we have hereunto set our hands in Congress. Done at Philadelphia in the State of Pennsylvania the ninth day of July in the year of our Lord one Thousand seven hundred and seventy-eight, and in the third year of the independence of America.

[Signatures Omitted]

Agreed to by Congress November 15, 1777.

In force after ratification by Maryland, March 1, 1781.

Exercise 3 (Text):

Re-read, *very closely*, the Constitution of 1789 and the Bill of Rights. As a preliminary matter, observe that this course started with a consideration of three written instruments that address the form of government: the Articles of Confederation, the Constitution of 1789, and the Bill of Rights. These documents along with the Declaration of Independence also assert important limitations on governmental power. In ways that we cannot fully appreciate, these instruments are extraordinary.

(1)   It is often remarked that the English had no written constitution. Against a history as English colonies, why did we adopt written constitutions? What purpose is served by reducing a constitution to writing?

For a recent review of the reasons Americans adopted a written Constitution, see Lee J. Strang, *The Clash of Rival and Incompatible Philosophical Traditions in Constitutional Interpretation: Originalism Grounded in the Central Western Philosophical Tradition*, 28 HARV. J.L. & PUB. POL'Y 909, 970–81 (2005).

The first of the branches of the central government that we will examine in detail is the judiciary. Please consider each of the following questions about the structure and power of the federal judiciary considering only the assigned texts. To the extent you infer an answer from text that is not explicit, identify the techniques you use to do so.

(2)   What does the U.S. Constitution indicate regarding whether the federal judiciary may properly review whether legislation or executive actions comply with the terms of the Constitution? Does it matter whether the legislative or executive actions under review are actions of federal or state governments? Are there some provisions of the Constitution that do not support judicial review? Are there provisions of the Constitution that are especially appropriate to enforcement through judicial review?

(3)   What does the U.S. Constitution indicate regarding which, if any, of the branches of the federal government have primacy in constitutional interpretation? Are each of the branches responsible for interpreting the Constitution? If so, do the branches have equal responsibility in such matters? Do they have equal authority?

(4)   What does the U.S. Constitution indicate are the limits on any federal judicial power to interpret the law, whether on constitutional or statutory matters?

(5)   What federal judiciary does the U.S. Constitution establish? What courts does the Constitution create? What judicial offices does it establish? What jurisdiction does it vest in those courts and offices?

(6)   What is the scope of a permissible federal judiciary under the Constitution? Who determines (and how) the number of federal courts, the number of federal judges on each such court, and the jurisdiction of each such court?

(7)   Who is qualified to serve as a federal judge? Who is disqualified? Could a non-lawyer serve as judge? Could a non-citizen serve as judge? Could a person simultaneously hold office as a federal judge and Member of Congress? Could a person simultaneously hold office as a federal judge and as Secretary of an Executive Department? Could a person simultaneously hold office as a federal judge and as judge of a state court?

(8)   What are the permissible means of appointing a federal judge? Could Congress authorize the Chief Justice of the U.S. Supreme Court to appoint federal district court judges?

(9)   What is the term of office of a federal judge?

(10)   What are the permissible means of removing a federal judge? Assume a federal judge is determined to be insane. How, if at all, may he be relieved of his duties absent a voluntary resignation? Assume a federal judge is in a coma. How, if at all, may he be relieved of his duties? Assume a federal judge is convicted of accepting bribes in exchange for favorable rulings? How, if at all, may he be relieved of his duties?

(11)   Other than the tenure provision and limitations on means of removal, how else does the Constitution protect the federal judiciary from influence by the other

branches of the federal government? Could Congress subject federal judges to a new payroll tax that was generally applicable to all federal employees? Would it matter if the tax were applicable to all employees regardless of employer?

(12) May Congress effectively remove judges from office by repealing the statute that creates their offices and/or courts?

(13) May Congress limit the issues that federal courts may address on appeal? May Congress limit the "original" (*i.e.*, trial level) jurisdiction of federal courts? May Congress do so with respect to the original jurisdiction of the U.S. Supreme Court? Are there some issues as to which Congress cannot limit federal judicial power, such as the availability of the writ of habeas corpus?

(14) May Congress grant federal courts additional jurisdiction beyond that specified in Article III? Does Article III merely specify a default set of jurisdictional boundaries in the absence of congressional action?

(15) May Congress revise legislation after the judiciary construes it? If so, may Congress make its revision applicable to pending cases? If so, may Congress make its revision retroactive to change the outcome in decided cases?

(16) Does the existence of a federal judiciary imply *exclusive* jurisdiction to adjudicate those cases involving an interpretation of the U.S. Constitution and/or federal statutes? If not, may Congress vest such exclusive jurisdiction in federal courts and exclude state courts from adjudicating such matters? May Congress require state courts to adjudicate cases involving an interpretation of the U.S. Constitution and/or federal statutes?

(17) Assuming a federal court has jurisdiction over a matter, may the court refrain from exercising that jurisdiction to resolve a concrete dispute between adverse parties on the basis of prudential considerations? If so, what considerations are sufficiently weighty?

(18) Does the constitutional text permit the federal judiciary to exercise jurisdiction over state governments as defendants? Does it matter whether the State contests such jurisdiction? Does it matter whether the plaintiff is the United States government, another State, a citizen of the State, or a citizen of another State? Does it matter what type of relief the plaintiff seeks?

(19) Does the constitutional text permit the federal judiciary to exercise jurisdiction over State governmental officials for actions in their official capacity? Does it matter whether the official contests such jurisdiction? Does it matter whether the plaintiff is the United States government, another State, a citizen of the State, or a citizen of another State? Does it matter what type of relief the plaintiff seeks?

(20) Does the constitutional text authorize Congress to permit the U.S. Supreme Court to sit in panels of Justices or must all Justices hear all cases together?

(21) Does the constitutional text permit Congress to assign duties to federal judges other than deciding individual cases? May Congress (or the President) assign judges the responsibility of negotiating specific treaty terms with foreign nations? May Congress (or the President) assign judges the responsibility of making initial determinations on claims for federal benefits subject to further review by Executive (or Legislative) officials? Does it matter whether the judge agrees to the additional duties?

In considering these questions, observe the extent to which a close reading of the *text* of the Constitution provides answers or at least a restricted range of permissible answers. Additional sources and interpretive methods to answer these questions will be introduced throughout the remainder of this Volume.

CHAPTER 2
ADDITIONAL FORMS OF HISTORICAL ARGUMENTS

The first chapter introduced three of the traditional forms of interpretation employed by lawyers: (1) the broad *structure* of government established by the Constitution, (2) the *historical setting* from which the Constitution emerged, and (3) the *text* of the Constitution itself. In addition to consideration of the historical setting that gave rise to the Constitution, there are several other sources that may more directly support arguments based upon history.

Drafting History. Records of the Constitutional Convention of 1787 illustrate the debates and compromises reflected in the text that was proposed for ratification. The Convention agreed to release no information regarding their deliberations until the work was completed. Even after the Convention completed its business, its journal and other papers were not made available to the public for decades. (The accompanying DVD-ROM contains the full text of James Madison's notes from the Constitutional Convention, as revised and expanded for publication in his retirement.) While these sources may be of historical value, what weight, if any, should be given to these sources in interpreting the Constitution?

Ratification History. In contrast to the drafting history, the ratification process was open to public view and participation. In addition to the records of the formal proceedings of conventions in various States, there was a heated public debate through a large number of speeches, pamphlets, essays, and newspaper articles. (The accompanying DVD-ROM contains the full text of many of the most significant essays and pamphlets from the ratification period, including The Federalist Papers.) To the extent those sources reflect a shared public understanding of the meaning of various provisions of the proposed Constitution, should they be given weight when interpreting the Constitution? Where the debate illustrates disagreement over the meaning of the Constitution, should greater weight be given to the views of those who prevailed in securing ratification (typically called "Federalists") or the opponents who failed to prevent ratification (typically called "Anti-Federalists")?

Early Practice. Once the Constitution was ratified and elections were held, the first Congress and President George Washington were confronted with the practical problems of implementing the Constitution in the absence of significant traditions and precedents. In light of the fact that President Washington had presided over the Constitutional Convention and many of the Convention's delegates served in the first Congress, should one presume that their formal actions in those offices reflect a proper understanding of the Constitution?

Exercise 4 (Ratification Debates):

Read the excerpts from the essays of Brutus (an Anti-Federalist) and Publius (three Federalists) regarding the structure and power of the judicial branch. These essays were published during the period New York was considering whether to ratify the Constitution. Reconsider the questions regarding judicial power posed in Exercise 3. Do the ratification materials change your answers to any of the questions?

Ratification Debates — Essays of Brutus

No. XI   The nature and extent of the judicial power of the United States, proposed to be granted by this constitution, claims our particular attention.

. . . [I]t is obvious, that we can form but very imperfect ideas of the manner in which this government will work, or the effect it will have in changing the internal police and mode of distributing justice at present subsisting in the respective states, without a thorough investigation of the powers of the judiciary and of the manner in which they will operate. . . . They are to be rendered totally independent, both of the people and the legislature, both with respect to their offices and salaries. No errors they may commit can be corrected by any power above them, if any such power there be, nor can they be removed from office for making ever so many erroneous adjudications.

The only causes for which they can be displaced, is, conviction of treason, bribery, and high crimes and misdemeanors.

. . . .

That we may be enabled to form a just opinion on this subject, I shall, in considering it,

[First] Examine the nature and extent of the judicial powers — and

[Second] Enquire, whether the courts who are to exercise them, are so constituted as to afford reasonable ground of confidence, that they will exercise them for the general good.

. . . .

In [Article III, section 2], it is said, "The judicial power shall extend to all cases in law and equity arising under this constitution, the laws of the United States, and treaties made, or which shall be made, under their authority, [etc.]."

. . . .

What latitude of construction this clause should receive, it is not easy to say. At first view, one would suppose, that it meant no more than this, that the courts under the general government should exercise, not only the powers of courts of law, but also that of courts of equity, in the manner in which those powers are usually exercised in the different states. But this cannot be the meaning, because the next clause authorizes the courts to take cognizance of all cases in law and equity arising under the laws of the United States; this last article, I conceive, conveys as much power to the general judicial as any of the state courts possess.

The cases arising under the constitution must be different from those arising under the laws, or else the two clauses mean exactly the same thing. . . .

. . . .

This article, therefore, vests the judicial with a power to resolve all questions that may arise on any case on the construction of the constitution, either in law or in equity.

[First]. They are authorised to determine all questions that may arise upon the meaning of the constitution in law. This article vests the courts with authority to give the constitution a legal construction, or to explain it according to the rules laid down for construing a law. — These rules give a certain degree of latitude of explanation. According to this mode of construction, the courts are to give such meaning to the constitution as comports best with the common, and generally received acceptation of the words in which it is expressed, regarding their ordinary and popular use, rather than their grammatical propriety. Where words are dubious, they will be explained by the context. The end of the clause will be attended to, and the words will be understood, as having a view to it; and the words will not be so understood as to bear no meaning or a very absurd one.

[Second]. The judicial are not only to decide questions arising upon the meaning of the constitution in law, but also in equity.

By this they are empowered, to explain the constitution according to the reasoning spirit of it, without being confined to the words or letter.

. . . .

[Grotius] observes, "That equity, thus depending essentially upon each individual case, there can be no established rules and fixed principles of equity laid down, without destroying its very essence, and reducing it to a positive law."

. . . .

They will give the sense of every article of the constitution, that may from time to time come before them. And in their decisions they will not confine themselves to any fixed or established rules, but will determine, according to what appears to them, the reason and spirit of the constitution. The opinions of the supreme court, whatever they may be, will have the force of law; because there is no power provided in the constitution, that can correct their errors, or controul their adjudications. From this court there is no appeal. And I conceive the legislature themselves, cannot set aside a judgment of this court, because they are authorised by the constitution to decide in the last resort. The legislature must be controlled by the constitution, and not the constitution by them. . . . The reason is plain; the judicial and executive derive their authority from the same source, that the legislature do theirs; and therefore in all cases, where the constitution does not make the one responsible to, or controllable by the other, they are altogether independent of each other.

. . . Every adjudication of the supreme court, on any question that may arise upon the nature and extent of the general government, will affect the limits of the state jurisdiction. In proportion as the former enlarge the exercise of their powers, will that of the latter be restricted.

That the judicial power of the United States, will lean strongly in favor of the general government, and will give such an explanation to the constitution, as will favor an extension of its jurisdiction, is very evident from a variety of considerations.

[First]. The constitution itself strongly countenances such a mode of construction. . . . The clause which vests the power to pass all laws which are proper and necessary, to carry the powers given into execution, it has been shown, leaves the legislature at liberty, to do every thing, which in their judgment is best. It is said, I know, that this clause confers no power on the legislature, which they would not have had without it — though I believe this is not the fact, yet admitting it to be, it implies that the constitution is not to receive an explanation strictly, according to its letter; but more power is implied than is expressed. And this clause, if it is to be considered, as explanatory of the extent of the powers given, rather than giving a new power, is to be understood as declaring, that in construing any of the articles conveying power, the spirit, intent and design of the clause, should be attended to, as well as the words in their common acceptation.

. . . .

[Second]. Not only will the constitution justify the courts in inclining to this mode of explaining it, but they will be interested in using this latitude of interpretation.

Every body of men invested with office are tenacious of power; they feel interested, and hence it has become a kind of maxim, to hand down their offices, with all its rights and privileges, unimpaired to their successors; the same principle will influence them to extend their power, and increase their rights; this of itself will operate strongly upon the courts to give such a meaning to the constitution in all cases where it can possibly be done, as will enlarge the sphere of their own authority. . . .

[Third]. Because they will have precedent to plead, to justify them in it. It is well known, that the courts in England, have by their own authority, extended their jurisdiction far beyond the limits set them in their original institution, and by the laws of the land.

. . . .

When the courts will have a precedent before them of a court which extended its jurisdiction in opposition to an act of the legislature, is it not to be expected that they will extend theirs, especially when there is nothing in the constitution expressly against it? and they are authorised to construe its meaning, and are not under any control?

This power in the judicial, will enable them to mold the government, into almost any shape they please. . . .

No. XII   In my last, I showed, that the judicial power of the United States under [Article I, Section 2, Paragraph 1], would be authorized to explain the constitution, not only according to its letter, but according to its spirit and intention; and having this power, they would strongly incline to give it such a construction as to extend the powers of the general government, as much as possible, to the diminution, and finally to the destruction, of that of the respective states.

I shall now proceed to shew how this power will operate in its exercise to effect these purposes. In order to perceive the extent of its influence, I shall consider,

First. How it will tend to extend the legislative authority.

Second. In what manner it will increase the jurisdiction of the courts, and

Third. The way in which it will diminish, and destroy, both the legislative and judicial authority of the United States.

First. Let us enquire how the judicial power will effect an extension of the legislative authority.

Perhaps the judicial power will not be able, by direct and positive decrees, ever to direct the legislature, because it is not easy to conceive how a question can be brought before them in a course of legal discussion, in which they can give a decision, declaring, that the legislature have certain powers which they have not exercised, and which, in consequence of the determination of the judges, they will be bound to exercise. But it is easy to see, that in their adjudications they may establish certain principles, which being received by the legislature, will enlarge the sphere of their power beyond all bounds.

It is to be observed, that the supreme court has the power, in the last resort, to determine all questions that may arise in the course of legal discussion, on the meaning and construction of the constitution. This power they will hold under the constitution, and independent of the legislature. . . .

In determining these questions, the court must and will assume certain principles, from which they will reason, in forming their decisions. These principles, whatever they may be, when they become fixed, by a course of decisions, will be adopted by the legislature, and will be the rule by which they will explain their own powers. This appears evident from this consideration, that if the legislature pass laws, which, in the judgment of the court, they are not authorised to do by the constitution, the court will not take notice of them; for it will not be denied, that the constitution is the highest or supreme law. And the courts are vested with the supreme and uncontrollable power, to determine, in all cases that come before them, what the constitution means; they cannot, therefore, execute a law, which, in their judgment, opposes the constitution, unless we can suppose they can make a superior law give way to an inferior. The legislature, therefore, will not go over the limits by which the courts may adjudge they are confined. And there is little room to doubt but that they will come up to those bounds, as often as occasion and opportunity may offer, and they may judge it proper to do it. For as on the one hand, they will not readily pass laws which they know the courts will not execute, so on the other, we may be sure they will not scruple to pass such as they know they will give effect, as often as they may judge it proper.

. . . .

To discover the spirit of the constitution, it is of the first importance to attend to the principal ends and designs it has in view. These are expressed in the preamble, in the following words, viz. "We, the people of the United States, in order to form a more perfect union, establish justice, insure domestic tranquility, provide for the common defence, promote the general welfare, and secure the blessings of liberty to ourselves and our posterity, do ordain and establish this constitution," &c. If the end of the government is to be learned from these words, which are clearly designed to declare it, it is obvious it has in view every object which is embraced by any government. The preservation of internal peace — the due administration of justice — and to provide for the defence of the community, seems to include all the objects of government; but if they do not, they are certainly comprehended in the words, "to provide for the general welfare." If it be further considered, that this constitution, if it is ratified, will not be a compact entered into by states, in their corporate capacities, but an agreement of the people of the United States, as one great body politic, no doubt can remain, but that the great end of the constitution, if it is to be collected from the preamble, in which its end is declared, is to constitute a government which is to extend to every case for which any government is instituted, whether external or internal. The courts, therefore, will establish this as a principle in expounding the constitution, and will give every part of it such an explanation, as will give latitude to every department under it, to take cognizance of every matter, not only that affects the general and national concerns of the union, but also of such as relate to the administration of private justice, and to regulating the internal and local affairs of the different parts.

. . . .

. . . I might proceed to the other clause, in the preamble, and it would appear by a consideration of all of them separately, as it does by taking them together, that if the spirit of this system is to be known from its declared end and design in the preamble, its spirit is to subvert and abolish all the powers of the state government, and to embrace every object to which any government extends.

As it sets out in the preamble with this declared intention, so it proceeds in the different parts with the same idea. Any person, who will peruse [Article I, Section 8] with attention, in which most of the powers are enumerated, will perceive that they either expressly or by implication extend to almost every thing about which any legislative power can be employed. But if this equitable mode of construction is applied to this part of the constitution; nothing can stand before it.

This will certainly give the first clause in that article a construction which I confess I think the most natural and grammatical one, to authorize the Congress to do any thing which in their judgment will tend to provide for the general welfare, and this amounts to the same thing as general and unlimited powers of legislation in all cases.

[continued]

. . . .

It is obvious that these courts will have authority to decide upon the validity of the laws of any of the states, in all cases where they come in question before them. Where the constitution gives the general government exclusive jurisdiction, they will adjudge all laws made by the states, in such cases void *ab initio*. Where the constitution gives them concurrent jurisdiction, the laws of the United States must prevail, because they are the supreme law. In such cases, therefore, the laws of the state legislatures must be repealed, restricted, or so construed, as to give full effect to the laws of the union on the same subject. From these remarks it is easy to see, that in proportion as the general government acquires power and jurisdiction, by the liberal construction which the judges may give the constitution, will those of the states lose its rights, until they become so trifling and unimportant, as not to be worth having. I am much mistaken, if this system will not operate to effect this with as much celerity, as those who have the administration of it will think prudent to suffer it. . . .

No. XIII [Article III, Section 2] extends its authority, to all cases, in law and equity, arising under the laws of the United States. This power, as I understand it, is a proper one. The proper province of the judicial power, in any government, is, as I conceive, to declare what is the law of the land. To explain and enforce those laws, which the supreme power or legislature may pass; but not to declare what the powers of the legislature are. I suppose the cases in equity, under the laws, must be so construed, as to give the supreme court not only a legal, but equitable jurisdiction of cases which may be brought before them, or in other words, so, as to give them, not only the powers which are now exercised by our courts of law, but those also, which are now exercised by our court of chancery. If this be the meaning, I have no other objection to the power, than what arises from the undue extension of the legislative power. For, I conceive that the judicial power should be commensurate with the legislative. Or, in other words, the supreme court should have authority to determine questions arising under the laws of the union.

. . . I presume every right which can be claimed under a treaty, must be claimed by virtue of some article or clause contained in it, which gives the right in plain and obvious words; or at least, I conceive, that the rules for explaining treaties, are so well ascertained, that there is no need of having recourse to an equitable construction. If under this power, the courts are to explain treaties, according to what they conceive are their spirit, which is nothing less than a power to give them whatever extension they may judge proper, it is a dangerous and improper power. The cases affecting ambassadors, public ministers, and consuls — of admiralty and maritime jurisdiction; controversies to which the United States are a party, and controversies between states, it is proper should be under the cognizance of the courts of the union, because none but the general government, can, or ought to pass laws on their subjects. But, I conceive the clause which extends the power of the judicial to controversies arising between a state and citizens of another state, improper in itself, and will, in its exercise, prove most pernicious and destructive.

It is improper, because it subjects a state to answer in a court of law, to the suit of an individual. This is humiliating and degrading to a government, and, what I believe, the supreme authority of no state ever submitted to.

The states are now subject to no such actions. All contracts entered into by individuals with states, were made upon the faith and credit of the states; and the individuals never had in contemplation any compulsory mode of obliging the government to fulfil its engagements.

The evil consequences that will flow from the exercise of this power, will best appear by tracing it in its operation. The constitution does not direct the mode in which an individual shall commence a suit against a state or the manner in which the judgement of the court shall be carried into execution, but it gives the legislature full power to pass all laws which shall be proper and necessary for the purpose. . . . We must, therefore, conclude that the legislature will pass laws which will be effectual in this head. An individual of one state will then have a legal remedy against a state for any demand he may have against a state to which he does not belong. Every state in the union is largely indebted to individuals. For the payment of these debts they have given notes payable to the bearer. At least this is the case in this state. Whenever a citizen of another state becomes possessed of one of these notes, he may commence an action in the supreme court of the general government; and I cannot see any way in which he can be prevented from recovering. It is easy to see, that when this once happens, the notes of the state will pass rapidly from the hands of citizens of the state to those of other states.

And when the citizens of other states possess them, they may bring suits against the state for them, and by this means, judgments and executions may be obtained against the state for the whole amount of the state debt. It is certain the state, with the utmost exertions it can make, will not be able to discharge the debt she owes, under a considerable number of years, perhaps with the best management, it will require twenty or thirty years to discharge it. This new system will protract the time in which the ability of the state will enable them to pay off their debt, because all the funds of the state will be transferred to the general government, except those which arise from internal taxes.

The situation of the states will be deplorable. By this system, they will surrender to the general government, all the means of raising money, and at the same time, will subject themselves to suits at law, for the recovery of the debts they have contracted in effecting the revolution.

The debts of the individual states will amount to a sum, exceeding the domestic debt of the United States; these will be left upon them, with power in the judicial of the general government, to enforce their payment, while the general government will possess an exclusive command of the most productive funds, from which the states can derive money, and a command of every other source of revenue paramount to the authority of any state.

. . . .

If the power of the judicial under this clause will extend to the cases above stated, it will, if executed, produce the utmost confusion, and in its progress, will crush the states beneath its weight. And if it does not extend to these cases, I confess myself utterly at a loss to give it any meaning. For if the citizen of one state, possessed of a written obligation, given in pursuance of a solemn act of the legislature, acknowledging a debt due to the bearer, and promising to pay it, cannot recover in the supreme court, I can conceive of no case in which they can recover. And it appears to me ridiculous to provide for obtaining judgment against a state, without giving the means of levying execution.

XIV

. . . .

The appellate jurisdiction granted to the supreme court, in [Article III, Section 2, paragraph 2], has justly been considered as one of the most objectionable parts of the constitution: under this power, appeals may be had from the inferior courts to the supreme, in every case to which the judicial power extends, except in the few instances in which the supreme court will have original jurisdiction.

By this article, appeals will lie to the supreme court, in all criminal as well as civil causes. . . . There is no criminal matter, to which the judicial power of the United States will extend; but such as are included under some one of the cases specified in this section. For this section is intended to define all the cases, of every description, to which the power of the judicial shall reach. But in all these cases it is declared, the supreme court shall have appellate jurisdiction, except in those which affect ambassadors, other public ministers and consuls, and those in which a state shall be a party. If then this section extends the power of the judicial, to criminal cases, it allows appeals in such cases. . . .

I believe it is a new and unusual thing to allow appeals in criminal matters. It is contrary to the sense of our laws, and dangerous to the lives and liberties of the citizen. As our law now stands, a person charged with a crime has a right to a fair and impartial trial by a jury of his country [sic], and their verdict is final. If he is acquitted no other court can call upon him to answer for the same crime. But by this system, a man may have had ever so fair a trial, have been acquitted by ever so respectable a jury of his country [sic]; and still the officer of the government who prosecutes, may appeal to the supreme court. The whole matter may have a second hearing. By this means, persons who may have disobliged those who execute the general government, may be subjected to intolerable oppression. They may be kept in long and ruinous confinement, and exposed to heavy and insupportable charges, to procure the attendence of witnesses, and provide the means of their defence, at a great distance from their places of residence.

I can scarcely believe there can be a considerate citizen of the United States, that will approve of this appellate jurisdiction, as extending to criminal cases, if they will give themselves time for reflection.

Whether the appellate jurisdiction as it respects civil matters, will not prove injurious to the rights of the citizens, and destructive of those privileges which have ever been held sacred by Americans, and whether it will not render the administration of justice intolerably burdensome, intricate, and dilatory, will best appear, when we have considered the nature and operation of this power.

It has been the fate of this clause, as it has of most of those, against which unanswerable objections have been offered, to be explained different ways, by the advocates and opponents to the constitution. I confess I do not know what the advocates of the system, would make it mean, for I have not been fortunate enough to see in any publication this clause taken up and considered. It is certain however, they do not admit the explanation which those who oppose the constitution give it, or otherwise they would not so frequently charge them with want of candor, for alleging that it takes away the trial by jury [—] appeals from an inferior to a superior court, as practiced in the civil law courts, are well understood. In these courts, the judges determine both on the law and the fact; and appeals are allowed from the inferior to the superior courts, on the whole merits: the superior tribunal will re-examine all the facts as well as the law, and frequently new facts will be introduced, so as many times to render the cause in the court of appeals very different from what it was in the court below.

If the appellate jurisdiction of the supreme court, be understood in the above sense, the term is perfectly intelligible. The meaning then is, that in all the civil causes enumerated, the supreme court shall have authority to re-examine the whole merits of the case, both with respect to the facts and the law which may arise under it, without the intervention of a jury; that this is the sense of this part of the system appears to me clear, from the express words of it, "in all the other cases before mentioned, the supreme court shall have appellate jurisdiction, both as to law and fact, &c." Who are the supreme court? Does it not consist of the judges? and they are to have the same jurisdiction of the fact as they are to have of the law. They will therefore have the same authority to determine the fact as they will have to determine the law, and no room is left for a jury on appeals to the supreme court.

If we understand the appellate jurisdiction in any other way, we shall be left utterly at a loss to give it a meaning; the common law is a stranger to any such jurisdiction: no appeals can lie from any of our common law courts, upon the merits of the case; the only way in which they can go up from an inferior to a superior tribunal is by habeas corpus before a hearing, or by certiorari, or writ of error, after they are determined in the subordinate courts; but in no case, when they are carried up, are the facts re-examined, but they are always taken as established in the inferior courts.

[continued]

It may still be insisted that this clause does not take away the trial by jury on appeals, but that this may be provided for by the legislature, under that paragraph which authorizes them to form regulations and restrictions for the court in the exercise of this power.

The natural meaning of this paragraph seems to be no more than this, that Congress may declare, that certain cases shall not be subject to the appellate jurisdiction, and they may point out the mode in which the court shall proceed in bringing up the causes before them, the manner of their taking evidence to establish the facts, and the method of the courts proceeding. But I presume they cannot take from the court the right of deciding on the fact, any more than they can deprive them of the right of determining on the law, when a cause is once before them; for they have the same jurisdiction as to fact, as they have as to the law. But supposing the Congress may under this clause establish the trial by jury on appeals, it does not seem to me that it will render this article much less exceptionable. An appeal from one court and jury, to another court and jury, is a thing altogether unknown in the laws of our state, and in most of the states in the union. A practice of this kind prevails in the eastern states . . . [and] this has proved so burdensome to the people in Massachusetts, that it was one of the principal causes which excited the insurrection in that state, in the year past; very few sensible and moderate men in that state but what will admit, that the inferior courts are almost entirely useless, and answer very little purpose, save only to accumulate costs against the poor debtors who are already unable to pay their just debts.

. . . .

. . . [I]t appears, that the administration of justice under the powers of the judicial will be dilatory; that it will be attended with such an heavy expense as to amount to little short of a denial of justice to the poor and middling class of people who in every government stand most in need of the protection of the law; and that the trial by jury, which has so justly been the boast of our fore fathers as well as ourselves is taken away under them.

These extraordinary powers in this court are the more objectionable, because there does not appear the least necessity for them, in order to secure a due and impartial distribution of justice.

The want of ability or integrity, or a disposition to render justice to every suitor, has not been objected against the courts of the respective states: so far as I have been informed, the courts of justice in all the states, have ever been found ready, to administer justice with promptitude and impartiality according to the laws of the land. . . .

. . . .

No pretext therefore, can be formed, from the conduct of the judicial courts which will justify giving such powers to the supreme general court, for their decisions have been such as to give just ground of confidence in them, that they will firmly adhere to the principles of rectitude, and there is no necessity of lodging these powers in the courts, in order to guard against the evils justly complained of, on the subject of security of property under this constitution. . . .

The courts of the respective states might therefore have been securely trusted, with deciding all cases between man and man, whether citizens of the same state or of different states, or between foreigners and citizens, and indeed for ought I see every case that can arise under the constitution or laws of the United States, ought in the first instance to be tried in the court of the state, except those which might arise between states, such as respect ambassadors, or other public ministers, and perhaps such as call in question the claim of lands under grants from different states. The state courts would be under sufficient control, if writs of error were allowed from the state courts to the supreme court of the union, according to the practice of the courts in England and of this state, on all cases in which the laws of the union are concerned, and perhaps to all cases in which a foreigner is a party.

This method would preserve the good old way of administering justice, would bring justice to every man's door, and preserve the inestimable right of trial by jury. It would be following, as near as our circumstances will admit, the practice of the courts in England, which is almost the only thing I would wish to copy in their government.

But as this system now stands, there is to be as many inferior courts as Congress may see fit to appoint, who are to be authorised to originate and in the first instance to try all the cases falling under the description of this article; there is no security that a trial by jury shall be had in these courts, but the trial here will soon become, as it is in Massachusetts' inferior courts, mere matter of form; for an appeal may be had to the supreme court on the whole merits. This court is to have power to determine in law and in equity, on the law and the fact, and this court is exalted above all other power in the government, subject to no control, and so fixed as not to be removable, but upon impeachment, which I shall hereafter shew, is much the same thing as not to be removable at all.

. . . .

The just way of investigating any power given to a government, is to examine its operation supposing it to be put in exercise. If upon enquiry, it appears that the power, if exercised, would be prejudicial, it ought not to be given. For to answer objections made to a power given to a government, by saying it will never be exercised, is really admitting that the power ought not to be exercised, and therefore ought not to be granted.

No. XV   I said in my last number, that the supreme court under this constitution would be exalted above all other power in the government, and subject to no control. . . .

The judges in England, it is true, hold their offices during their good behavior, but then their determinations are subject to correction by the house of lords; and their power is by no means so extensive as that of the proposed supreme court of the union. — I believe they in no instance assume the authority to set aside an act of parliament under the idea that it is inconsistent with their constitution. They consider themselves bound to decide according to the existing laws of the land, and never undertake to control them by adjudging that they are inconsistent with the constitution — much less are they vested with the power of giving an *equitable* construction to the constitution.

The judges in England are under the control of the legislature, for they are bound to determine according to the laws passed by them. But the judges under this constitution will controul the legislature, for the supreme court are authorised in the last resort, to determine what is the extent of the powers of the Congress; they are to give the constitution an explanation, and there is no power above them to set aside their judgment. The framers of this constitution appear to have followed that of the British, in rendering the judges independent, by granting them their offices during good behavior, without following the constitution of England, in instituting a tribunal in which their errors may be corrected; and without adverting to this, that the judicial under this system have a power which is above the legislative, and which indeed transcends any power before given to a judicial by any free government under heaven.

. . . There is no power above them, to control any of their decisions. There is no authority that can remove them, and they cannot be controlled by the laws of the legislature. In short, they are independent of the people, of the legislature, and of every power under heaven. . . .

The great reason assigned, why the judges in Britain ought to be commissioned during good behavior, is this, that they may be placed in a situation, not to be influenced by the crown, to give such decisions, as would tend to increase its powers and prerogatives. . . . But these reasons do not apply to this country, we have no hereditary monarch; those who appoint the judges do not hold their offices for life, nor do they descend to their children. The same arguments, therefore, which will conclude in favor of the tenor of the judge's offices for good behavior, lose a considerable part of their weight when applied to the state and condition of America. But much less can it be shown, that the nature of our government requires that the courts should be placed beyond all account more independent, so much so as to be above control.

I have said that the judges under this system will be *independent* in the strict sense of the word: To prove this I will shew — That there is no power above them that can control their decisions, or correct their errors. There is no authority that can remove them from office for any errors or want of capacity, or lower their salaries, and in many cases their power is superior to that of the legislature.

[First.] There is no power above them that can correct their errors or control their decisions — The adjudications of this court are final and irreversible, for there is no court above them to which appeals can lie, either in error or on the merits. — In this respect it differs from the courts in England, for there the house of lords is the highest court, to whom appeals, in error, are carried from the highest of the courts of law.

[Second.] They cannot be removed from office or suffer a diminution of their salaries, for any error in judgement or want of capacity.

. . . .

The only clause in the constitution which provides for the removal of judges from office, is that which declares, that "the president, vice-president, and all civil officers of the United States, shall be removed from office, on impeachment for, and conviction of treason, bribery, or other high crimes and misdemeanors." By this paragraph, civil officers, in which the judges are included, are removable only for crimes. . . . Errors in judgement, or want of capacity to discharge the duties of the office, can never be supposed to be included in these words, *high crimes and misdemeanors*. A man may mistake a case in giving judgment, or manifest that he is incompetent to the discharge of the duties of a judge, and yet give no evidence of corruption or want of integrity. To support the charge, it will be necessary to give in evidence some facts that will shew, that the judges committed the error from wicked and corrupt motives.

[Third.] The power of this court is in many cases superior to that of the legislature. I have shown, in a former paper, that this court will be authorised to decide upon the meaning of the constitution, and that, not only according to the natural and obvious meaning of the words, but also according to the spirit and intention of it. In the exercise of this power they will not be subordinate to, but above the legislature. For all the departments of this government will receive their powers, so far as they are expressed in the constitution, from the people immediately, who are the source of power. The legislature can only exercise such powers as are given them by the constitution, they cannot assume any of the rights annexed to the judicial, for this plain reason, that the same authority which vested the legislature with their powers, vested the judicial with theirs — both are derived from the same source, both therefore are equally valid, and the judicial hold their powers independently of the legislature, as the legislature do of the judicial. — The supreme court then have a right, independent of the legislature, to give a construction to the constitution and every part of it, and there is no power provided in this system to correct their construction or do it away. If, therefore, the legislature pass any laws, inconsistent with the sense the judges put upon the constitution, they will declare it void; and therefore in this respect their power is superior to that of the legislature. In England the judges are not only subject to have their decisions set aside by the house of lords, for error, but in cases where they give an explanation to the laws or constitution of the country, contrary to the sense of the parliament, though the parliament will not set aside the judgement of the court, yet, they have authority, by a new law, to explain a former one, and by this means to prevent a reception of such decisions. But no such power is in the legislature. The judges are supreme — and no law, explanatory of the constitution, will be binding on them.

. . . .

Perhaps nothing could have been better conceived to facilitate the abolition of the state governments than the constitution of the judicial. They will be able to extend the limits of the general government gradually, and by insensible degrees, and to accommodate themselves to the temper of the people. Their decisions on the meaning of the constitution will commonly take place in cases which arise between individuals, with which the public will not be generally acquainted; one adjudication will form a precedent to the next, and this to a following one. These cases will immediately affect individuals only; so that a series of determinations will probably take place before even the people will be informed of them. In the mean time all the art and address of those who wish for the change will be employed to make converts to their opinion. . . . In this situation, the general legislature, might pass one law after another, extending the general and abridging the state jurisdictions, and to sanction their proceedings would have a course of decisions of the judicial to whom the constitution has committed the power of explaining the constitution. — If the states remonstrated, the constitutional mode of deciding upon the validity of the law, is with the supreme court, and neither people, nor state legislatures, nor the general legislature can remove them or reverse their decrees.

Had the construction of the constitution been left with the legislature, they would have explained it at their peril; if they exceed their powers, or sought to find, in the spirit of the constitution, more than was expressed in the letter, the people from whom they derived their power could remove them, and do themselves right; and indeed I can see no other remedy that the people can have against their rulers for encroachments of this nature. A constitution is a compact of a people with their rulers; if the rulers break the compact, the people have a right and ought to remove them and do themselves justice; but in order to enable them to do this with the greater facility, those whom the people choose at stated periods, should have the power in the last resort to determine the sense of the compact; if they determine contrary to the understanding of the people, an appeal will lie to the people at the period when the rulers are to be elected, and they will have it in their power to remedy the evil; but when this power is lodged in the hands of men independent of the people, and of their representatives, and who are not, constitutionally, accountable for their opinions, no way is left to control them but *with a high hand and an outstretched arm.*

Brutus

Ratification Debates — Essays of Publius

No. 78 (Alexander Hamilton) *A View of the Constitution of the Judicial Department, in Relation to the Tenure of good Behavior*

We proceed now to an examination of the judiciary department of the proposed government.

In unfolding the defects of the existing confederation, the utility and necessity of a federal judicature have been clearly pointed out. . . . The only questions which have been raised being relative to the manner of constituting it, and to its extent. . . .

. . . .

According to the plan of the convention, all the judges who may be appointed by the United States are to hold their offices *during good behaviour* . . . . The standard of good behavior for the continuance in office of the judicial magistracy is certainly one of the most valuable of the modern improvements in the practice of government. In a monarchy it is an excellent barrier to the despotism of the prince: In a republic it is a no less excellent barrier to the encroachments and oppressions of the representative body. And it is the best expedient which can be devised in any government, to secure a steady, upright and impartial administration of the laws.

Whoever attentively considers the different departments of power must perceive, that in a government in which they are separated from each other, the judiciary, from the nature of its functions, will always be the least dangerous to the political rights of the constitution; because it will be least in a capacity to annoy or injure them. The executive not only dispenses the honors, but holds the sword of the community. The legislative not only commands the purse, but prescribes the rules by which the duties and rights of every citizen are to be regulated. The judiciary on the contrary has no influence over either the sword or the purse, no direction either of the strength or of the wealth of the society, and can take no active resolution whatever. It may truly be said to have neither FORCE NOR WILL, but merely judgment; and must ultimately depend upon the aid of the executive arm even for the efficacy of its judgments.

. . . I agree, that "there is no liberty, if the power of judging be not separated from the legislative and executive powers." And it proves, in the last place, that as liberty can have nothing to fear from the judiciary alone, but would have every thing to fear from its union with either of the other departments; that as all the effects of such a union must ensue from a dependence of the former on the latter, notwithstanding a nominal and apparent separation; that as from the natural feebleness of the judiciary, it is in continual jeopardy of being overpowered, awed or influenced by its co-ordinate branches; and that as nothing can contribute so much to its firmness and independence, as permanency in office, this quality may therefore be justly regarded as an indispensable ingredient in its constitution; and in a great measure, as the citadel of the public justice and the public security.

The complete independence of the courts of justice is peculiarly essential in a limited constitution. By a limited constitution I understand one which contains certain specified exceptions to the legislative authority; such for instance as that it shall pass no bills of attainder, no *ex post facto* laws, and the like. Limitations of this kind can be preserved in practice no other way than through the medium of the courts of justice; whose duty it must be to declare all acts contrary to the manifest tenor of the constitution void. Without this, all the reservations of particular rights or privileges would amount to nothing.

Some perplexity respecting the right of the courts to pronounce legislative acts void, because contrary to the constitution, has arisen from an imagination that the doctrine would imply a superiority of the judiciary to the legislative power. It is urged that the authority which can declare the acts of another void, must necessarily be superior to the one whose acts may be declared void. As this doctrine is of great importance in all the American constitutions, a brief discussion of the grounds on which it rests cannot be unacceptable.

There is no position which depends on clearer principles, than that every act of a delegated authority, contrary to the tenor of the commission under which it is exercised, is void. No legislative act therefore contrary to the constitution can be valid. To deny this would be to affirm that the deputy is greater than his principal; that the servant is above his master; that the representatives of the people are superior to the people themselves; that men acting by virtue of powers may do not only what their powers do not authorize, but what they forbid.

If it be said that the legislative body are themselves the constitutional judges of their own powers, and that the construction they put upon them is conclusive upon the other departments, it may be answered, that this cannot be the natural presumption, where it is not to be collected from any particular provisions in the constitution. It is not otherwise to be supposed that the constitution could intend to enable the representatives of the people to substitute their *will* to that of their constituents. It is far more rational to suppose that the courts were designed to be an intermediate body between the people and the legislature, in order, among other things, to keep the latter within the limits assigned to their authority. The interpretation of the laws is the proper and peculiar province of the courts. A constitution is in fact, and must be, regarded by the judges as a fundamental law. It therefore belongs to them to ascertain its meaning as well as the meaning of any particular act proceeding from the legislative body. If there should happen to be an irreconcilable variance between the two, that which has the superior obligation and validity ought of course to be preferred; or in other words, the constitution ought to be preferred to the statute, the intention of the people to the intention of their agents.

. . . .

This exercise of judicial discretion in determining between two contradictory laws, is exemplified in a familiar instance. It not uncommonly happens, that there are two statutes existing at one time, clashing in whole or in part with each other . . . . So far as they can by any fair construction be reconciled to each other; reason and law conspire to dictate that this should be done: Where this is impracticable, it becomes a matter of necessity to give effect to one, in the exclusion of the other. . . .

But in regard to the interfering acts of a superior and subordinate authority, of an original and derivative power, the nature and reason of the thing . . . teach us that the prior act of a superior ought to be preferred to the subsequent act of an inferior and subordinate authority; and that, accordingly, whenever a particular statute contravenes the constitution, it will be the duty of the judicial tribunals to adhere to the latter, and disregard the former.

It can be of no weight to say, that the courts on the pretense of a repugnancy, may substitute their own pleasure to the constitutional intentions of the legislature. . . .

. . . .

This independence of the judges is equally requisite to guard the constitution and the rights of individuals from the effects of those ill humors which the arts of designing men, or the influence of particular conjunctures sometimes disseminate among the people themselves, and which, though they speedily give place to better information and more deliberate reflection, have a tendency in the mean time to occasion dangerous innovations in the government, and serious oppressions of the minor party in the community. . . . Until the people have by some solemn and authoritative act annulled or changed the established form, it is binding upon themselves collectively, as well as individually; and no presumption, or even knowledge of their sentiments, can warrant their representatives in a departure from it, prior to such an act. But it is easy to see that it would require an uncommon portion of fortitude in the judges to do their duty as faithful guardians of the constitution, where legislative invasions of it had been instigated by the major voice of the community.

But it is not with a view to infractions of the constitution only that the independence of the judges may be an essential safeguard against the effects of occasional ill humors in the society. These sometimes extend no farther than to the injury of the private rights of particular classes of citizens, by unjust and partial laws. . . .

That inflexible and uniform adherence to the rights of the constitution and of individuals, which we perceive to be indispensable in the courts of justice, can certainly not be expected from judges who hold their offices by a temporary commission. Periodical appointments, however regulated, or by whomsoever made, would in some way or other be fatal to their necessary independence. If the power of making them was committed either to the executive or legislative, there would be danger of an improper complaisance to the branch which possessed it; if to both, there would be an unwillingness to hazard the displeasure of either; if to the people, or to persons chosen by them for the special purpose, there would be too great a disposition to consult popularity, to justify a reliance that nothing would be consulted but the constitution and the laws.

There is yet a further and a weightier reason for the permanency of the judicial offices; which is deducible from the nature of the qualifications they require. . . . To avoid an arbitrary discretion in the courts, it is indispensable that they should be bound down by strict rules and precedents, which serve to define and point out their duty in every particular case that comes before them . . . that the records of those precedents must unavoidably swell to a very considerable bulk, and must demand long and laborious study to acquire a competent knowledge of them. Hence it is that there can be but few men in the society, who will have sufficient skill in the laws to qualify them for the stations of judges. . . . [In addition,] a temporary duration in office, which would naturally discourage such characters from quitting a lucrative line of practice to accept a seat on the bench, would have a tendency to throw the administration of justice into hands less able, and less well qualified to conduct it with utility and dignity. . . .

Upon the whole there can be no room to doubt that the convention acted wisely in copying from the models of those constitutions which have established *good behavior* as the tenure of their judicial offices in point of duration; and that so far from being blameable on this account, their plan would have been inexcusably defective if it had wanted this important feature of good government. . . .

No. 79 (Alexander Hamilton) *A further View of the Judicial Department, in Relation to the Provisions for the Support and Responsibility of the Judges.*

Next to permanency in office, nothing can contribute more to the independence of the judges than a fixed provision for their support. . . . The plan of the convention accordingly has provided, that the judges of the United States "shall at *stated times* receive for their services a compensation, which shall not be *diminished* during their continuance in office."

. . . It will readily be understood that the fluctuations in the value of money, and in the state of society rendered a fixed rate of compensation in the constitution inadmissible. . . . It will be observed that a difference has been made by the convention between the compensation of the president and of the judges. That of the former can neither be increased nor diminished. That of the latter can only not be diminished. This probably arose from the difference in the duration of the respective offices. . . . [W]ith regard to the judges, who, if they behave properly, will be secured in their places for life, it may well happen, especially in the early stages of the government, that a stipend, which would be very sufficient at their first appointment, would become too small in the progress of their service.

. . . .

The precautions for their responsibility are comprised in the article respecting impeachments. They are liable to be impeached for malconduct by the house of representatives, and tried by the senate, and if convicted, may be dismissed from office and disqualified for holding any other. This is the only provision on the point, which is consistent with the necessary independence of the judicial character, and is the only one which we find in our own constitution in respect to our own judges.

The want of a provision for removing the judges on account of inability, has been a subject of complaint. But all considerate men will be sensible that such a provision would either not be practiced upon, or would be more liable to abuse than calculated to answer any good purpose. . . .

. . . In a republic, where fortunes are not affluent, and pensions not expedient, the dismiss[al] of men from stations in which they have served their country long and usefully, on which they depend for subsistence, and from which it will be too late to resort to any other occupation for a livelihood, ought to have some better apology to humanity, than is to be found in the imaginary danger of a superannuated bench.

No. 80 (Alexander Hamilton) *A further View of the Judicial Department, in Relation to the Extent of its Powers.*

To judge with accuracy of the proper extent of the federal judicature, it will be necessary to consider in the first place what are its proper objects.

It seems scarcely to admit of controversy that the judiciary authority of the union ought to extend to these several descriptions of causes: [First], to all those which arise out of the laws of the United States, passed in pursuance of their just and constitutional powers of legislation; [Second], to all those which concern the execution of the provisions expressly contained in the articles of union; [Third], to all those in which the United States are a party; [Fourth], to all those which involve the PEACE of the CONFEDERACY, whether they relate to the intercourse between the United States and foreign nations, or to that between the States themselves; [Fifth], to all those which originate on the high seas, and are of admiralty or maritime jurisdiction; and lastly, to all those in which the state tribunals cannot be supposed to be impartial and unbiased.

The first point depends upon this obvious consideration that there ought always to be a constitutional method of giving efficacy to constitutional provisions. . . . The states, by the plan of the convention are prohibited from doing a variety of things; some of which are incompatible with the interests of the union, and others with the principles of good government. . . . No man of sense will believe that such prohibitions would be scrupulously regarded, without some effectual power in the government to restrain or correct the infractions of them. This power must either be a direct negative on the state laws, or an authority in the federal courts, to over-rule such as might be in manifest contravention of the articles of union. There is no third course that I can imagine. The latter appears to have been thought by the convention preferable to the former, and I presume will be most agreeable to the states.

As to the second point, it is impossible by any argument or comment to make it clearer than it is in itself. If there are such things as political axioms, the propriety of the judicial power of a government being coextensive with its legislative, may be ranked among the number. The mere necessity of uniformity in the interpretation of the national laws, decides the question. Thirteen independent courts of final jurisdiction over the same causes, arising upon the same laws, is a hydra in government, from which nothing but contradiction and confusion can proceed.

Still less need be said in regard to the third point. Controversies between the nation and its members or citizens, can only be properly referred to the national tribunals. Any other plan would be contrary to reason, to precedent, and to decorum.

The fourth point rests on this plain proposition, that the peace of the WHOLE ought not to be left at the disposal of a PART. The union will undoubtedly be answerable to foreign powers for the conduct of its members. And the responsibility for an injury ought ever to be accompanied with the faculty of preventing it. As the denial or perversion of justice by the sentences of courts, as well as in any other manner, is with reason classed among the just causes of war, it will follow that the federal judiciary ought to have cognizance of all causes in which the citizens of other countries are concerned. . . .

The power of determining causes between two states, between one state and the citizens of another, and between the citizens of different states, is perhaps not less essential to the peace of the union than that which has been just examined. . . .

A method of terminating territorial disputes between the states, under the authority of the federal head, was not unattended to, even in the imperfect system by which they have been hitherto held together. But there are many other sources, besides interfering claims of boundary, from which bickerings and animosities may spring up among the members of the union. . . . Whatever practices may have a tendency to disturb the harmony between the states, are proper objects of federal superintendence and control.

. . . .

The fifth point will demand little animadversion. The most bigoted idolizers of state authority have not thus far shown a disposition to deny the national judiciary the cognizance of maritime causes. These so generally depend on the laws of nations, and so commonly affect the rights of foreigners, that they fall within the considerations which are relative to the public peace. The most important part of them are by the present confederation submitted to federal jurisdiction.

The reasonableness of the agency of the national courts in cases in which the state tribunals cannot be supposed to be impartial, speaks for itself. . . . Claims to land under grants of different states, founded upon adverse pretensions of boundary, are of this description. The courts of neither of the granting states could be expected to be unbiased. The laws may have even prejudged the question, and tied the courts down to decisions in favor of the grants of the state to which they belonged. And even where this had not been done, it would be natural that the judges, as men, should feel a strong predilection to the claims of their own government.

Having thus laid down and discussed the principles which ought to regulate the constitution of the federal judiciary, we will proceed to test, by these principles, the particular powers of which, according to the plan of the convention, it is to be composed. . . .

First. To all cases in law and equity *arising under the constitution* and *the laws of the United States.* . . . It has been asked, what is meant by "cases arising under the constitution," in contradistinction from those "arising under the laws of the United States"? The difference has been already explained. All the restrictions upon the authority of the state legislatures, furnish examples of it. They are not, for instance, to emit paper money; but the interdiction results from the constitution, and will have no connection with any law of the United States. Should paper money, notwithstanding, be emitted, the controversies concerning it would be cases arising under the constitution and not the laws of the United States, in the ordinary signification of the terms. This may serve as a sample of the whole.

It has also been asked, what need of the word "equity"? . . . There is hardly a subject of litigation between individuals, which may not involve those ingredients of *fraud, accident, trust,* or *hardship,* which would render the matter an object of equitable, rather than of legal jurisdiction, as the distinction is known and established in several of the states. It is the peculiar province, for instance, of a court of equity to relieve against what are called hard bargains . . . .

. . . .

From this review of the particular powers of the federal judiciary, as marked out in the constitution, it appears, that they are all conformable to the principles which ought to have governed the structure of that department, and which were necessary to the perfection of the system. If some partial inconveniences should appear to be connected with the incorporation of any of them into the plan, it ought to be recollected that the national legislature will have ample authority to make such *exceptions* and to prescribe such regulations as will be calculated to obviate or remove these inconveniences. . . .

No. 81 (Alexander Hamilton) *A further View of the Judicial Department, in Relation to the Distribution of its Authority.*

Let us now return to the partition of the judiciary authority between different courts, and their relations to each other.

. . . .

That there ought to be one court of supreme and final jurisdiction is a proposition which has not been, and is not likely to be contested. . . . The only question that seems to have been raised concerning it, is whether it ought to be a distinct body or a branch of the legislature. The same contradiction is observable in regard to this matter, which has been remarked in several other cases. The very men who object to the senate as a court of impeachments, on the ground of an improper intermixture of powers, advocate, by implication at least, the propriety of vesting the ultimate decision of all causes in the whole, or in a part of the legislative body.

The arguments, or rather suggestions, upon which this charge is founded, are to this effect: "The authority of the proposed supreme court of the United States, which is to be a separate and independent body, will be superior to that of the legislature. The power of construing the laws, according to the *spirit* of the constitution, will enable that court to mold them into whatever shape it may think proper; especially as its decisions will not be in any manner subject to the revision or correction of the legislative body. This is as unprecedented as it is dangerous. . . . [T]he errors and usurpations of the supreme court of the United States will be uncontrollable and remediless." This, upon examination, will be found to be made up altogether of false reasoning upon misconceived fact.

In the first place, there is not a syllable in the plan under consideration which *directly* empowers the national courts to construe the laws according to the spirit of the constitution, or which gives them any greater latitude in this respect, than may be claimed by the courts of every State. I admit however, that the constitution ought to be the standard of construction for the laws, and that wherever there is an evident opposition, the laws ought to give place to the constitution. . . .

But perhaps the force of the objection may be thought to consist in the particular organization of the proposed supreme court; in its being composed of a distinct body of magistrates, instead of being one of the branches of the legislature, as in the government of Great Britain and that of this state. To insist upon this point, the authors of the objection must renounce the meaning they have labored to annex to the celebrated maxim, requiring a separation of the departments of power. . . . From a body which had even a partial agency in passing bad laws, we could rarely expect a disposition to temper and moderate them in the application. . . . Still less could it be expected, that men who had infringed the constitution, in the character of legislators, would be disposed to repair the breach in the character of judges. Nor is this all: — Every reason, which recommends the tenure of good behavior for judicial offices, militates against placing the judiciary power in the last resort in a body composed of men chosen for a limited period. . . . And there is a still greater absurdity in subjecting the decisions of men selected for their knowledge of the laws, acquired by long and laborious study, to the revision and control of men, who for want of the same advantage cannot but be deficient in that knowledge. . . . [O]n account of the natural propensity of such bodies to party divisions, there will be no less reason to fear, that the pestilential breath of faction may poison the fountains of justice. . . .

. . . .

. . . The theory, neither of the British, nor the State constitutions, authorizes the revisal of a judicial sentence, by a legislative act. Nor is there any thing in the proposed constitution more than in either of them, by which it is forbidden. In the former as well as in the latter, the impropriety of the thing, on the general principles of law and reason, is the sole obstacle. A legislature without exceeding its province cannot reverse a determination once made, in a particular case; though it may prescribe a new rule for future cases. This is the principle, and it applies in all its consequences, exactly in the same manner and extent, to the state governments, as to the national government, now under consideration. Not the least difference can be pointed out in any view of the subject.

. . . .

Having now examined, and I trust removed the objections to the distinct and independent organization of the supreme court, I proceed to consider the propriety of the power of constituting inferior courts, and the relations which will subsist between these and the former.

. . . .

I am not sure but that it will be found highly expedient and useful to divide the United States into four or five, or half a dozen districts; and to institute a federal court in each district, in lieu of one in every state. The judges of these courts, with the aid of the state judges, may hold circuits for the trial of causes in the several parts of the respective districts. Justice through them may be administered with ease and dispatch; and appeals may be safely circumscribed within a very narrow compass. This plan appears to me at present the most eligible of any that could be adopted, and in order to it, it is necessary that the power of constituting inferior courts should exist in the full extent in which it is to be found in the proposed constitution.

. . . .

The supreme court is to be invested with original jurisdiction, only "in cases affecting ambassadors, other public ministers and consuls, and those in which a STATE shall be a party." . . . In cases in which a state might happen to be a party, it would ill suit its dignity to be turned over to an inferior tribunal.

Though it may rather be a digression from the immediate subject of this paper, I shall take occasion to mention here, a supposition which has excited some alarm upon very mistaken grounds: It has been suggested that an assignment of the public securities of one state to the citizens of another, would enable them to prosecute that state in the federal courts for the amount of those securities. A suggestion which the following considerations prove to be without foundation.

It is inherent in the nature of sovereignty, not to be amenable to the suit of an individual *without its consent*. This is the general sense and the general practice of mankind; and the exemption, as one of the attributes of sovereignty, is now enjoyed by the government of every state in the union. Unless therefore, there is a surrender of this immunity in the plan of the convention, it will remain with the states, and the danger intimated must be merely ideal. The circumstances which are necessary to produce an alienation of state sovereignty, were discussed in considering the article of taxation, and need not be repeated here. A recurrence to the principles there established will satisfy us, that there is no color to pretend that the state governments, would by the adoption of that plan, be divested of the privilege of paying their own debts in their own way, free from every constraint but that which flows from the obligations of good faith. The contracts between a nation and individuals are only binding on the conscience of the sovereign, and have no pretensions to a compulsive force. They confer no right of action, independent of the sovereign will. To what purpose would it be to authorize suits against states, for the debts they owe? How could recoveries be enforced? It is evident that it could not be done without waging war against the contracting state; and to ascribe to the federal courts, by mere implication, and in destruction of a pre-existing right of the state governments, a power which would involve such a consequence, would be altogether forced and unwarrantable.

. . . .

. . . The appellate jurisdiction of the supreme court (may it have been argued) will extend to causes determinable in different modes, some in the course of the COMMON LAW, and others in the course of the *civil law*. In the former, the revision of the law only, will be, generally speaking, the proper province of the supreme court; in the latter, the re-examination of the fact is agreeable to usage, and in some cases, of which prize causes are an example, might be essential to the preservation of the public peace. It is therefore necessary, that the appellate jurisdiction should, in certain cases, extend in the broadest sense to matters of fact. It will not answer to make an express exception of cases, which shall have been originally tried by a jury, because in the courts of some of the states, *all causes* are tried in this mode; and such an exception would preclude the revision of matters of fact, as well where it might be proper, as where it might be improper. To avoid all inconveniences, it will be safest to declare generally, that the supreme court shall possess appellate jurisdiction, both as to law and *fact*, and that this jurisdiction shall be subject to such *exceptions* and regulations as the national legislature may prescribe. This will enable the government to modify it in such a manner as will best answer the ends of public justice and security.

. . . The legislature of the United States would certainly have full power to provide that in appeals to the supreme court there should be no re-examination of facts where they had been tried in the original causes by juries. . . .

The amount of the observations hitherto made on the authority of the judicial department is this — that it has been carefully restricted to those causes which are manifestly proper for the cognizance of the national judicature, that in the partition of this authority a very small portion of original jurisdiction has been reserved to the supreme court, and the rest consigned to the subordinate tribunals — that the supreme court will possess an appellate jurisdiction both as to law and fact in all the cases referred to them, both subject to any *exceptions* and *regulations* which may be thought advisable; that this appellate jurisdiction does in no case *abolish* the trial by jury, and that an ordinary degree of prudence and integrity in the national councils will insure us solid advantages from the establishment of the proposed judiciary, without exposing us to any of the inconveniences which have been predicted from that source.

The First Congress

One of the most important tasks of the First Congress was to enact legislation providing for federal offices other than those elected under provisions in the Constitution itself. That is, except for the President (George Washington), Vice President (John Adams), and members of the Senate and House of Representatives, there were no other offices — let alone individuals serving as "officers" — in the federal government.

Exercise 5:

Examine the following statutes establishing the first Departments and the federal judiciary. They are presented here in chronological order of enactment.

(1)   Examine the constitutional text pertinent to the creation of federal offices and the designation of persons to fill such offices. Do these statutes enacted by the First Congress comply with the Constitution?

(2)   What is the significance of the specified manner of appointment to, and removal from, office?

(3)   What is the significance, if any, of denominating an entity a "Department" or an "Executive Department"?

(4)   Re-examine the constitutional text pertinent to the federal judicial power and the Federal Judiciary Act of 1789 (the final statute in this chapter). This statute was the first bill in the first session of the Senate. The bill was drafted by a Senator who had been a delegate to the Constitutional Convention. Is the 1789 Act consistent with the Constitution?

(5)   Does the Federal Judiciary Act of 1789 authorize the federal judiciary to exercise the full scope of power permitted by the Constitution? Does the Act exceed the scope of power permitted by the Constitution?

(6)   Reconsider the questions regarding judicial power posed in Exercises 3 and 4. Does the 1789 Act change your answers to any of the questions? Should it? For an example of recent scholarship relying on the practice of the First Congress to illuminate the original meaning of the Constitution, see Lee J. Strang, *Originalism, the Declaration of Independence, and the Constitution: A Unique Role in Constitutional Interpretation?*, 111 PENN. ST. L. REV. 413, 473–74 (2006).

AN ACT FOR ESTABLISHING AN EXECUTIVE DEPARTMENT, TO BE DENOMINATED THE DEPARTMENT OF FOREIGN AFFAIRS.

Section 1.   *Be it enacted by the Senate and House of Representatives of the United States of America in Congress assembled,* That there shall be an Executive department, to be denominated the Department of Foreign Affairs, and that there shall be a principal officer therein, to be called the Secretary for the Department of Foreign Affairs, who shall perform and execute such duties as shall from time to time be enjoined on or intrusted to him by the President of the United States, agreeable to the Constitution, relative to correspondences, commissions or instructions to or with public ministers or consuls, from the United States, or to negotiations with public ministers from foreign states or princes, or to memorials or other applications from foreign public ministers or other foreigners, or to such other matters respecting foreign affairs, as the President of the United States shall assign to the said department; and furthermore, that the said principal officer shall conduct the business of the said department in such manner as the President of the United States shall from time to time order or instruct.

Section 2. *And be it further enacted,* That there shall be in the said department, an inferior officer, to be appointed by the said principal officer, and to be employed therein as he shall deem proper, and to be called the chief Clerk in the Department of Foreign Affairs, and who, whenever the said principal officer shall be removed from office by the President of the United States, or in any other case of vacancy, shall during such vacancy have the charge and custody of all records, books and papers appertaining to the said department.

Section 3. *And be it further enacted,* That the said principal officer, and every other person to be appointed or employed in the said department, shall, before he enters on the execution of his office or employment, take an oath or affirmation, well and faithfully to execute the trust committed to him.

Section 4. *And be it further enacted,* That the Secretary for the Department of Foreign Affairs, to be appointed in consequence of this act, shall forthwith after his appointment, be entitled to have the custody and charge of all records, books and papers in the office of Secretary for the Department of Foreign Affairs, heretofore established by the United States in Congress assembled.

Approved: July 27, 1789 — 1 Stat. 28

AN ACT TO ESTABLISH THE TREASURY DEPARTMENT.

Section 1. *Be it enacted by the Senate and House of Representatives of the United States of America in Congress assembled,* That there shall be a Department of Treasury, in which shall be the following officers, namely: a Secretary of the Treasury, to be deemed head of the department; a Comptroller, an Auditor, a Treasurer, a Register, and an Assistant to the Secretary of the Treasury, which assistant shall be appointed by the said Secretary.

Section 2. *And be it further enacted,* That it shall be the duty of the Secretary of the Treasury to digest and prepare plans for the improvement and management of the revenue, and for the support of public credit; to prepare and report estimates of the public revenue, and the public expenditures; to superintend the collection of revenue; to decide on the forms of keeping and stating accounts and making returns, and to grant under the limitations herein established, or to be hereafter provided, all warrants for monies to be issued from the Treasury, in pursuance of appropriations by law; to execute such services relative to the sale of the lands belonging to the United States, as may be by law required of him; to make report, and give information to either branch of the legislature, in person or in writing (as he may be required), respecting all matters referred to him by the Senate or House of Representatives, or which shall appertain to his office; and generally to perform all such services relative to the finances, as he shall be directed to perform.

Section 3. *And be it further enacted,* That it shall be the duty of the Comptroller to superintend the adjustment and preservation of the public accounts; to examine all accounts settled by the Auditor, and certify the balances arising thereon to the Register; to countersign all warrants drawn by the Secretary of the Treasury, which shall be warranted by law; to report to the Secretary the official forms of all papers to be issued in the different offices for collecting the public revenue, and the manner and form of keeping and stating the accounts of the several persons employed therein. He shall moreover provide for the regular and punctual payment of all monies which may be collected, and shall direct prosecutions for all delinquencies of officers of the revenue, and for debts that are, or shall be due to the United States.

Section 4. *And be it further enacted,* That it shall be the duty of the Treasurer to receive and keep the monies of the United States, and to disburse the same upon warrants drawn by the Secretary of the Treasury, countersigned by the Comptroller, recorded by the Register, and not otherwise . . . .

Section 5. *And be it further enacted,* That it shall be the duty of the Auditor to receive all public accounts, and after examination to certify the balance, and transmit the accounts with the vouchers and certificate to the Comptroller for his decision thereon: *Provided,* That if any person whose account shall be so audited, be dissatisfied therewith, he may within six months appeal to the Comptroller against such settlement.

Section 6. *And be it further enacted,* That it shall be the duty of the Register to keep all accounts of the receipts and expenditures of the public money . . . .

Section 7. *And be it further enacted,* That whenever the Secretary shall be removed from office by the President of the United States, or in any other case of vacancy in the office of Secretary, the Assistant shall, during the vacancy, have the charge and custody of the records, books, and papers appertaining to the said office.

Section 8. *And be it further enacted,* That no person appointed to any office instituted by this act, shall directly or indirectly be concerned or interested in carrying on the business of trade or commerce, or be owner in whole or in part of any sea-vessel, or purchase by himself, or another in trust for him, any public lands or other public property, or be concerned in the purchase or disposal of any public securities of any State, or of the United States, or take or apply to his own use, any emolument or gain for negotiating or transacting any business in the said department, other than what shall be applied by law; and if any person shall offend against any of the prohibitions of this act, he shall be deemed guilty of a high misdemeanor, and forfeit to the United States the penalty of three thousand dollars, and shall upon conviction be removed from office, and forever thereafter incapable of holding any office under the United States: *Provided,* That if any other person than a public prosecutor shall give information of any such offence, upon which a prosecution and conviction shall be had, one half the aforesaid penalty of three thousand dollars, when recovered, shall be for the use of the person giving such information.

Approved: September 2, 1789 — 1 Stat. 65

AN ACT TO PROVIDE FOR THE SAFE-KEEPING OF THE ACTS, RECORDS AND SEAL OF THE UNITED STATES, AND FOR OTHER PURPOSES.

Section 1. *Be enacted by the Senate and House of Representatives of the United States of America in Congress assembled,* That the Executive department, denominated the Department of Foreign Affairs, shall hereafter be denominated the Department of State, and the principal officer therein shall hereafter be called the Secretary of State.

Section 2. *And be it further enacted,* That whenever a bill, order, resolution, or vote of the Senate and House of Representatives, having been approved and signed by the President of the United States, or not having been returned by him with his objections, shall become a law, or take effect, it shall forthwith thereafter be received by the said Secretary from the President; and whenever a bill, order, resolution, or vote, shall be returned by the President with his objections, and shall, on being reconsidered, be agreed to be passed, and be approved by two-thirds of both Houses of Congress, and thereby become a law or take effect, it shall, in such case, be received by the said Secretary from the President of the Senate, or the Speaker of the House of Representatives, in whichsoever House it shall last have been so approved; and the said Secretary shall, as soon as conveniently may be, after he shall receive the same, cause every such law, order, resolution, and vote, to be published in at least three of the public newspapers printed within the United States, and shall also cause one printed copy to be delivered to each Senator and Representative of the United States, and two printed copies duly authenticated to be sent to the Executive authority of each State; and he shall carefully preserve the originals, and shall cause the same to be recorded in books to be provided for the purpose.

Section 3.   *And be it further enacted,* That the seal heretofore used by the United States in Congress assembled, shall be, and hereby is declared to be, the seal of the United States.

Section 4.   *And be it further enacted,* That the said Secretary shall keep the said seal, and shall make out and record, and shall affix the said seal to all civil commissions, to officers of the United States, to be appointed by the President by and with the advice and consent of the Senate, or by the President alone. *Provided,* That the said seal not be affixed to any commission, before the same shall have been signed by the President of the United States, nor to any other instrument or act, without the special warrant of the President therefor.

Section 5.   *And be it further enacted,* That the said Secretary shall cause a seal of office to be made for the said department of such device as the President of the United States shall approve, and all copies of records and papers in the said office, authenticated under the said seal, shall be evidence equally as the original record or paper.

Section 6.   *And be it further enacted,* That there shall be paid to the Secretary, for the use of the United States, the following fees of office . . . .

Section 7.   *And be it further enacted,* That the Secretary shall forthwith after his appointment be entitled to have the custody and charge of the said seal of the United States, and also of all books, records and papers, remaining in the office of the late Secretary of the United States in Congress assembled; and such of the said books, records and papers, as may appertain to the Treasury department, or War department, shall be delivered over to the principal officers in the said departments respectively, as the President of the United States shall direct.

Approved: September 15, 1789 — 1 Stat. 68

AN ACT TO ESTABLISH THE JUDICIAL COURTS OF THE UNITED STATES.

Section 1.   *Be it enacted by the Senate and House of Representatives of the United States of America in Congress assembled,* That the supreme court of the United States shall consist of a chief justice and five associate justices, any four of whom shall be a quorum, and shall hold annually at the seat of government two sessions, the one commencing the first Monday of February, and the other the first Monday of August. That the associate justices shall have precedence according to the date of their commissions . . . .

Section 2.   *And be it further enacted,* That the United States shall be and they hereby are divided into thirteen districts . . . .

Section 3.   *And be it further enacted,* That there be a court called a District Court, in each of the afore mentioned districts, to consist of one judge, who shall reside in the district for which he is appointed, and shall be called a District Judge, and shall hold annually four sessions . . . .

Section 4.   *And be it further enacted,* That the before mentioned districts . . . shall be divided into three circuits, and be called the eastern, middle, and the southern circuit. . . . [T]here shall be held annually in each district of said circuits, two courts, which shall be called Circuit Courts, and shall consist of any two justices of the Supreme Court, and the district judge of such districts, any two of whom shall constitute a quorum: *Provided,* That no district judge shall give a vote in any case of appeal or error from his own decision . . . .

. . . .

Section 7.   *And be it further enacted,* That the Supreme Court, and the district courts shall have power to appoint clerks for their respective courts . . . . And the said clerks shall also severally give bond, with sufficient sureties, (to be approved of by the Supreme and district courts respectively) to the United States, in the sum of two thousand dollars, faithfully to discharge the duties of his office, and seasonably to record the decrees, judgments and determinations of the court of which he is clerk.

. . . .

Section 9.   *And be it further enacted,* That the district courts shall have, exclusively of the courts of the several States, cognizance of all crimes and offences that shall be cognizable under the authority of the United States, committed within their respective districts, or upon the high seas; where no other punishment than whipping, not exceeding thirty stripes, a fine not exceeding one hundred dollars, or a term of imprisonment not exceeding six months, is to be inflicted; and shall also have exclusive original cognizance of all civil causes of admiralty and maritime jurisdiction . . .; and shall also have exclusive original cognizance of all seizures on land, or other waters than as aforesaid, made, and of all suits for penalties and forfeitures incurred, under the laws of the United States. And shall also have cognizance, concurrent with the courts of the several States, or the circuit courts, as the case may be, of all causes where an alien sues for a tort only in violation of the law of nations or a treaty of the United States. And shall also have cognizance, concurrent as last mentioned, of all suits at common law where the United States sue, and the matter in dispute amounts, exclusive of costs, to the sum of one hundred dollars. And shall also have jurisdiction exclusively of the courts of the several States, of all suits against consuls or vice-consuls, except for offences above the description aforesaid. And the trial of issues in fact, in the district courts, in all causes except civil causes of admiralty and maritime jurisdiction, shall be by jury.

. . . .

Section 11.   *And be it further enacted,* That the circuit courts shall have original cognizance, concurrent with the courts of the several States, of all suits of a civil nature at common law or in equity, where the matter in dispute exceeds, exclusive of costs, the sum or value of five hundred dollars, and the United States are plaintiffs, or petitioners; or an alien is a party, or the suit is between a citizen of the State where the suit is brought, and a citizen of another State. And shall have exclusive cognizance of all crimes and offences cognizable under the authority of the United States, except where this act otherwise provides, or the laws of the United States shall otherwise direct, and concurrent jurisdiction with the district courts of the crimes and offences cognizable therein. But no person shall be arrested in one district for trial in another . . . . And no civil suit shall be brought before either of said courts against an inhabitant of the United States, by any original process in any other district than that whereof he is an inhabitant, or in which he shall be found at the time of serving the writ, nor shall any district or circuit court have cognizance of any suit to recover the contents of any promissory note or other chose in action in favour of an assignee, unless a suit might have been prosecuted in such court to recover the said contents if no assignment had been made, except in cases of foreign bills of exchange. And the circuit courts shall also have appellate jurisdiction from the district courts under the regulations and restrictions herein after provided.

Section 12.   *And be it further enacted,* That if a suit be commenced in any state court against an alien, or by a citizen of the state in which the suit is brought against a citizen of another state, and the matter in dispute exceeds the aforesaid sum or value of five hundred dollars, exclusive of costs, to be made to appear to the satisfaction of the court; and the defendant shall, at the time of entering his appearance in such state court, file a petition for the removal of the cause for trial into the next circuit court, to be held in the district where the suit is pending . . . the cause shall there proceed in the same manner as if it had been brought there by original process . . . . [A]nd the trial of issues in fact in the circuit courts shall, in all suits, except those of equity, and of admiralty, and maritime jurisdiction, be by a jury.

Section 13.   *And be it further enacted,* That the Supreme Court shall have exclusive jurisdiction of all controversies of a civil nature, where a state is a party, except between a state and its citizens; and except also between a state and citizens of other states, or aliens, in which latter case it shall have original but not exclusive jurisdiction. And shall have exclusively all such jurisdiction of suits or proceedings against ambassadors, or other public ministers . . . as a court of law can have or exercise consistently with the law of nations; and original, but not exclusive jurisdiction of all suits brought by ambassadors, or other public ministers, or in which a consul, or vice consul, shall be a party. And the trial of issues in fact in the Supreme Court, in all actions at law against citizens of the United States, shall be by jury. The Supreme Court shall also have appellate jurisdiction from the circuit courts and courts of the several states, in the cases herein after specially provided for; and shall have power to issue writs of prohibition to the district courts, when proceeding as courts of admiralty and maritime jurisdiction, and writs of *mandamus,* in cases warranted by the principles and usages of law, to any courts appointed, or persons holding office, under the authority of the United States.

Section 14.   *And be it further enacted,* That all the before-mentioned courts of the United States, shall have the power to issue writs of *scire facias, habeas corpus,* and all other writs not specifically provided for by statute, which may be necessary for the exercise of their respective jurisdictions, and agreeable to the principles and usages of law . . . .

. . . .

Section 16.   *And it be further enacted,* That suits in equity shall not be sustained in either of the courts of the United States, in any case where plain, adequate and complete remedy may be had at law.

Section 17. *And be it further enacted,* That all the said courts of the United States shall have power to grant new trials, in cases where there has been a trial by jury for reasons which new trials have usually been granted in the courts of law . . . .

. . . .

Section 22. *And be it further enacted,* That final decrees and judgments in civil actions in a district court, where the matter in dispute exceeds the sum or value of fifty dollars, exclusive of costs, may be re-examined, and reversed or affirmed in a circuit court . . . upon a writ of error. And upon a like process, may final judgments and decrees in civil actions, and suits in equity in a circuit court, brought there by original process . . . or removed there by appeal from a district court where the matter in dispute exceeds the sum or value of two thousand dollars, exclusive of costs, be re-examined and reversed or affirmed in the Supreme Court . . . .

. . . .

Section 25. *And be it further enacted,* That a final judgment or decree in any suit, in the highest court of law or equity of a State in which a decision in the suit could be had, where is drawn in question the validity of a treaty or statute of, or an authority exercised under the United States, and the decision is against their validity; or where is drawn in question the validity of a statute of, or an authority exercised under any State, on the ground of their being repugnant to the constitution, treaties or laws of the United States, and the decision is in favour of such their validity, or where is drawn in question the construction of any clause of the constitution, or of a treaty, or statute of, or commission held under the United States, and the decision is against the title, right, privilege or exemption specially set up or claimed by either party, under such clause of the said Constitution, treaty, statute or commission, may be re-examined and reversed or affirmed in the Supreme Court of the United States upon a writ of error . . . in the same manner and under the same regulations, and the writ shall have the same effect, as if the judgment or decree complained of had been rendered or passed in a circuit court . . . .

. . . .

Section 27. *And be it further enacted,* That a marshal shall be appointed in and for each district for the term of four years, but shall be removable from office at pleasure, whose duty it shall be to attend the district and circuit courts when sitting therein . . . . And to execute throughout the district, all lawful precepts directed to him . . . and to appoint as there shall be occasion, one or more deputies, who shall be removable from office by the judge of the district court . . . .

Section 28. *And be it further enacted,* . . . . And in case of the death of any marshal, his deputy or deputies shall continue in office, unless otherwise specially removed; and shall execute the same in the name of the deceased, until another marshal shall be appointed and sworn . . . .

Section 29. *And be it further enacted,* That in cases punishable with death, the trial shall be had in the county where the offence was committed, or where that cannot be done without great inconvenience, twelve petit jurors at least shall be summoned from thence. . . .

. . . .

Section 34. *And be it further enacted,* That the laws of the several states, except where the constitution, treaties or statutes of the United States shall otherwise require or provide, shall be regarded as rules of decision in trials at common law in the courts of the United States in cases where they apply.

Section 35. *And be it further enacted,* That in all the courts of the United States, the parties may plead and manage their own causes personally or by the assistance of such counsel or attorneys at law as by the rules of the said courts respectively shall be permitted to manage and conduct causes therein. And there shall be appointed in each district a meet person learned in the law to act as attorney for the United States in such district . . . . And he shall receive as a compensation for his services such fees as shall be taxed therefor in the respective courts before which the suits or prosecutions shall be. And there shall also be appointed a meet person, learned in the law, to act as attorney-general for the United States, who shall be sworn or affirmed to a faithful execution of his office; whose duty it shall be to prosecute and conduct all suits in the Supreme Court in which the United States shall be concerned, and to give his advice and opinion upon questions of law when required by the President of the United States, or when requested by the heads of any of the departments, touching any matters that may concern their departments, and shall receive such compensation for his services as shall by law be provided.

Approved: September 24, 1789 — 1 Stat. 73

CHAPTER 3
THE EARLY JUDICIARY

The first chapter introduced three of the traditional forms of interpretation employed by lawyers: (1) the broad *structure* of government established by the Constitution, (2) the *historical setting* from which the Constitution emerged, and (3) the *text* of the Constitution itself. The second chapter introduced additional historical materials that may influence constitutional interpretation, including the drafting history, ratification history, and early practice of Congress and the President. Early practice may support another form of constitutional interpretation: (4) one based upon *tradition* (or historical precedent). To what extent — apart from structure, pre-ratification history, and text — should constitutional interpretation be influenced by a tradition of viewing matters in a certain fashion? In law, certain forms of argument based upon tradition (or historical precedent) attract attention: lawyers most often rely upon (5) *judicial precedent*.

As used throughout this Volume, the term *tradition* generally refers to interpretations based on actions after ratification while the term *history* (or historical setting) generally refers to matters up to and including ratification. The term *precedent* generally refers to judicial determinations while the term *tradition* generally refers to an established understanding reached outside the judicial context.

In reading early judicial decisions of the Supreme Court, consider whether they establish a judicial precedent for accepting (or rejecting) certain forms of argument when interpreting the Constitution.

LETTER FROM SECRETARY OF STATE THOMAS JEFFERSON TO THE JUSTICES OF THE U.S. SUPREME COURT

Philadelphia
July 18, 1793

Gentlemen:

The war which has taken place among the powers of Europe produces frequent transactions within our ports and limits, on which questions arise of considerable difficulty, and of greater importance to the peace of the United States. These questions depend for their solution on the construction of our treaties, on the laws of nature and nations, and on the laws of the land, and are often presented under circumstances *which do not give a cognisance of them to the tribunals of the country*. Yet their decision is so little analogous to the ordinary functions of the executive, as to occasion much embarrassment and difficulty to them. The President therefore would be much more relieved if he found himself free to refer questions of this description to the opinions of the judges of the Supreme Court of the United States, whose knowledge of the subject would secure us against errors dangerous to the peace of the United States, and their authority to insure the respect of all parties. He has therefore asked the attendance of such of the judges as would be collected in time for the occasion, to know, in the first place, their opinion, whether the public may, with propriety, be availed of their *advice on these questions*? And if they may, to present, for their advice, the abstract questions which have already occurred, or may soon occur, from which they will themselves strike out such as any circumstances might, in their opinion, forbid them to

61

pronounce on. I have the honour to be with sentiments of the most perfect respect, gentlemen,

Your most obedient and humble servant,

Thos. Jefferson

LETTER FROM CHIEF JUSTICE JOHN JAY AND THE ASSOCIATE JUSTICES OF THE U.S. SUPREME COURT TO PRESIDENT WASHINGTON

Philadelphia
August 8, 1793

Sir:

We have considered the previous question stated in a letter written by your direction to us by the Secretary of State on [July 18, on the topic of] the lines of separation drawn by the Constitution between the three departments of the government. These being in certain respects checks upon each other, and our being judges of a court in the last resort, are considerations which afford strong arguments against the propriety of our extra-judicially deciding the questions alluded to, especially as the power given by the Constitution to the President, of calling on the heads of departments for opinions, seems to have been *purposely* as well as expressly united to the *executive* departments.

We exceedingly regret every event that may cause embarrassment to your administration, but we derive consolation from the reflection that your judgment will discern what is right, and that your usual prudence, decision, and firmness will surmount every obstacle to the preservation of the rights, peace, and dignity of the United States.

We have the honor to be, with perfect respect, sir, your most obedient and humble servants.

Federal Pensions for Disabled Veterans of the Revolutionary War

Congress established pensions for disabled veterans of the Revolutionary War.[1] Congress assigned the federal circuit courts responsibility for making initial determinations on individual claims for pensions.[2] Those determinations, however, were not binding upon the Secretary of War who administered the pensions. If the Secretary of War disapproved a claim approved by the circuit courts, he was obligated to report the matter to Congress so it could determine whether to award a pension despite the denial.[3]

The federal circuit courts at that time consisted of one or two Supreme Court justices sitting together with a district court judge.

---

[1] *See* Act of March 23, 1792, 1 Stat. 243.

[2] *Id.* § 2, 1 Stat. at 244.

[3] *Id.* § 4, 1 Stat. at 24.

On April 5, 1792, the Circuit Court for the District of New York — including Chief Justice John Jay and Associate Justice William Cushing — formally stated upon the record:

> That neither the legislative nor executive branches can constitutionally assign to the judicial any duties, but such as are properly judicial, and to be performed in a judicial manner: —

> That the duties assigned to the circuit courts by this act are not of that description; and that the act itself does not appear to contemplate them as such, inasmuch as it subjects the decisions of these courts, made pursuant to those duties, first to the consideration and suspension of the secretary at war, and then to the revision of the legislature.

> As therefore the business assigned to this court by the act is not judicial, nor directed to be performed judicially, the act can only be considered as appointing commissioners for the purposes mentioned in it by official instead of personal descriptions . . . .

> That as the objects of this act are exceedingly benevolent, and do real honor to the humanity and justice of congress, and as the judges desire to manifest on all proper occasions, and in every proper manner, their high respect for the national legislature, they will execute this act in the capacity of commissioners.[4]

By letter dated April 10, 1792, the judges protested the matter to President Washington.

On April 11, 1792, the Circuit Court for the District of Pennsylvania — including Associate Justices James Wilson and John Blair, Jr. — read the pension claim of William Hayburn and determined not to address the matter.[5] By letter dated April 18, 1792, the judges protested the matter to President Washington.

> Upon due consideration, we have been unanimously of opinion, that, under this act, the circuit court, held for the Pennsylvania district, could not proceed; . . . Be assured, that, though it became necessary, it was far from being pleasant. To be obliged to act contrary either to the obvious directions of congress, or to a constitutional principle, in our judgment, equally obvious, excited feelings in us, which we hope never to experience again.[6]

In the few intervening days, on April 13, 1792, Congress received Hayburn's request for relief. Hayburn's petition observed: "This being the first instance in which a court of justice had declared a law of Congress to be unconstitutional, the novelty of the case produced a variety of opinions with respect to the measures to be taken on the occasion."[7] Representative Elias Boudinot confirmed to the House of Representatives that Hayburn fairly characterized the position of the Circuit Court for the District of Pennsylvania.

---

[4] The text of this decision is set forth in Max Farrand, *The First Hayburn Case, 1792*, 13 Am. Hist. Rev. 281, 281–82 (1908). The Supreme Court memorialized this understanding of the matter in *United States v. Ferreira*, 54 U.S. 40, 49–50 (1851).

[5] *See* Farrand, *supra* note 4, at 283. This matter is known as the first *Hayburn* case.

[6] *See id.* In *Ferreira*, the Court emphasized that the refusal was based on the view that the circuit court was not exercising "a judicial power then subject to revision of the Secretary of War and Congress." 54 U.S. at 50.

[7] *See* Farrand, *supra* note 4, at 284.

There is some suggestion that some Members of Congress may have considered impeachment of the judges of the Circuit Court for the District of Pennsylvania.

> Never was the word 'impeachment' so hackneyed, as it has been since the spirited sentence passed by our judges on an unconstitutional law. The high-fliers, in and out of Congress, and the very humblest of their humble retainers talk of nothing but impeachment! impeachment! impeachment! as if forsooth Congress were wrapped up in the cloak of infallibility, which has been torn from the shoulders of the Pope; and that it was damnable heresy and sacrilege to doubt the constitutional orthodoxy of any decision of theirs, once written on calf-skin![8]

The Circuit Court for the District of North Carolina — including Justice James Iredell — limited their handling of pension requests, by purporting to act solely in the capacity of commissioners.[9] By letter dated June 8, 1792, they also protested to President Washington.[10]

When the U.S. Supreme Court convened for its August 1792 Term, Attorney General Randolph petitioned the Court to issue a writ of mandamus to the Circuit Court for the District of Pennsylvania, directing it to consider the merits of Hayburn's pension request.[11] The Court took the matter under advisement until its next session but, due to intervening legislation, never ruled on the matter.[12]

On February 28, 1793, Congress repealed the administrative provisions of the 1792 Act.[13] Under the new legislation, the duty of initially reviewing evidence of eligibility for a pension was assigned to the district court judge in each district or by "any three persons specially authorized by commission from said judge." Another provision of the 1793 Act imposed the duty upon

> the Secretary of War, in conjunction with the Attorney General, to take such measures as may be necessary to obtain an adjudication of the Supreme Court of the United States, on the validity of any such rights claimed under the act aforesaid, by the determination of certain persons styling themselves Commissioners.[14]

In response to that statutory directive, the United States brought suit against Yale Todd to recover sums paid to him as a pension based upon a determination by the judges of the Circuit Court for the District of Connecticut — including Chief Justice Jay and Justice Cushing — acting as commissioners.[15] By that point in time, every Justice of the U.S. Supreme Court, except Thomas Johnson, "had formally expressed his opinion, in writing, that the duty imposed, when the decision was subject to the revision of a Secretary and of Congress, could not be executed by the court as a judicial power: and the only question upon which there appears to have

---

[8] *See id.* at 285 (observing "that the word 'impeachment' was several times mentioned in the House of Representatives although no motion was made on the subject").

[9] *See Ferreira*, 54 U.S at 50.

[10] *See* Farrand, *supra* note 4, at 282.

[11] *Hayburn's Case*, 2 U.S. 409, 410 (1792).

[12] *Id.*

[13] Act of Feb. 28, 1793, § 1, 1 Stat. 324, 324.

[14] *Id.* § 3, 1 Stat. at 325.

[15] *See* Farrand, *supra* note 4, at 282.

been any difference of opinion, was whether it might not be construed as conferring the power on the judges personally as commissioners."[16]

On February 12, 1794, the U.S. Supreme Court ruled against Todd.[17]

> Chief Justice Jay and Justice[s] Cushing, Wilson, Blair, and Paterson, were present at the decision. No opinion was filed stating the grounds of the decision. Nor is any dissent from the judgment entered on the record. It would seem, therefore, to have been unanimous, and that Chief Justice Jay and Justice Cushing became satisfied, on further reflection, that the power given in the act of 1792 to the Circuit Court as a court, could not be construed to give it to the judges out of court as commissioners.[18]

With that ruling and the earlier revision of the statute, the controversy came to an end.

Exercise 6:

Consider the following matters in connection with the exchange of correspondence between the Washington Administration and the Supreme Court as well as the history of the Revolutionary War pension cases:

(1) What limitation on the judicial power, if any, is articulated by the Supreme Court in response to the Washington Administration? What argument does the Court rely upon to support its position? What additional limitations, if any, are suggested by the Court's reasoning?

(2) Does the summary of the Revolutionary War pension cases illustrate that as early as 1794, the U.S. Supreme Court had declared federal legislation to be inconsistent with the Constitution? If so, what is the scope of that precedent?

(3) If the Court had declared a federal statute void as inconsistent with the Constitution, what *specifically* was the problem with the statute?

(a) Was it that Congress may not mandate that federal judges adjudicate such claims?

(b) Was it that Congress may not authorize federal judges to undertake such duties, even on a voluntary basis outside their judicial capacity?

(c) Was it that if federal judges were required to adjudicate such claims, the Executive Branch must be obligated to accept the adjudication as conclusive?

(d) Was it that if federal judges were required to adjudicate such claims, Congress could not retain discretion to revise the pension law with respect to claims not then finally adjudicated?

(e) Was it that if federal judges were required to adjudicate such claims, Congress could not award benefits to a claimant after the Executive Branch determined the claimant did not qualify? Why should Congress not be permitted to create an additional pension for a particularly worthy individual (by a "private law") even if he did not qualify under the public law as viewed by the Executive?

---

[16] *Ferreira,* 54 U.S. at 51.

[17] *See* Farrand, *supra* note 4, at 282 (citing *Ferreira,* 54 U.S. at 52, note appended by order of Chief Justice Taney, summarizing "the result of the opinions expressed" seriatim in the *Todd* case to be that the power vested in the circuit courts by the 1792 Act was unconstitutional).

[18] *Ferreira,* 54 U.S. 40, 52, note appended by order of Chief Justice Taney.

If your instructor assigns Volume 2, reconsider this question before reading *INS v. Chadha.*

A Note on Early Supreme Court Decisions

The Supreme Court adopted the English practice of each individual judge writing a separate opinion. In these *seriatim* opinions, no judge speaks for any fellow judge. As a result, there is no opinion of "the Court" or even of "a majority." Only by synthesizing the views stated in each of the separate opinions can one ascertain which propositions garnered the support of a majority of the Court. The order in which the separate opinions are printed does not (unlike modern practice) indicate whether opinions even support the ultimate judgment of the Court.

CALDER v. BULL
3 U.S. 386 (1798)

[Calder and Bull had competing claims to a decedent's estate. After a probate court ruled in the matter for Calder and the statutory time for appeal expired, the Connecticut legislature set aside the decree and granted a new hearing before the probate court with right to appeal from that court's new ruling. The probate court then ruled for Bull, and the Connecticut appellate courts affirmed that determination. Calder then sought review by the U.S. Supreme Court, arguing that the Connecticut legislature violated the federal Constitution's prohibition on ex post facto laws.]

JUSTICE CHASE.

. . . .

It appears to me a self-evident proposition, that the several State Legislatures retain all the powers of legislation, delegated to them by the State Constitutions; which are not EXPRESSLY taken away by the Constitution of the United States. The establishing courts of justice, the appointment of Judges, and the making regulations for the administration of justice, within each State, according to its laws, on all subjects not entrusted to the Federal Government, appears to me to be the peculiar and exclusive province, and duty of the State Legislatures: All the powers delegated by the people of the United States to the Federal Government are defined, and NO CONSTRUCTIVE powers can be exercised by it, and all the powers that remain in the State Governments are indefinite . . . .

. . . The sole enquiry is, whether this resolution or law of Connecticut, having such operation, is an ex post facto law, within the prohibition of the Federal Constitution?

. . . An ACT of the Legislature (for I cannot call it a law) contrary to the great first principles of the social compact, cannot be considered a rightful exercise of legislative authority. The obligation of a law in governments established on express compact, and on republican principles must be determined by the nature of the power, on which it was founded. A few instances will suffice to explain what I mean. A law that punished a citizen for an innocent action, or, in other words, for an act, which, when done, was in violation of no existing law . . . .

. . . .

The Constitution of the United States, article I, section 9, prohibits the Legislature of the United States from passing any ex post facto law; and, in section 10, lays several restrictions on the authority of the Legislatures of the several states; and, among them, "that no state shall pass any ex post facto law." . . .

I shall endeavour to show what law is to be considered an ex post facto law, within the words and meaning of the prohibition in the Federal Constitution. . . . [T]he plain and obvious meaning and intention of the prohibition is this; that the Legislatures of the several states, shall not pass laws, after a fact is done by a subject, or citizen, which shall have relation to such fact, and shall punish him for having done it. The prohibition considered in this light, is an additional bulwark in favour of the personal security of the subject, to protect his person from punishment by legislative acts, having a retrospective operation. I do not think it was inserted to secure the citizen in his private rights, of either property, or contracts. The prohibitions not to make anything but gold and silver coin a tender in payment of debts, and not to pass any law impairing the obligation of contracts, were inserted to secure private rights; but the restriction not to pass any ex post facto law, was to secure the person of the subject from injury, or punishment, in consequence of such law. If the prohibition against making ex post facto laws was intended to secure personal rights from being affected, or injured, by such laws, and the prohibition is sufficiently extensive for that object, the other restraints, I have enumerated, were unnecessary, and therefore improper; for both of them are retrospective.

. . . The expressions "ex post facto laws," are technical, they had been in use long before the Revolution, and had acquired an appropriate meaning, by Legislators, Lawyers, and Authors. The celebrated and judicious Sir William Blackstone, in his commentaries, considers an ex post facto law precisely in the same light I have done. His opinion is confirmed by his successor, Mr. Wooddeson; and by the author of the Federalist . . . .

I also rely greatly on the definition, or explanation of EX POST FACTO LAWS, as given by the Conventions of Massachusetts, Maryland, and North Carolina; in their several Constitutions, or forms of Government.

. . . .

Without giving an opinion, at this time, whether this Court has jurisdiction to decide that any law made by Congress, contrary to the Constitution of the United States, is void; I am fully satisfied that this court has no jurisdiction to determine that any law of any state Legislature, contrary to the Constitution of such state, is void. . . .

. . . .

I am of opinion, that the decree of the Supreme Court of Errors of Connecticut be affirmed, with costs.

JUSTICE PATERSON.

The Constitution of Connecticut is made up of usages, and it appears that its Legislature have, from the beginning, exercised the power of granting new trials. . . . This usage makes up part of the Constitution of Connecticut, and we are bound to consider it as such, unless it be inconsistent with the Constitution of the United States. . . . The question, then, which arises on the pleadings in this cause, is, whether the resolution of the Legislature of Connecticut, be an ex post facto law, within the meaning of the Constitution of the United States? I am of opinion, that it is not. The words, ex post facto, when applied to a law, have a technical meaning, and, in legal phraseology, refer to crimes, pains, and penalties. Judge Blackstone's description of the terms is clear and accurate. . . .

On inspecting such of our state Constitutions, as take notice of laws made ex post facto, we shall find, that they are understood in the same sense.

. . . .

Again, the words of the Constitution of the United States are, "That no State shall pass any bill of attainder, ex post facto law, or law impairing the obligation of contracts." Article I, section 10.

Where is the necessity or use of the latter words, if a law impairing the obligation of contracts, be comprehended within the terms ex post facto law? . . .

. . . [O]n full consideration, I am convinced, that ex post facto laws must be limited in the manner already expressed; they must be taken in their technical, which is also their common and general, acceptation, and are not to be understood in their literal sense.

JUSTICE IREDELL.

If . . . a government, composed of Legislative, Executive, and Judicial departments, were established, by a Constitution, which imposed no limits on the legislative power, the consequence would inevitably be, that whatever the legislative power chose to enact, would be lawfully enacted, and the judicial power could never interpose to pronounce it void. It is true that some speculative jurists have held, that a legislative act against natural justice must, in itself, be void; but I cannot think that, under such a government, any Court of Justice would possess a power to declare it so. . . .

In order, therefore, to guard against so great an evil, it has been the policy of all the American states, which have, individually, framed their state constitutions since the revolution, and of the people of the United States, when they framed the Federal Constitution, to define with precision the objects of the legislative power, and to restrain its exercise within marked and settled boundaries. If any act of Congress, or of the Legislature of a state, violates those constitutional provisions, it is unquestionably void; though, I admit, that as the authority to declare it void is of a delicate and awful nature, the Court will never resort to that authority, but in a clear and urgent case. If, on the other hand, the Legislature of the Union, or the Legislature of any member of the Union, shall pass a law, within the general scope of their constitutional power, the Court cannot pronounce it to be void, merely because it is, in their judgment, contrary to the principles of natural justice. . . .

. . . [I]n the present instance, the act or resolution of the Legislature of Connecticut, cannot be regarded as an ex post facto law; for, the true construction of the prohibition extends to criminal, not to civil, cases. . . .

JUSTICE CUSHING.

The case appears to me to be clear of all difficulty, taken either way. If the act is a judicial act, it is not touched by the Federal Constitution: and, if it is a legislative act, it is maintained and justified by the ancient and uniform practice of the state of Connecticut.

Judgment affirmed.

Exercise 7:

In the various opinions in *Calder v. Bull*, identify the interpretive methods employed. Identify any of the five forms of argument that are employed by the Court.

(1)   For arguments based upon constitutional text, what techniques do the Justices use other than examining the plain meaning of the words?

(2)   For arguments based upon history, what sources do the Justices consider?

In addition, consider:

(3)   What role, if any, does "natural law" play in judicial review? Is the Court's answer to that question consistent with the views expressed in the ratification debates?

For one scholar's answer to the question, see Lee J. Strang, *Originalism, the Declaration of Independence, and the Constitution: A Unique Role in Constitutional Interpretation?*, 111 PENN. ST. L. REV. 413, 439–74 (2006) (asserting that the Declaration of Independence is not a source of "natural rights" enforceable by federal courts).

(4)   Does *Hayburn's Case* or *Calder v. Bull* establish a precedent for judicial review by federal courts? To the extent either case does so, under what circumstances is judicial review supported by early precedent? Is the exercise of judicial review consistent with the structure and text of the Constitution? Is it consistent with views expressed in the ratification debates? Is it consistent with the views of the First Congress?

(5)   Why did the Court decline to consider whether Calder asserted a violation of the Connecticut Constitution?

(6)   How does *Calder v. Bull* answer the question of whether the constitutional prohibition on *ex post facto* laws prohibits legislatures (federal or state) from revising laws and making the new law applicable to pending cases?

(7)   Are there terms in Article III that should be construed as "terms of art" with an established meaning in law?

Hidden Meaning in "Terms of Art" in Article III?

The Supreme Court's treatment of the meaning of the *ex post facto* clause suggests that there may be other terms in the Constitution that should also be understood to have a specialized meaning not evident from the plain words. This Volume addresses the judiciary and so this is an appropriate point to pause and consider whether there are terms in Article III that should be construed as terms of art.

Does the phrase "the judicial power" convey any particular meaning?

The U.S. Supreme Court has, at times, described the judicial power of Article III as equivalent to that exercised by certain English courts at the time of the drafting of the U.S. Constitution.

Writing for four Justices on an issue that evenly split the Court, Justice Frankfurter explained:

> In endowing this Court with "judicial Power" the Constitution presupposed an historic content for that phrase and relied on assumption by the judiciary of authority only over issues which are appropriate for disposition by judges. . . . Both by what they said and by what they implied, the framers of the Judiciary Article [*i.e.*, Article III] gave merely outlines of what were to them the familiar operations of the English judicial system and its manifestations on this side of the Ocean before the Union. Judicial power could come into play only in matters that were the traditional concern of the courts at Westminster and only if they arose in ways that to the expert feel of lawyers constituted "Cases" or "Controversies."

Coleman v. Miller, 307 U.S. 433, 460 (1939) (Frankfurter, J.). A majority of the Court has endorsed that view in several subsequent cases. *See, e.g., Vermont Agency of Natural Resources v. United States ex rel. Stevens*, 529 U.S. 765, 774 (2000); *FEC v. Akins*, 524 U.S. 11, 24 (1998).

For an argument that "the judicial power" was commonly understood in this sense at the time of drafting and ratification of the Constitution, see Randy E. Barnett, *The Original Meaning of the Judicial Power,* 12 Sup. Ct. Econ. R. 115 (2004). And for an argument that "the judicial power" was understood to also include strong adherence to precedent, see Lee J. Strang, *An Originalist Theory of Precedent: Originalism, Nonoriginalist Precedent, and the Common Good,* 36 N.M. L. Rev. 419, 447–71 (2006).

Does judicial tenure "during good behavior" convey any particular meaning?

Article III, Section 1 provides that all judges, not only those of the U.S. Supreme Court, hold their office "during good behaviour." To the modern reader it may not be clear whether that term is the equivalent of (1) tenure for life subject only to removal by impeachment on the bases specified in Article II, Section 4, or (2) tenure for as long as the President approves of the behavior of the judge (that is, tenure at the pleasure of the President). Certainly an examination of the ratification materials (or even a representative sample like the excerpts in Chapter 2) illustrates a broad consensus among the Anti-Federalists and Federalists on this point. There was a shared understanding that Article III granted judges substantial independence from the influence of the other branches of the central government even if the opposing parties disagreed as to whether that was a wise provision. That view implicitly rejects a reading of tenure during good behavior as subjecting judges to any but the most limited removal provisions.

One need not rely on such reasoning to resolve any ambiguity regarding constitutionally-granted judicial tenure. Tenure during "good behavior" may be understood as a term of art having originated under English law. The early patents (equivalent to commissions) of English judges of the courts of King's Bench and Common Pleas almost uniformly provided tenure "during the pleasure of the king" with a few exceptions when tenure was granted "for life, even without a limitation as to good behaviour." As a judge holding office only during the pleasure of the King, Sir Edward Coke — "the most learned lawyer of his time" — was removed in 1616 by James I (who reigned 1603–1625). His successor Charles I (who reigned 1625–1648) continued to appoint such judges with such tenure provisions and to exercise his power of removal. Parliament then petitioned Charles I "praying that tenure during good behavior be substituted for that during pleasure" and Charles I complied with his promise to do so. The record of the Commonwealth period and after the Restoration of Charles II was mixed, but removals of judges by James II (who reigned 1685–1688) "passed all precedent and all decency." Following the "Glorious Revolution" of 1688, the judges were appointed during good behavior and no judges were removed during the joint reign of William and Mary or the reign of William (who reigned until 1702). The Act of Settlement of 1701 provided that judges would be appointed to a tenure of good behavior. As a consequence, the King surrendered the power to unilaterally remove judges even though judges were still subject to removal by impeachment.[1]

When a later King treated judges as serving only at his pleasure, the Colonists identified that practice as one of the grievances in the Declaration of Indepen-

---

[1] The quotations and much of the substance of this paragraph is drawn from *The Tenure of English Judges,* in C.W. McIlwain, Constitutionalism and the Changing World 296–307 (1939). Other mechanisms for removing judges existed, but none placed authority in the King acting alone rather than in conjunction with judicial process or special authorization by both Houses of Parliament. *See id.* at 302–303.

dence.[2] That background may suggest that tenure during good behavior was designed to accomplish a greater degree of judicial independence from control by the executive authority.

The Continued Debate Over Sovereignty

The concept of sovereignty was central during the ratification debates. Gordon Wood observes that most supporters of the proposed Constitution "soon realized that this problem of sovereignty was the most powerful obstacle to the acceptance of the new Constitution the opponents could have erected."[1] "Both sides in the debate over the Constitution soon came to focus on this, 'the principle question,' 'the source of the greatest objection, which can be made to its adoption' — 'whether this system proposes a consolidation or a confederation of the states.' "[2] None of the Federalists' responses in terms of " 'joint jurisdictions' and 'coequal sovereignties' convincingly refuted the Antifederalist doctrine of a supreme and indivisible sovereignty."

Where could sovereignty possibly reside under the Constitution where it would be the supreme and indivisible authority? Once sovereignty was located, what were the implications for governmental structures that were not sovereign?

More thoroughly than anyone else, James Wilson explained an entirely new concept that seemed to solve the theoretical puzzle of sovereignty. His speeches on the issue during Pennsylvania's consideration of the proposed Constitution[3] removed a major obstacle to ratification not only in Pennsylvania but in the eleven other States that subsequently considered ratification. Only Delaware had ratified the Constitution before Pennsylvania.

As one of the original Justices of the U.S. Supreme Court, Wilson relied upon his concept of sovereignty in one of the Court's earliest controversial decisions.

CHISHOLM v. GEORGIA
2 U.S. 419 (1793)

[An individual citizen of South Carolina who served as executor to a testator who also was a citizen of South Carolina instituted this action against the State of Georgia seeking damages for common law breach of contract. The marshall for the District of Georgia served process upon the Governor and Attorney General of the State. Counsel for Georgia asserted that the federal court lacked jurisdiction and requested that the action be dismissed. The Supreme Court delivered its opinions seriatim.]

JUSTICE IREDELL.

. . . .

This is the first instance wherein the important question involved in this cause has come regularly before the Court. In the Maryland case it did not because the Attorney-General of the State voluntarily appeared. . . . [Even under those

---

[2] *See* Declaration of Independence, part II(D).

[1] GORDON S. WOOD, THE CREATION OF THE AMERICAN REPUBLIC, 1776–1787, at 529 (1998).

[2] *Id.*

[3] On October 6, 1787 — less than a month after the Constitutional Convention adjourned — Wilson delivered his famous State House Yard Speech. *See* 1 COLLECTED WORKS OF JAMES WILSON 171–178 (Kermit L. Hall & Mark David Hall eds. 2007). As one of the first public statements in support of ratification, the speech had significant influence. Wilson also delivered several important speeches in the Pennsylvania ratification convention. *See id.* at 178–284.

circumstances, if that case had resulted in a jury verdict against Maryland,] it would have been our duty, previous to giving judgment, to have well considered whether we were warranted in giving it. . . . I am now decidedly of opinion that no such action as this before the Court can legally be maintained.

The action [is for common law breach of contract]. . . . [Counsel for Chisholm] must know, that in England, certain judicial proceedings not inconsistent with the sovereignty, may take place against the Crown, but that an action [for breach of contract] will not lie. . . .

. . . [If an action against a State for breach of contract may be brought against a non-consenting State,] it must be in virtue of the Constitution of the United States, and of some law of Congress conformable thereto. . . . The Constitution . . . provides for the jurisdiction wherein a State is a party . . . . And it also provides, that in all cases in which a State shall be a party, the Supreme Court shall have original jurisdiction.

[Section 13 of the Federal Judiciary Act of 1789 vests original, but not exclusive, jurisdiction in the Supreme Court in an action against a State by a citizen of another State.]

. . . .

. . . I conceive, that all the Courts of the United States must receive, not merely their organization as to the number of Judges of which they are to consist; but all their authority, as to the manner of their proceeding, from the Legislature only. This appears to me to be one of those cases, with many others, in which an article of the Constitution cannot be effectuated without the intervention of the Legislative authority. . . . Having a right thus to establish the Court, and it being capable of being established in no other manner, I conceive it necessarily follows, that they are also to direct the manner of its proceedings. Upon this authority, there is, that I know, but one limit: that is, "that they shall not exceed their authority." If they do, I have no hesitation to say, that any act to that effect would be utterly void, because it would be inconsistent with the Constitution, which is a fundamental law paramount to all others, which we are not only bound to consult, but sworn to observe; and, therefore, where there is an interference, being superior in obligation to the other, we must unquestionably obey that in preference. . . .

. . . The authority contended for is certainly not one of those necessarily incident to all Courts merely as such.

. . . .

. . . [T]he Legislature did not chuse to leave to our own discretion the path to justice, but has prescribed one of its own. In doing so, it has, I think, wisely, referred us to principles and usages of law already well known, and by their precision calculated to guard against that innovating spirit of Courts of Justice

. . . .

. . . I believe there is no doubt that neither the State now in question, nor in any other in the Union, any particular legislative mode, authorizing a compulsory suit for the recovery of money against a State, was in being either when the Constitution was adopted, or at the time the judicial act was passed. . . .

. . . [I]t is certain that in regard to any common law principle which can influence the question before us no alteration has been made by any statute, which could occasion the least material difference, or have any partial effect. No other part of the common law of England, it appears to me, can have any reference to this subject, but that part of it which prescribes remedies against the crown. Every

State in the Union in every instance where its sovereignty has not been delegated to the United States, I consider to be as completely sovereign, as the United States are in respect to the powers surrendered. . . .

. . . [Under the Judiciary Act of 1789,] this Court hath a concurrent jurisdiction only . . . . It follows, therefore, unquestionably, I think, that looking at the act of Congress, which I consider on this occasion the limit of our authority (whatever further might be constitutionally enacted) we can exercise no authority in the present instance consistently with the clear intention of the act, but such as a proper State Court would have been at least competent to exercise at the time the act was passed.

. . . [N]o such remedy could, under any circumstances, I apprehend, be allowed in any of the American States, in none of which it is presumed any Court of Justice hath any express authority over the revenues of the State such as has been attributed to the Court of Exchequer in England.

. . . .

. . . [In England,] in all cases of petition of right, of whatever nature is the demand, I think it is clear beyond all doubt, that there must be some endorsement or order of the King himself to warrant any further proceedings. The remedy, in the language of Blackstone, being a matter of grace, and not on compulsion.

. . . .

Now let us consider the case of a debt due from a State. . . . [S]o far as analogy is to take place, such Petition in a State could only be presented to the sovereign power, which surely the Governor is not. The only constituted authority to which such an application could with any propriety be made, must undoubtedly be the Legislature, whose express consent, upon the principle of analogy, would be necessary to any further proceeding. . . .

. . . .

. . . A State does not owe its origin to the Government of the United States, in the highest or in any of its branches. It was in existence before it. It derives its authority from the same pure and sacred source itself: The voluntary and deliberate choice of the people. . . . A State is altogether exempt from the jurisdiction of the Courts of the United States, or from any other exterior authority, unless, in the special instances where the general Government has power derived from the Constitution itself. . . . A State, though subject in certain specified particulars to the authority of the Government of the United States, is in every other respect totally independent upon it. The people of the State created, the people of the State can only change, its Constitution. Upon this power there is no other limitation but that imposed by the Constitution of the United States; that is must be of the Republican form. . . .

. . . .

. . . My opinion being, that even if the Constitution would admit of the exercise of such a power, a new law is necessary for the purpose, since no part of the existing law applies, this alone is sufficient to justify my determination in the present case. So much, however, has been said on the Constitution, that it may not be improper to intimate that my present opinion is strongly against any construction of it, which will admit, under any circumstances, a compulsive suit against a State for the recovery of money. I think every word in the Constitution may have its full effect without involving this consequences, and that nothing but express words, or an insurmountable implication (neither of which I consider, can be found in this case) would authorise the deduction of so high a power. . . .

JUSTICE BLAIR.

. . . The Constitution of the United States is the only fountain from which I shall draw; the only authority to which I shall appeal. . . . What then do we find there requiring the submission of individual States to the judicial authority of the United States? This is expressly extended, among other things, to controversies between a State and citizens of another State. Is then the case before us one of that description? Undoubtedly it is . . . . It seems to me, that if this Court should refuse to hold jurisdiction of a case where a State is Defendant, it would renounce part of the authority conferred, and, consequently, part of the duty imposed on it by the Constitution; because it would be a refusal to take cognizance of a case where a State is a party. Nor does the jurisdiction of this Court, in relation to a State, seem to me to be questionable, on the ground that Congress has not provided any form of execution, or pointed out any mode of making the judgment against a State effectual . . . . Let us go on as far as we can; and if, at the end of the business, notwithstanding the powers given us in [Section 14 of the Federal Judiciary Act of 1789], we meet difficulties insurmountable to us, we must leave it to those departments of Government which have higher powers . . . . I see no reason for confining the Plaintiff to proceed by way of petition; indeed there would even seem to be an impropriety in proceeding in that mode. When sovereigns are sued in their own Courts, such a method may have been established as the most respectful form of demand; but we are not now in a State-Court; and if sovereignty be an exemption from suit in any other then the sovereign's own Courts, it follows that when a State, by adopting the Constitution, has agreed to be amendable to the judicial power of the United States, she has, in that respect, given up her right of sovereignty.

. . . .

JUSTICE WILSON.

This is a case of uncommon magnitude. One of the parties to it is a State; certainly respectable, claiming to be sovereign. The question to be determined is, whether this State, so respectable, and whose claim soars so high, is amenable to the jurisdiction of the Supreme Court of the United States? This question, important in itself, will depend on others, more important still; and, may, perhaps, be ultimately resolved into one, no less radical than this "do the people of the United States form a Nation?"

. . . .

I.

I am, first, to examine this question by the principles of general jurisprudence. . . .

To the Constitution of the United States the term SOVEREIGN, is totally unknown. There is but one place where it could have been used with propriety. But, even in that place it would not, perhaps, have comported with the delicacy of those, who ordained and established that Constitution. They might have announced themselves "SOVEREIGN" people of the United States: But serenely conscious of the fact, they avoided the ostentatious declaration.

. . . .

Let a State be considered as subordinate to the People: But let every thing else be subordinate to the State. . . . By a State I mean, a complete body of free persons united together for their common benefit, to enjoy peaceably what is their own, and to do justice to others. It is an artificial person. . . . It may be bound by contracts; and for damages arising from the breach of those contracts. . . .

. . . Is there any part of this description, which intimates, in the remotest manner, that a State, any more than the men who compose it, ought not to do justice and fulfil engagements? . . . The only reason, I believe, why a free man is bound by human laws, is, that he binds himself. Upon the same principles, upon which he becomes bound by the laws, he becomes amenable to the Courts of Justice, which are formed and authorised by those laws. If one free man, an original sovereign, may do all this; why may not an aggregate of free men, a collection of original sovereigns, do likewise? . . . Who, or what, is a sovereign? What is his or its sovereignty? On this subject, the errors and the mazes are endless and inexplicable. . . .

. . . As a citizen, I know the Government of that State [i.e., Georgia] to be republican; and my short definition of such a Government is, one constructed on this principle, that the Supreme Power resides in the body of the people. As a Judge of this Court, I know, and can decide upon the knowledge, that the citizens of Georgia, when they acted upon the large scale of the Union, as a part of the "People of the United States," did not surrender the Supreme or Sovereign Power to that State; but, as to the purposes of the Union, retained it to themselves. As to the purposes of the Union, therefore, Georgia is NOT a sovereign State. If the Judicial decision of this case forms one of those purposes; the allegation, that Georgia is a sovereign State, is unsupported by the fact. . . .

. . . [I]n the case of the King, the sovereignty had a double operation. While it vested him with jurisdiction over others, it excluded all others from jurisdiction over him. With regard to him, there was no superior power; and, consequently, on feudal principles, no right or jurisdiction. . . . Hence it is, that no suit or action can be brought against the King, even in civil matters; because no Court can have jurisdiction over him: for all jurisdiction implies superiority of power. This last position is only a branch of a much more extensive principle . . . . The principle is, that all human law must be prescribed by a superior. . . . Suffice it, at present to say, that another principle, very different in its nature and operations, forms, in my judgment, the basis of sound and genuine jurisprudence; laws derived from the pure source of equality and justice must be founded on the CONSENT of those, whose obedience they require. The sovereign, when traced to this source, must be found in the man.

. . . I have examined the question before us, by the principles of general jurisprudence. In those principles I find nothing, which tends to evince an exemption of the State of Georgia, from the jurisdiction of the Court. I find everything to have a contrary tendency.

II.

I am, in the second place, to examine this question by the laws and practices of different States and Kingdoms. . . .

. . . .

In England, according to Sir William Blackstone, no suit can be brought against the King, even in civil matters. So, in that Kingdom, is the law, at this time, received. But it was not always so. . . . Until the time of Edward I [who reigned from 1272 to 1307] the King might have been sued as a common person. . . .

III.

I am, thirdly, and chiefly, to examine the important question now before us, by the Constitution of the United States, and the legitimate result of that valuable instrument. . . .

. . . With the strictness of propriety,. . . our national scene opens with the most magnificent object, which the nation could present. "The PEOPLE of the United States" are the first personages introduced. Who were those people? They were the citizens of thirteen States, each of which had a separate Constitution and Government, and all of which were connected together by articles of confederation. . . . In order, therefore, to form a more perfect union, to establish justice, to ensure domestic tranquility, to provide for the common defence, and to secure the blessings of liberty, those people, among whom were the people of Georgia, ordained and established the present Constitution. By that Constitution Legislative power is vested, Executive power is vested, Judicial power is vested.

The question now opens fairly to our view, could the people of those States, among whom were those of Georgia, bind those States, and Georgia among the others, by the Legislative, Executive, and Judicial power so vested? If the principles, on which I have founded myself, are just and true; this question must unavoidably receive an affirmative answer. . . .

The next question under this head, is, Has the Constitution done so? . . . [T]he people of the United States intended to bind the several States, by the Legislative power of the national Government.

. . . Did the people of the United States intend to bind the several States by the Executive power of the national Government? The affirmative answer to the former question directs, unavoidably, an affirmative answer to this. . . . When the laws are plain, and the application of them is uncontroverted, they are enforced immediately by the Executive authority of the Government. When the application of them is doubtful or intricate, the interposition of the judicial authority becomes necessary. The same principle, therefore, which directed us from the first [*i.e.*, legislative] to the second [*i.e.*, executive] step, will direct us from the second to the third [*i.e.*, judicial] and last step of our deduction. Fair and conclusive deduction, then, evinces that the people of the United States did vest this Court with jurisdiction over the State of Georgia. The same truth may be deduced from the declared objects, and the general texture of the Constitution of the United States. One of its declared objects is, to form an union more perfect, than, before that time, had been formed. . . . Another declared object is, "to establish justice." This points, in a particular manner, to the Judicial authority. . . . A third declared object is "to ensure domestic tranquility." This tranquility is most likely to be disturbed by controversies between States. These consequences will be most peaceably and effectually decided by the establishment and by the exercise of a superintending judicial authority. . . .

Whoever considers, in a combined and comprehensive view, the general texture of the Constitution, will be satisfied, that the people of the United States intended to form themselves into a nation for national purposes. They instituted, for such purposes, a national Government, complete in all of its parts, with powers Legislative, Executive and Judiciary; and, in all those powers, extending over the whole nation. Is it congruous, that, with regard to such purposes, any man or body of men, any person natural or artificial, should be permitted to claim successfully an entire exemption from the jurisdiction of the national Government? . . .

But, in my opinion, this doctrine rests not upon the legitimate result of fair and conclusive deduction from the Constitution: It is confirmed, beyond all doubt, by the direct and explicit declaration of the Constitution itself. "The judicial power of the United States shall extend, to controversies between two States." Two States are supposed to have a controversy between them: This controversy is supposed to be brought before those vested with the judicial power of the United States: Can the most consummate degree of professional ingenuity devise a mode by which this "controversy between two States" can be brought before a Court of law; and yet neither of those States be a Defendant? "The judicial power of the United States shall extend to controversies, between a state and citizens of another State." Could the strictest legal language; could even that language, which is peculiarly appropriated to an art, deemed, by a great master, to be one of the most honorable, laudable, and profitable things in our law; could this strict and appropriated language, describe, with more precise accuracy, the case now depending before the tribunal? . . .

JUSTICE CUSHING.

The grand and principal question in this case is, whether a State can, by the Federal Constitution, be sued by an individual citizen of another State?

The point turns not upon the law or practice of England, although perhaps it may be in some measure elucidated thereby, nor upon the law of any other country whatever; but upon the Constitution established by the people of the United States; and peculiarly upon the extent of powers given to the Federal Judicial in the second section of the third article of the Constitution. . . . The judicial power, then, is expressly extended to "controversies between a State and citizens of another State." When a citizen makes a demand against a State, of which he is not a citizen, it is as really a controversy between a State and a citizen of another State, as if such State made a demand against such a citizen. The case, then, seems clearly to fall within the letter of the Constitution. It may be suggested that it could not be intended to subject a State to be a Defendant, because it would effect the sovereignty of States. If that be the case, what shall we do with the immediate preceding clause; "controversies between two or more States," where a State must of necessity be Defendant? . . . Why was not an exception made if one was intended?

. . . One design of the general Government was for managing the great affairs of peace and war and the general defence; which were impossible to be conducted, with safety, by the States separately. Incident to these powers, and for preventing controversies between foreign powers or citizens from rising to extremeties and to an appeal to the sword, a national tribunal was necessary, amicably to decide them, and thus ward off such fatal, public calamity. Thus, States at home and their citizens, and foreign States and their citizens, are put together without distinction upon the same footing, as far as may be, as to controversies between them. So also, with respect to controversies between a State and citizens of another State (at home) comparing all the clauses together, the remedy is reciprocal; the claim to justice equal. . . .

But still it may be insisted, that this will reduce States to mere corporations, and take away all sovereignty. . . . As to individual States and the United States, the Constitution marks the boundary of powers. Whatever power is deposited with the Union by the people for their own necessary security, is so far a curtailing of the power and prerogatives of States. This is, as it were, a self-evident proposition; at least it cannot be contested. Thus the power of declaring war, making peace, raising and supporting armies for public defence, levying duties, excises and taxes, if necessary, with many other powers, are lodged in Congress; and are a most essential abridgement of State sovereignty. . . . So that, I think, no argument of force can be taken from the sovereignty of States. Where it has been abridged, it was thought necessary for the greater indispensable good of the whole. If the Constitution is found inconvenient in practice in this or any other particular, it is well that a regular mode is pointed out for amendment. . . .

One other objection has been suggested, that if a State may be sued by a citizen of another State, then the United States may be sued by a citizen of any of the States, or, in other words, by any of their citizens. If this be a necessary consequence, it must be so. I doubt the consequence, from the different wording of the different clauses, connected with other reasons. When speaking of the United States, the Constitution says "controversies to which the United States shall be a party" not controversies between the United States and any of their citizens . . . . But I do not think it necessary to enter fully into the question, whether the United States are liable to be sued by an individual citizen in order to decide the point before us. Upon the whole, I am of opinion, that the Constitution warrants a suit against a State, by an individual citizen of another State.

. . . .

CHIEF JUSTICE JAY.

The question we are now to decide has been accurately stated, viz., Is a State suable by individual citizens of another State?

It is said, Georgia refuses to appear and answer to the Plaintiff in this action, because she is a sovereign State, and therefore not liable to such actions. . . .

. . . .

[First, in] determining the sense in which Georgia is a sovereign State, it may be useful to turn our attention to the political situation we were in, prior to the Revolution, and to the political rights which emerged from the Revolution. . . .

The Revolution, or rather the Declaration of Independence, found the people already united for general purposes, and at the same time providing for their more domestic concerns by State conventions and other temporary arrangements. . . . [T]hirteen sovereignties were considered as emerged from the principles of the Revolution, combined with local convenience and considerations; the people nevertheless continued to consider themselves, in a national point of view, as one people; and they continued without interruption to manage their national concerns accordingly; afterwards, in the hurry of the war, and in the warmth of mutual confidence, they made a confederation of the States, the basis of a general Government. Experience disappointed the expectations they had formed from it; and then the people, in their collective and national capacity, established the present Constitution. . . . Here we see the people acting as sovereigns of the whole country; and in the language of sovereignty, establishing a Constitution by which it was their will, that the State Governments should be bound, and to which the State Constitutions should be made to conform. Every State Constitution is a compact made by and between the citizens of a State to govern themselves in a certain manner; and the Constitution of the United States is likewise a compact made by the people of the United States to govern themselves as to general objects, in a certain manner. By this great compact however, many prerogatives were transferred to the national Government . . . .

. . . .

It will be sufficient to observe briefly, that the sovereignties in Europe, and particularly in England, exist on feudal principles. . . . The same feudal ideas run through all their jurisprudence, and constantly remind us of the distinction between the Prince and the subject. No such ideas obtain here; at the Revolution, the sovereignty devolved on the people; and they are truly the sovereigns of the country . . . .

. . . .

. . . The second object of enquiry now presents itself, viz. whether suability is compatible with State sovereignty.

. . . Will it be said, that the fifty odd thousand citizens in Delaware being associated under a State Government, stand in rank so superior to the forty odd thousand of Philadelphia, associated under their charter, that although it may become the latter to meet an individual on an equal footing in a Court of Justice, yet that such a procedure would not comport with the dignity of the former? . . .

. . . [A]ny one State in the Union may sue another State, in this Court . . . . It is plain then, that a State may be sued, and hence it plainly follows, that suability and state sovereignty are not incompatible. . . . [Moreover, the] State of Georgia is at this moment prosecuting an action in this Court against two citizens of South Carolina.

The only remnant of objection therefore that remains is, that the State is not bound to appear and answer as a Defendant at the suit of an individual: but why it is unreasonable that she should be so bound, is hard to conjecture . . . .

Let us now proceed to enquire whether Georgia has not, by being a party to the national compact, consented to be suable by individual citizens of another State. . . .

. . . .

Let us now turn to the Constitution. The people therein declare, that their design in establishing it, comprehended six objects. . . . To form a more perfect union. . . . To establish justice. . . .

. . . Even this cursory review of the judicial powers of the United States, leaves the mind strongly impressed with the importance of them to the preservation of the tranquillity, the equal sovereignty, and the equal right of the people.

The question now before us renders it necessary to pay particular attention to that part of the second section, which extends the judicial power "to controversies between a state and citizens of another state." . . .

This extension of power is remedial, because it is to settle controversies. It is therefore, to be construed liberally. . . . If the Constitution really meant to extend these powers only to those controversies in which a State might be a Plaintiff, to the exclusion of those in which citizens had demands against a State, it is inconceivable that it should have attempted to convey that meaning in words, not only so incompetent, but also repugnant to it; if it meant to exclude a certain class of these controversies, why were they not expressly excepted; on the contrary, not even an intimation of such intention appears in any part of the Constitution. . . .

The exception contended for, would contradict and do violence to the great and leading principles of a free and equal national government, one of the great objects of which is, to ensure justice to all . . . . It would be strange, indeed, that the joint and equal sovereigns of this country, should, in the very Constitution by which they professed to establish justice, so far deviate from the plain path of equality and impartiality, as to give to the collective citizens of one State, a right of suing individual citizens of another State, and yet deny to those citizens a right of suing them. . . . Words are to be understood in their ordinary and common acceptation, and the word party being in common usage, applicable both to Plaintiff and

Defendant, we cannot limit it to one of them in the present case. We find the Legislature of the United States expressing themselves in the like general and comprehensive manner; they speak in [Section 13 of the Federal Judiciary Act of 1789] of controversies where a State is a party . . . .

I perceive, and therefore candor urges me to mention, a circumstance, which seems to favor the opposite side of the question. It is this: the same section of the Constitution which extends the judicial power to controversies "between a State and the citizens of another State," does also extend that power to controversies to which the United States are a party. Now, it may be said, if the word party comprehends both Plaintiff and Defendant, it follows, that the United States may be sued by any citizen, between whom and them there may be a controversy. This appears to me to be fair reasoning; but the same principles of candour which urge me to mention this objection, also urge me to suggest an important difference between the two cases. It is this: in all cases of actions against States or individual citizens, the National Courts are supported in all their legal and Constitutional proceedings and judgments, by the arm of the Executive power of the United States; but in cases of actions against the United States, there is no power which the Courts can call to their aid. From this distinction important conclusions are deducible, and they place the case of a State, and the case of the United States, in very different points of view.

. . . .

. . . [This interpretation] brings into action, and enforces this great and glorious principle, that the people are the sovereign of this country, and consequently that fellow citizens and joint sovereigns cannot be degraded by appearing with each other in their own Courts to have their controversies determined. . . .

For the reasons before given, I am clearly of opinion, that a State is suable by citizens of another State . . . .

Exercise 8:

In the various opinions in *Chisholm v. Georgia*, identify the interpretive methods employed. Identify any of the five forms of argument that are employed by the Court.

(1)   For arguments based upon constitutional text, what techniques do the Justices use other than examining the plain meaning of the words?

(2)   For arguments based upon history, what sources do the Justices consider?

In addition, consider:

(3)   What is the holding of the Court in *Chisholm v. Georgia* with regard to whether States may be required to defend in federal court actions for damages instituted by citizens of another State?

(4)   With respect to those Justices who supported federal jurisdiction over Georgia, upon what constitutional text did they rely? Was that text different than text considered in connection with Exercises 3 or 4 or 5? Was the text relied upon in *Chisholm* construed by Brutus and/or Hamilton in the ratification debates?

(5)   With respect to those Justices who supported federal jurisdiction over Georgia, did they adequately distinguish the case of suits against the United States? That is, if the Constitution does not guarantee unconsenting States immunity from suits brought by private individuals, is there any basis to conclude that the Constitution guarantees such immunity to the government of the United States?

(6)   Did the majority of the Court embrace a different view of the structure of the Constitution than identified in Exercise 1?

(7)   How did a majority of the Court answer the question about the location of "sovereignty" under the U.S. Constitution?

(8)   With respect to those Justices who supported federal jurisdiction over Georgia, did they agree that each State benefitted from immunity to suit by individuals before the Constitution? After ratification of the Constitution, could each State continue to assert such immunity in actions filed in its own court system? What, if anything, in the ratification debates and Judiciary Act of 1789 shed light on these questions?

(9)   Read the Eleventh Amendment. After ratification of that Amendment, under what conditions may a State be required to defend itself in federal court?

CHAPTER 4

THE ELEVENTH AMENDMENT IN THE NINETEENTH CENTURY

Exercise Three examined the text of the Constitution of 1789 with respect to the question of immunity of the States in suits brought by private individuals in federal court. *Exercise Four* revisited the question with additional information regarding the shared public understanding of the Constitution as reflected in debates on the ratification of the Constitution. The Supreme Court addressed the issue in *Chisholm v. Georgia* (in the previous Chapter). The Eleventh Amendment was promptly adopted in reaction to that decision. *Exercise Eight* examined the text of the Eleventh Amendment to determine the resulting scope of state immunity from suits brought by private individuals in federal court.

The Constitution is not a static instrument. Through the addition of Amendments contemplated by Article V, previous provisions may be modified or superceded altogether. The ratification of the Eleventh Amendment provides the opportunity to examine the role of Amendments in the process of interpreting the Constitution.

The Supreme Court addressed the meaning of the Eleventh Amendment in several cases in the first century after its ratification. Two of those cases are presented here.

Observe that beginning with the appointment of John Marshall as Chief Justice, in 1801, the Court abandoned its earlier practice of *seriatim* opinions. When a majority of Justices agreed with the judgment and reasoning, a single opinion would be published as the "Opinion of the Court."

COHENS v. VIRGINIA
19 U.S. 264 (1821)

[Congress established the Corporation of the City of Washington and authorized it, among other things, to conduct lotteries to raise funds for public improvement projects. Cohens, a citizen of Virginia, sold tickets for the lottery while in Virginia.

The Commonwealth of Virginia criminally prosecuted Cohens in state court for violation of a state statute prohibiting the sale of lottery tickets. In his defense, Cohens asserted that a federal statute authorized him to sell the lottery tickets. The highest state court in which the matter was cognizable ruled against Cohens.

Cohens then sought review of the state court judgment by the U.S. Supreme Court via a writ of error. Virginia argued that the Court lacked jurisdiction to review the matter.]

CHIEF JUSTICE MARSHALL delivered the Opinion of the Court.

. . . .

In support of this motion, three points have been made, and argued with the ability which the importance of the question merits. The points are —

[First, that] a State is a defendant.

[Second, that] no writ of error lies from this Court to a State Court.

[Third, . . .] that the want of jurisdiction was shown by the subject matter of the case. [Or, alternatively,] that the jurisdiction was not given by the [Judiciary Act of 1789]. . . .

The questions presented to the Court by the two first points made at the bar are of great magnitude, and may be truly said vitally to affect the Union. . . . They maintain that the constitution of the United States has provided no tribunal for the final construction of itself, or of the laws or treaties of the nation; but that this power may be exercised in the last resort by the Courts of every State in the Union. That the constitution, laws, and treaties, may receive as many constructions as there are States; and that this is not a mischief, or, if a mischief, is irremediable. . . .

If such be the constitution, it is the duty of the Court to bow with respectful submission to its provisions. If such be not the constitution, it is equally the duty of this Court to say so; and to perform that task which the American people have assigned to the judicial department.

[I]

The first question to be considered is, whether the jurisdiction of this Court is excluded by the character of the parties, one of them being a State, and the other a citizen of that State?

[A]

[Article III, section 2] of the constitution defines the extent of the judicial power of the United States. Jurisdiction is given to the Courts of the Union in two classes of cases. In the first, their jurisdiction depends on the character of the cause, whoever may be the parties. This class comprehends "all cases in law and equity arising under this constitution, the laws of the United States, and treaties made, or which shall be made, under their authority." This clause extends the jurisdiction of the Court to all the cases described, without making in its terms any exception whatever, and without regard to the condition of the party. . . .

In the second class, the jurisdiction depends entirely on the character of the parties. . . . If these be the parties, it is entirely unimportant what may be the subject of controversy. Be it what it may, these parties have a constitutional right to come into the Courts of the Union.

. . . .

. . . [If Virginia contends] that a case arising under the constitution, or a law, must be one in which a party comes into Court to demand something conferred on him by the constitution or a law, we think the construction too narrow. A case in law or equity consists of the right of the one party, as well as of the other, and may truly be said to arise under the constitution or a law of the United States, whenever its correct decision depends on the construction of either. Congress seems to have intended to give its own construction of this part of the constitution in [section 25 of the Federal Judiciary Act of 1789]; and we perceive no reason to depart from that construction.

. . . .

. . . [Virginia asserts] the general proposition, that a sovereign independent State is not suable, except by its own consent.

This general proposition will not be controverted. But its consent is not requisite in each particular case. It may be given in a general law. . . .

The American States, as well as the American people, have believed a close and firm Union to be essential to their liberty and to their happiness. They have been taught by experience, that this Union cannot exist without a government for the whole; and they have been taught by the same experience that this government would be a mere shadow, that must disappoint all their hopes, unless invested with large portions of that sovereignty which belongs to independent States. Under the influence of this opinion, and thus instructed by experience, the American people, in the conventions of their respective States, adopted the present constitution.

If it could be doubted, whether from its nature, it were not supreme in all cases where it is empowered to act, that doubt would be removed by the declaration, that "this constitution, and the laws of the United States, which shall be made in pursuance thereof, and all treaties made, or which shall be made, under the authority of the United States, shall be the supreme law of the land; and the judges in every State shall be bound thereby; any thing in the constitution or laws of any State to the contrary notwithstanding."

This is the authoritative language of the American people . . . . The general government, though limited as to its objects, is supreme with respect to those objects. . . .

To this supreme government ample powers are confided; and if it were possible to doubt the great purposes for which they were so confided, the people of the United States have declared, that they are given "in order to form a more perfect union, establish justice . . . and secure the blessings of liberty to themselves and their posterity."

With the ample powers confided to this supreme government, for these interesting purposes, are connected many express and important limitations on the sovereignty of the States, which are made for the same purposes. . . . The maintenance of these principles in their purity, is certainly among the great duties of government. One of the instruments by which this duty may be peaceably performed, is the judicial department. It is authorized to decide all cases of every description, arising under the constitution or laws of the United States. From this general grant of jurisdiction, no exception is made of those cases in which a State may be a party. . . . We think a case arising under the constitution or laws of the United States, is cognizable in the Courts of the Union, whoever may be the parties to that case.

Had any doubt existed with respect to the just construction of this part of the section, that doubt would have been removed by the enumeration of those cases to which the jurisdiction of the federal Courts is extended, in consequence of the character of the parties. . . .

One of the express objects, then, for which the judicial department was established, is the decision of controversies between States, and between a State and individuals. The mere circumstance, that a State is a party, gives jurisdiction to the Court. How, then, can it be contended, that the very same instrument, in the very same section, should be so construed, as that this same circumstance should withdraw a case from the jurisdiction of the Court, where the constitution or laws of the United States are supposed to have been violated? The constitution gave to every person having a claim upon a State, a right to submit his case to the Court of the nation. . . .

. . . [That understanding is supported by the principle] that the judicial power of every well constituted government must be co-extensive with the legislative, and must be capable of deciding every judicial question which grows out of the constitution and laws.

If any proposition may be considered as a political axiom, this, we think, may be so considered. In reasoning upon it as an abstract question, there would, probably, exist no contrariety of opinion respecting it. Every argument, proving the necessity of the department, proves also the propriety of giving this extent to it. . . .

. . . .

. . . Different States may entertain different opinions on the true construction of the constitutional powers of Congress. We know, that at one time, the assumption of the debts contracted by the several States, during the war of our revolution, was deemed unconstitutional by some of them. We know, too, that at other times, certain taxes, imposed by Congress, have been pronounced unconstitutional. . . . When we observe the importance which that constitution attaches to the independence of judges, we are the less inclined to suppose that it can have intended to leave these constitutional questions to tribunals where this independence may not exist, in all cases where a State shall prosecute an individual who claims the protection of an act of Congress. These prosecutions may take place even without a legislative act. A person making a seizure under an act of Congress, may be indicted as a trespasser, if force has been employed, and of this a jury may judge. How extensive may be the mischief if the first decisions in such cases should be final!

These collisions may take place in times of no extraordinary commotion. But a constitution is framed for ages to come, and is designed to approach immortality as nearly as human institutions can approach it. Its course cannot always be tranquil. It is exposed to storms and tempests, and its framers must be unwise statesmen indeed, if they have not provided it, as far as its nature will permit, with the means of self-preservation from the perils it may be destined to encounter. No government ought to be so defective in its organization, as not to contain within itself the means of securing the execution of its own laws against other dangers than those which occur every day. Courts of justice are the means most usually employed; and it is reasonable to expect that a government should repose on its own Courts, rather than on others. . . . Is it so improbable that [the Framers] should confer on the judicial department the power of construing the constitution and laws of the Union in every case, in the last resort, and of preserving them from all violation from every quarter, so far as judicial decisions can preserve them, that this improbability should essentially affect the construction of the new system? We are . . . truly told, that the great change which is to give efficacy to the present system, is its ability to act on individuals directly, instead of acting through the instrumentality of State governments. But, ought not this ability, in reason and sound policy, to be applied directly to the protection of individuals employed in the execution of the laws, as well as to their coercion? Your laws reach the individual without the aid of any other power; why may they not protect him from punishment for performing his duty in executing them?

. . . .

It is very true that, whenever hostility to the existing system shall become universal, it will be also irresistible. The people made the constitution, and the people can unmake it. It is the creature of their will, and lives only by their will. But this supreme and irresistible power to make or to unmake, resides only in the whole body of the people; not in any sub-division of them. The attempt of any of the parts to exercise it is usurpation, and ought to be repelled by those to whom the people have delegated their power of repelling it.

. . . .

It has been also urged, as an additional objection to the jurisdiction of the Court, that cases between a State and one of its own citizens, do not come within the general scope of the constitution; and were obviously never intended to be made cognizable in the federal Courts. . . .

This is very true, so far as jurisdiction depends on the character of the parties; and the argument would have great force if urged to prove that this Court could not establish the demand of a citizen upon his State, but it is not entitled to the same force when urged to prove that this Court cannot inquire whether the constitution or laws of the United States protect a citizen from a prosecution instituted against him by a State. If jurisdiction depended entirely on the character of the parties, and was not given where the parties have not an original right to come into Court, that part of [Article III, section 2], which extends the judicial power to all cases arising under the constitution and laws of the United States, would be mere surplusage. It is to give jurisdiction where the character of the parties would not give it, that this very important part of the clause was inserted. . . . If the constitution or laws may be violated by proceedings instituted by a State against its own citizens, and if that violation may be such as essentially to affect the constitution and the laws, such as to arrest the progress of government in its constitutional course, why should these cases be excepted from that provision which expressly extends the judicial power of the Union to *all* cases arising under the constitution and laws?

After bestowing on this subject the most attentive consideration, the Court can perceive no reason founded on the character of the parties for introducing an exception which the constitution has not made; and we think that the judicial power, as originally given, extends to all cases arising under the constitution or a law of the United States, whoever may be the parties.

[B]

It has also been contended, that this jurisdiction, if given, is original, and cannot be exercised in the appellate form.

[1]

The words of the constitution are, "in all cases . . . in which a State shall be a party, the Supreme Court shall have original jurisdiction. In all the other cases before mentioned, the Supreme Court shall have appellate jurisdiction."

This distinction between original and appellate jurisdiction, excludes, we are told, in all cases, the exercise of the one where the other is given.

The constitution gives the Supreme Court original jurisdiction in certain enumerated cases, and gives it appellate jurisdiction in all others. Among those in which jurisdiction must be exercised in the appellate form, are cases arising under the constitution and laws of the United States. These provisions are equally obligatory, and are to be equally respected. If a State be a party, the jurisdiction of this Court is original; if the case arise under a constitution or a law, the jurisdiction is appellate. But a case to which a State is a party may arise under the constitution or a law of the United States. What rule is applicable to such a case? . . .

. . . When, then, the constitution declares the jurisdiction, in cases where a State shall be a party, to be original, and in all cases arising under the constitution or a law, to be appellate — the conclusion seems irresistible, that its framers designed to include in the first class those cases in which jurisdiction is given, because a State is a party; and to include in the second, those in which jurisdiction is given, because the case arises under the constitution or a law.

This reasonable construction is rendered necessary by other considerations.

That the constitution or a law of the United States, is involved in a case, and makes a part of it, may appear in the progress of a cause, in which the Courts of the Union, but for that circumstance, would have no jurisdiction, and which of consequence could not originate in the Supreme Court. In such a case, the jurisdiction can be exercised only in its appellate form. To deny its exercise in this form is to deny its existence, and would be to construe a clause, dividing the power of the Supreme Court, in such a manner, as in a considerable degree to defeat the power itself. . . .

. . . .

The constitution declares, that in cases where a State is a party, the Supreme Court shall have original jurisdiction; but does not say that its appellate jurisdiction shall not be exercised in cases where, from their nature, appellate jurisdiction is given, whether a State be or be not a party. . . .

. . . .

. . . It has been generally held, that the State Courts have a concurrent jurisdiction with the federal Courts, in cases to which the judicial power is extended, unless the jurisdiction of the federal Courts be rendered exclusive by the words of [Article III]. If the words, "to all cases," give exclusive jurisdiction in cases affecting foreign ministers, they may also give exclusive jurisdiction, if such be the will of Congress, in cases arising under the constitution, laws, and treaties of the United States. Now, suppose an individual were to sue a foreign minister in a State Court, and that Court were to maintain its jurisdiction, and render judgment against the minister, could it be contended, that this Court would be incapable of revising such judgment, because the constitution had given it original jurisdiction in the case? If this could be maintained, then a clause inserted for the purpose of excluding the jurisdiction of all other Courts than this, in a particular case, would have the effect of excluding jurisdiction of this Court in that very case, if the suit were to be brought in another Court, and that Court were to assert jurisdiction. . . .

. . . The truth is, that where the words confer only appellate jurisdiction, original jurisdiction is most clearly not given; but where the words admit of appellate jurisdiction, the power to take cognizance of the suit originally, does not necessarily negative the power to decide upon it on an appeal, if it may originate in a different Court.

It is, we think, apparent that to give this distributive clause the interpretation contended for, to give to its affirmative words a negative operation, in every possible case, would, in some instances, defeat the obvious intention of [Article III]. . . . Every part of the [A]rticle must be taken into view, and that construction adopted which will consist with its words, and promote its general intention. The Court may imply a negative from affirmative words, where the implication promotes, not where it defeats the intention.

. . . The original jurisdiction of this Court cannot be enlarged, but its appellate jurisdiction may be exercised in every case cognizable under [Article III] of the constitution, in the federal Courts, in which original jurisdiction cannot be exercised . . . .

[2]

[Virginia asserts], in opposition to this rule of construction, some *dicta* of the Court, in the case of *Marbury v. Madison.*

It is a maxim not to be disregarded, that general expressions, in every opinion, are to be taken in connection with the case in which those expressions are used. If they go beyond the case, they may be respected, but ought not to control the judgment in a subsequent suit when the very point is presented for decision. The reason for this maxim is obvious. The question actually before the Court is investigated with care, and considered in its full extent. Other principles which may serve to illustrate it, are considered in their relation to the case decided, but their possible bearing on all other cases is seldom completely investigated.

In the case of *Marbury v. Madison,* the single question before the Court, so far as that case can be applied to this, was, whether the legislature could give this Court original jurisdiction in a case in which the constitution had clearly not given it, and in which no doubt respecting the construction of [Article III] could possibly be raised. The Court decided, and we think very properly, that the legislature could not give original jurisdiction in such a case. But, in the reasoning of the Court in support of this decision, some expressions are used which go far beyond it. The counsel for Marbury had insisted on the unlimited discretion of the legislature in the apportionment of the judicial power; and it is against this argument that the reasoning of the Court is directed. . . .

. . . [The *Marbury*] Court lays down a principle which is generally correct, in terms much broader than the reasoning with which that decision is supported, but in some instances contradictory to its principle. . . .

. . . The general expressions in the case of *Marbury v. Madison* must be understood with the limitations which are given them in this opinion; limitations which in no degree affect the decision in that case, or the tenor of its reasoning.

. . . .

It is most true that this Court will not take jurisdiction if it should not: but it is equally true, that it must take jurisdiction if it should. The judiciary cannot, as the legislature may, avoid a measure because it approaches the confines of the constitution. We cannot pass it by because it is doubtful. With whatever doubts, with whatever difficulties, a case may be attended, we must decide it, if it be brought before us. We have no more right to decline the exercise of jurisdiction which is given, than to usurp that which is not given. . . .

. . . .

. . . [Article III] does not extend the judicial power to every violation of the constitution which may possibly take place, but to "a case in law or equity," in which a right, under such law, is asserted in a Court of justice. If the question cannot be brought into a Court, then there is no case in law or equity, and no jurisdiction is given by the words of the article. But if, in any controversy depending in a Court, the cause should depend on the validity of such a law, that would be a case arising under the constitution, to which the judicial power of the United States would extend. . . .

We think, then, that, as the constitution originally stood, the appellate jurisdiction of this Court, in all cases arising under the constitution, laws, or treaties of the United States, was not arrested by the circumstance that a State was a party.

[3]

This leads to a consideration of the [Eleventh] Amendment.

It is in these words: "The judicial power of the United States shall not be construed to extend to any suit in law or equity commenced or prosecuted against one of the United States, by citizens of another State, or by citizens or subjects of any foreign State."

[a]

It is a part of our history, that, at the adoption of the constitution, all the States were greatly indebted; and the apprehension that these debts might be prosecuted in the federal Courts, formed a very serious objection to that instrument. Suits were instituted; and the Court maintained its jurisdiction. The alarm was general; and, to quiet the apprehensions that were so extensively entertained, this amendment was proposed in Congress, and adopted by the State legislatures. That its motive was not to maintain the sovereignty of a State from the degradation supposed to attend a compulsory appearance before the tribunal of the nation, may be inferred from the terms of the amendment. It does not comprehend controversies between two or more States, or between a State and a foreign State. The jurisdiction of the Court still extends to these cases; and in these a State may still be sued. We must ascribe the amendment, then, to some other cause than the dignity of a State. There is no difficulty in finding this cause. Those who were inhibited from commencing a suit against a State, or from prosecuting one which might be commenced before the adoption of the amendment, were persons who might probably be its creditors. There was not much reason to fear that foreign or sister States would be creditors to any considerable amount, and there was reason to retain the jurisdiction of the Court in those cases, because it might be essential to the preservation of peace. The amendment, therefore, extended to suits commenced or prosecuted by individuals, but not to those brought by States.

The first impression made on the mind by this amendment is, that it was intended for those cases, and for those only, in which some demand against a State is made by an individual in the Courts of the Union. If we consider the causes to which it is to be traced, we are conducted to the same conclusion. . . .

The words of the amendment appear to the Court to justify and require this construction. . . .

. . . .

[b]

To commence a suit, is to demand something by the institution of process in a Court of justice; and to prosecute the suit, is, according to the common acceptation of language, to continue that demand. By a suit commenced by an individual against a State, we should understand process sued out by that individual against the State, for the purpose of establishing some claim against it by the judgment of a Court; and the prosecution of that suit is its continuance. Whatever may be the stages of its progress, the actor is still the same. . . . The object of the amendment was not only to prevent the commencement of future suits, but to arrest the prosecution of those which might be commenced when this article should form a part of the constitution. . . .

A writ of error is defined to be, a commission by which the judges of one Court are authorized to examine a record upon which a judgment was given in another

Court, and, on such examination, to affirm or reverse the same according to law. . . .

. . . .

Under the [Judiciary Act of 1789], the effect of a writ of error is simply to bring the record into Court, and submit the judgment of the inferior tribunal to re-examination. . . . Where, then, a State obtains a judgment against an individual, and the Court, rendering such judgment overrules a defence set up under the constitution or laws of the United States, the transfer of this record into the Supreme Court, for the sole purpose of inquiring whether the judgment violates the constitution or laws of the United States, can, with no propriety, we think, be denominated a suit commenced or prosecuted against the State whose judgment is so far re-examined. Nothing is demanded from the State. No claim against it of any description is asserted or prosecuted. . . . Whether it be by writ of error or appeal, no claim is asserted, no demand is made by the original defendant; he only asserts the constitutional right to have his defence examined by that tribunal whose province it is to construe the constitution and laws of the Union.

. . . .

[This conclusion is further supported] by a reference to the course of this Court in suits instituted by the United States. The universally received opinion is, that no suit can be commenced or prosecuted against the United States; that the [Judiciary Act of 1789] does not authorize such suits. Yet writs of error, accompanied with citations, have uniformly issued for the removal of judgments in favor of the United States into a superior Court, where they have, like those in favor of an individual, been re-examined, and affirmed or reversed. It has never been suggested, that such writ of error was a suit against the United States, and, therefore, not within the jurisdiction of the appellate court.

. . . .

[c]

But should we in this be mistaken, the error does not affect the case now before the Court. If this writ of error be a suit in the sense of the [Eleventh Amendment], it is not a suit commenced or prosecuted "by a citizen of another State, or by a citizen or subject of any foreign State." It is not then within the amendment, but is governed entirely by the constitution as originally framed, and we have already seen, that in its origin, the judicial power was extended to all cases arising under the constitution or laws of the United States, without respect to parties.

[II]

The second objection to the jurisdiction of the Court is, that its appellate power cannot be exercised, in any case, over the judgment of a State Court.

This objection is sustained chiefly by arguments drawn from the supposed total separation of the judiciary of a State from that of the Union, and their entire independence of each other. . . .

. . . .

That the United States form, for many, and for most important purposes, a single nation, has not yet been denied. . . . The people have declared, that in the exercise of all powers given for these objects, it is supreme. It can, then, in effecting these objects, legitimately control all individuals or governments within the American territory. The constitution and laws of a State, so far as they are repugnant to the constitution and laws of the United States, are absolutely void. These States are constituent parts of the United States. They are members of one great empire — for some purposes sovereign, for some purposes subordinate.

. . . .

The propriety of entrusting the construction of the constitution, and laws made in pursuance thereof, to the judiciary of the Union, has not, we believe, as yet, been drawn into question. It seems to be a corollary from this political axiom, that the federal Courts should either possess exclusive jurisdiction in such cases, or a power to revise the judgment rendered in them, by the State tribunals. . . .

. . . .

[A]

[The words of Article III] give to the Supreme Court appellate jurisdiction in all cases arising under the constitution, laws, and treaties of the United States. The words are broad enough to comprehend all cases of this description, in whatever Court they may be decided. In expounding them, we may be permitted to take into view those considerations to which Courts have always allowed great weight in the exposition of laws.

[B]

The framers of the constitution would naturally examine the state of things existing at the time; and their work sufficiently attests that they did so. All acknowledge that they were convened for the purpose of strengthening the confederation by enlarging the powers of government, and by giving efficacy to those which it before possessed, but could not exercise. They inform us themselves, in the instrument they presented to the American public, that one of its objects was to form a more perfect union. Under such circumstances, we certainly should not expect to find, in that instrument, a diminution of the powers of the actual government.

[Under the Articles of Confederation,] Congress established Courts which received appeals in prize causes decided in the Courts of the respective States. . . . These Courts did exercise appellate jurisdiction over those cases decided in the State Courts, to which the judicial power of the federal government extended.

. . . .

The Convention which framed the Constitution, on turning their attention to the judicial power, found it limited to a few objects, but exercised, with respect to some of those objects, in its appellate form, over the judgments of the State Courts. They extend it, among other objects, to all cases arising under the constitution, laws, and treaties of the United States; and in a subsequent clause declare, that in such cases, the Supreme Court shall exercise appellate jurisdiction. Nothing seems to be given which would justify the withdrawal of a judgment rendered in a State Court, on the constitution, laws, or treaties of the United States, from this appellate jurisdiction.

[C]

Great weight has always been attached, and very rightly attached, to contemporaneous exposition. No question, it is believed, has arisen to which this principle applies more unequivocally than to that now under consideration.

[1]

The opinion of the *Federalist* has always been considered as of great authority. It is a complete commentary on our constitution; and is appealed to by all parties in the questions to which that instrument has given birth. Its intrinsic merit entitles it to this high rank; and the part two of its authors performed in framing the constitution, put it very much in their power to explain the views with which it was framed. These essays having been published while the constitution was before the nation for adoption or rejection, and having been written in answer to objections founded entirely on the extent of its powers, and on its diminution of State sovereignty, are entitled to the more consideration where they frankly avow that the power objected to is given, and defend it.

In discussing the extent of the judicial power, the *Federalist* says, "Here another question occurs: what relation would subsist between the national and State Courts in these instances of concurrent jurisdiction? I answer, that an appeal would certainly lie from the latter, to the Supreme Court of the United States. The constitution in direct terms gives an appellate jurisdiction to the Supreme Court in all the enumerated cases of federal cognizance in which it is not to have an original one, without a single expression to confine its operation to the inferior federal courts. The objects of the appeal, not the tribunals from which it is to be made, are alone contemplated. . . . Either this must be the case, or the local Courts must be excluded from a concurrent jurisdiction in matters of national concern, else the judicial authority of the Union may be eluded at the pleasure of every plaintiff or prosecutor. . . . Agreeable to the remark already made, the national and State systems are to be regarded as ONE WHOLE. The Courts of the latter will of course be natural auxiliaries to the execution of the laws of the Union, and an appeal from them will as naturally lie to that tribunal which is destined to unite and assimilate the principles of natural justice, and the rules of national decision. . . . To confine, therefore, the general expressions which give appellate jurisdiction to the Supreme Court, to appeals from the subordinate federal Courts, instead of allowing their extension to the State Courts, would be to abridge the latitude of the terms, in subversion of the intent, contrary to every sound rule of interpretation."

[2]

A contemporaneous exposition of the constitution, certainly of not less authority than that which has been just cited, is the [Judiciary Act of 1789] itself. We know that in the Congress which passed that act were many eminent members of the Convention which formed the constitution. Not a single individual, so far as is known, supposed that part of the act which gives the Supreme Court appellate jurisdiction over the judgments of the State Courts in the cases therein specified, to be unauthorized by the constitution.

[3]

While on this part of the argument, it may be also material to observe that the uniform decisions of this Court on the point now under consideration, have been assented to, with a single exception, by the Courts of every State in the Union whose judgments have been revised . . . .

. . . .

. . . Let the nature and objects of our Union be considered; let the great fundamental principles, on which the fabric stands, be examined; and we think the result must be, that there is nothing so extravagantly absurd in giving to the Court of the nation the power of revising the decisions of local tribunals on questions which affect the nation, as to require that words which import this power should be restricted by a forced construction. The question then must depend on the words themselves; and on their construction we shall be the more readily excused for not adding to the observations already made, because the subject was fully discussed and exhausted in the case of *Martin v. Hunter.*

[III]

We come now to the third objection, which, though differently stated by the counsel, is substantially the same. One gentleman has said that the [Judiciary Act of 1789] does not give jurisdiction in the case.

. . . .

If [Section 25 of the Judiciary Act of 1789] be inspected, it will at once be perceived that it comprehends expressly the case under consideration.

. . . They deny that the act of Congress, on which [Cohens] relies, is a law of the United States; or, if a law of the United States, is within [Article VI, Clause 2 of the U.S. Constitution].

In the enumeration of the powers of Congress, which is made in [Article I, section 8], we find that of exercising exclusive legislation over such District as shall become the seat of government. This power, like all others which are specified, is conferred on Congress as the legislature of the Union . . . . In legislating for the District, they necessarily preserve the character of the legislature of the Union; for, it is in that character alone that the constitution confers on them this power of exclusive legislation. This proposition need not be enforced.

[Article VI, Clause 2 of the U.S. Constitution] declares, that "This constitution, and the laws of the United States, which shall be made in pursuance thereof, shall be the supreme law of the land."

This clause which gives exclusive jurisdiction is, unquestionably, a part of the constitution, and, as such, binds all the United States. Those who contend that acts of Congress, made in pursuance of this power, do not, like acts made in pursuance of other powers, bind the nation, ought to show some safe and clear rule which shall support this construction, and prove that an act of Congress, clothed in all the forms which attend other legislative acts, and passed in virtue of a power conferred on, and exercised by Congress, as the legislature of the Union, is not a law of the United States, and does not bind them.

One of the gentlemen sought to illustrate his proposition that Congress, when legislating for the District, assumed a distinct character, and was reduced to a mere local legislature, whose laws could possess no obligation out of the ten miles square . . . .

. . . .

Since Congress legislates in the same forms, and in the same character, in virtue of powers of equal obligation, conferred in the same instrument, when exercising its exclusive powers of legislation, as well as when exercising those which are limited, we must inquire whether there be any thing in the nature of this exclusive legislation, which necessarily confines the operation of the laws made in virtue of this power to the place with a view to which they are made.

. . . .

The solution, and the only solution of the difficulty, is, that the power vested in Congress, as the legislature of the United States, to legislate exclusively within any place ceded by a State, carries with it, as an incident, the right to make that power effectual. . . .

Whether any particular law be designed to operate without the District or not, depends on the words of that law. . . .

The whole merits of this case, then, consist in the construction of the constitution and the act of Congress. . . .

The counsel for the State of Virginia have, in support of this motion, urged many arguments of great weight against the application of the act of Congress to such a case as this; but those arguments go to the construction of the constitution, or of the law, or of both; and seem, therefore, rather calculated to sustain their cause upon its merits, than to prove a failure of the jurisdiction in the Court.

. . . .

Motion [to dismiss] denied.

. . . .

[In a subsequent opinion addressing the merits of the dispute, the Court concluded that Congress did not evidence any intent to authorize sale of the lottery tickets beyond the boundaries of the District of Columbia.]

Exercise 9:

Consider the following matters in connection with *Cohens v. Virginia:*

(1)   Do you agree that when a defendant in an action pending in state court raises a defense based on a federal statute, the case is one which "arises under" federal law within the meaning of Article III? If not, is there any other textual basis for Supreme Court review of the matter?

(2)   Do you agree that when a defendant in an action pending in state court raises a defense based on a federal statute, the case is one which Congress authorized the Supreme Court to review? If so, where is the statutory authorization? Is that authorization phrased any differently than the trial court jurisdiction of federal courts?

(3)   Does the fact that one party to the case is the State of Virginia take the matter outside the scope of Article III? Why or why not? Does the Court's analysis of that question follow or reject *Chisholm v. Georgia?*

(4)   How does the Court describe its power to construe the Constitution? Is it one of several coordinate branches each charged with a similar duty? Or, does the Court assert a special or superior role in interpreting the Constitution?

(5)   How does the Court define *dicta?* Throughout the remainder of the course, remain watchful of when the Court produces *dicta* and when it distinguishes precedents as mere *dicta.*

(6)   Observe the Court's description of its duty to exercise its jurisdiction. Should the Court be required to exercise its jurisdiction? What, if any, basis is there for the Court to decline to exercise jurisdiction?

(7)   Does the Court describe the case or controversy requirement in a manner consistent with your understanding of the justiciability doctrines? Is the description consistent with the early Court's views expressed in the letters to President Washington and in the decisions in the Revolutionary War pension cases?

(8)   What precedent does *Cohens* establish regarding the scope of the Eleventh Amendment?

(9)   What sources does the Court draw upon in its historical analysis? Which sources, if any, does the Court accord great weight?

(10)   Applying the Court's own definition of *dicta*, what is the holding of *Cohens*?

HANS v. STATE OF LOUISIANA
134 U.S. 1 (1890)

JUSTICE BRADLEY delivered the Opinion of the Court.

This is an action brought in the circuit court of the United States, in December, 1884, against the state of Louisiana, by Hans, a citizen of that state, to recover the amount of certain coupons annexed to bonds of the state, issued under the provisions of an act of the legislature approved January 24, 1874. . . . [Hans alleges that the State's actions in failing to make payment on the bonds] are in contravention of said contract, and . . . that said state thereby sought to impair the validity thereof with [Hans], in violation of article I, section 10, of the constitution of the United States, and the effect so given to said state constitution does impair said contract. . . .

[Hans served process upon the Governor. The State's attorney general objected to the federal court's jurisdiction, asserting that Hans] cannot sue the state without its permission; the constitution and laws do not give this honorable court jurisdiction of a suit against the state . . . . [The circuit court granted the State's motion to dismiss and Hans sought review by this Court.] [T]he question is presented whether a state can be sued in a circuit court of the United States by one of its own citizens upon a suggestion that the case is one that arises under the constitution or laws of the United States.

The ground taken is that under the constitution, as well as under the act of congress passed to carry it into effect, a case is within the jurisdiction of the federal courts, without regard to the character of the parties, if it arises under the constitution or laws of the United States, or, which is the same thing, if it necessarily involves a question under said constitution or laws. The language relied on is that clause of the third article of the constitution, which declares that "the judicial power of the United States shall extend to all cases in law and equity arising under this constitution, the laws of the United States, and treaties made, or which shall be made, under their authority;" and the corresponding clause of the act conferring jurisdiction upon the circuit court . . . in the act of March 3, 1875 . . . . It is said that these jurisdictional clauses make no exception arising from the character of the parties, and therefore that a state can claim no exemption from suit, if the case is really one arising under the constitution, laws, or treaties of the United States. It is conceded that, where the jurisdiction depends alone upon the character of the parties, a controversy between a state and its own citizens is not embraced within it . . . .

That a state cannot be sued by a citizen of another state, or of a foreign state, on the mere ground that the case is one arising under the constitution or laws of the United States, is clearly established by the decisions of this court in several recent cases. . . . This court held that the suits [against state officers for nonpayment of the State's debts] were virtually against the states themselves, and were consequently violative of the eleventh amendment of the constitution, and could not be maintained. It was not denied that they presented cases arising under the constitution; but, notwithstanding that, they were held to be prohibited by the amendment referred to.

In the present case [Hans] contends that he, being a citizen of Louisiana, is not embarrassed by the obstacle of the eleventh amendment, inasmuch as that amendment only prohibits suits against a state which are brought by the citizens of another state, or by citizens or subjects of a foreign state. It is true the amendment does so read, and, if there were no other reason or ground for abating his suit, it might be maintainable; and then we should have this anomalous result, that, in cases arising under the constitution or laws of the United States, a state may be sued in the federal courts by its own citizens, though it cannot be sued for a like cause of action by the citizens of other states, or of a foreign state; and may be thus sued in the federal courts, although not allowing itself to be sued in its own courts. If this is the necessary consequence of the language of the constitution and the law, the result is no less startling and unexpected than was the original decision of this court, that, under the language of the constitution and of the judiciary act of 1789, a state was liable to be sued by a citizen of another state or of a foreign country. That decision was made in the case of *Chisholm v. Georgia* and created such a shock of surprise throughout the country that, at the first meeting of congress thereafter, the eleventh amendment to the constitution was almost unanimously proposed, and was in due course adopted by the legislatures of the states. This amendment, expressing the will of the ultimate sovereignty of the whole country, superior to all legislatures and all courts, actually reversed the decision of the supreme court. It did not in terms prohibit suits by individuals against the states, but declared that the constitution should not be construed to import any power to authorize the bringing of such suits. [Based on that language, the Court declared that all federal courts lacked authority to continue to exercise jurisdiction over any cases of that description then-pending in federal court.]

This view of the force and meaning of the amendment is important. It shows that, on this question of the suability of the states by individuals, the highest authority of this country was in accord rather with the minority than with the majority of the court in the decision of the case of *Chisholm v. Georgia;* and this fact lends additional interest to the able opinion of Mr. Justice Iredell on that occasion. The other justices were more swayed by a close observance of the letter of the constitution, without regard to former experience and usage . . . . Justice Iredell, on the contrary, contended that it was not the intention to create new and unheard of remedies, by subjecting sovereign states to actions at the suit of individuals (which he conclusively showed was never done before) but only, by proper legislation, to invest the federal courts with jurisdiction to hear and determine controversies and cases, between the parties designated, that were properly susceptible of litigation in courts. Looking back from our present standpoint at the decision in *Chisholm v. Georgia,* we do not greatly wonder at the effect which it had on the country. Any such power as that of authorizing the federal judiciary to entertain suits by individuals against the states had been expressly disclaimed, and even resented, by the great defenders of the constitution while it was on its trial before the American people. . . .

The eighty-first number of the Federalist, written by [Alexander] Hamilton, has the following profound remarks:

> . . . It is inherent in the nature of sovereignty not to be amenable to the suit of an individual without its consent. This is the general sense and the general practice of mankind; and the exemption, as one of the attributes of sovereignty, is now enjoyed by the government of every state in the Union. . . . [T]here is no color to pretend that the state governments would, by the adoption of that plan, be divested of the privilege of paying their own debts in their own way, free from every constraint but that which flows from the obligations of good faith. . . . [T]o ascribe to the federal courts by mere implication, and in destruction of a pre-existing right of the

state governments, a power which would involve such a consequence, would be altogether forced and unwarrantable.

. . . [L]ooking at the subject as Hamilton did, and as Mr. Justice Iredell did, in the light of history and experience and the established order of things, [their] views were clearly right, as the people of the United States in their sovereign capacity subsequently decided.

But Hamilton was not alone . . . . In the Virginia convention the same objections were raised. . . . [In response, James] Madison said:

> Its jurisdiction [the federal jurisdiction] in controversies between a state and citizens of another state is so much objected to, and perhaps without reason. It is not in the power of individuals to call any state into court. . . . It appears to me that this [clause] can have no operation but this: to give a citizen a right to be heard in the federal courts, and, if a state should condescend to be a party, this court may take cognizance of it.

[John] Marshall, in answer to the same objection, said:

> With respect to disputes between a state and the citizens of another state, its jurisdiction has been decried with unusual vehemence. I hope no gentleman will think that a state will be called at the bar of the federal court. . . . It is not rational to suppose that the sovereign power should be dragged before a court. The intent is to enable states to recover claims of individuals residing in other states. . . . I see a difficulty in making a state defendant which does not prevent its being plaintiff.

It seems to us that these views of those great advocates and defenders of the constitution were most sensible and just, and they apply equally to the present case as to that then under discussion. The letter is appealed to now, as it was then, as a ground for sustaining a suit brought by an individual against a state. The reason against it is as strong in this case as it was in that. It is an attempt to strain the constitution and the law to a construction never imagined or dreamed of. Can we suppose that, when the eleventh amendment was adopted, it was understood to be left open for citizens of a state to sue their own state in the federal courts, while the idea of suits by citizens of other states, or of foreign states, was indignantly repelled? Suppose that congress, when proposing the eleventh amendment, had appended to it a proviso that nothing therein contained should prevent a state from being sued by its own citizens in cases arising under the constitution or laws of the United States, can we imagine that it would have been adopted by the states? The supposition that it would is almost an absurdity on its face.

The truth is that the cognizance of suits and actions unknown to the law, and forbidden by the law, was not contemplated by the constitution when establishing the judicial power of the United States. Some things, undoubtedly, were made justifiable which were not known as such at the common law; such, for example, as controversies between states as to boundary lines, and other questions admitting of judicial solution. . . . The establishment of this new branch of jurisdiction seemed to be necessary from the extinguishment of diplomatic relations between the states. . . .

The suability of a state, without its consent, was a thing unknown to the law. This has been so often laid down and acknowledged by courts and jurists that it is hardly necessary to be formally asserted. It was fully shown by an exhaustive examination of the old law by Mr. Justice Iredell in his opinion in *Chisholm v. Georgia;* and it has been conceded in every case since, where the question has, in any way, been presented, even in the cases which have gone furthest in sustaining suits against the officers or agents of states. . . . "It may be accepted as a point of departure unquestioned," said Mr. Justice Miller in *Cunningham v. Railroad Co.,* "that neither a state nor the United States can be sued as defendant in any court in this country without their consent, except in the limited class of cases in which a state may be made a party in the supreme court of the United States by virtue of the original jurisdiction conferred on this court by the constitution."

Undoubtedly, a state may be sued by its own consent . . . . Chief Justice Taney, delivering the opinion of the court, said: "It is an established principle of jurisprudence in all civilized nations that the sovereign cannot be sued in its own courts, or in any other, without its consent and permission; but it may, if it thinks proper, waive this privilege, and permit itself to be made a defendant in a suit by individuals, or by another state. And, as this permission is altogether voluntary on the part of the sovereignty, it follows that it may prescribe the terms and conditions on which it consents to be sued, and the manner in which the suit shall be conducted, and may withdraw its consent whenever it may suppose that justice to the public requires it." . . .

But besides the presumption that no anomalous and unheard-of proceedings or suits were intended to be raised up by the constitution, — anomalous and unheard of when the constitution was adopted, — an additional reason why the jurisdiction claimed for the circuit court does not exist is the language of the act of congress by which its jurisdiction is conferred. The words are these: "The circuit courts of the United States shall have original cognizance, concurrent with the courts of the several states, of all suits of a civil nature, at common law or in equity, . . . arising under the constitution or laws of the United States, or treaties," etc. "concurrent with the courts of the several states." Does not this qualification show that congress, in legislating to carry the constitution into effect, did not intend to invest its courts with any new and strange jurisdictions? The state courts have no power to entertain suits by individuals against a state without its consent. Then how does the circuit court, having only concurrent jurisdiction, acquire any such power? It is true that the same qualification existed in the Judiciary Act of 1789, which was before the court in *Chisholm v. Georgia,* and the majority of the court did not think that it was sufficient to limit the jurisdiction of the circuit court. Justice Iredell thought differently. In view of the manner in which that decision was received by the country, the adoption of the eleventh amendment, the light of history, and the reason of the thing, we think we are at liberty to prefer Justice Iredell's views in this regard.

. . . It is not necessary that we should enter upon an examination of the reason or expediency of the rule which exempts a sovereign state from prosecution in a court of justice at the suit of individuals. This is fully discussed by the writers on public law. It is enough for us to declare its existence. . . . [T]o deprive the legislature of the power of judging what the honor and safety of the state may require, even at the expense of a temporary failure to discharge the public debts, would be attended with greater evils than such failure can cause. The judgment of the circuit court is affirmed.

JUSTICE HARLAN, concurring.

I concur with the court in holding that a suit directly against a state by one of its citizens is not one to which the judicial power of the United States extends, unless the state itself consents to be sued. Upon this ground alone I assent to the judgment. But I cannot give my assent to many things said in the opinion. The comments made upon the decision in *Chisholm v. Georgia* do not meet my approval. They are not necessary to the determination of the present case. Besides, I am of opinion that the decision in that case was based upon a sound interpretation of the constitution as that instrument then was.

Exercise 10:

Consider the following matters in connection with *Hans v. Louisiana:*

(1)   Why did Congress propose a constitutional amendment in response to *Chisholm* rather than simply limit the jurisdiction granted by the Federal Judiciary Act of 1789? Could Congress have accomplished the same end by limiting the scope of diversity jurisdiction — as it already had in the 1789 Act — in yet one additional manner, namely that unconsenting States would not be subject to such jurisdiction in actions commenced by individuals?

(2)   What is the holding of the Court with regard to whether States may be required to defend in federal court actions for damages instituted by individuals? Does the form of relief sought by an individual matter?

(3)   After ratification of the Eleventh Amendment, under what conditions may a State be required to defend itself in federal court? Are all plaintiffs covered by the language of the Eleventh Amendment? Are all the bases of federal court jurisdiction specified in Article III covered by the language of the Eleventh Amendment?

(4)   What interpretive methods and sources did the Court draw upon to answer the preceding questions?

(5)   Is *Hans v. Louisiana* consistent with *Cohens v. Virginia*? Can the holdings of the two cases be rationalized if *dicta* alone is distinguished?

(6)   Recall Chief Justice Marshall's analysis in *Cohens v. Virginia* as to whether the fact that one party to the case was the State of Virginia took the matter outside the scope of Article III. Was the analysis there consistent with the statement of John Marshall at the Virginia ratifying convention (quoted in *Hans v. Louisiana*)?

(7)   Does *Hans v. Louisiana* reject the theory of sovereignty articulated by Justice Wilson in *Chisholm v. Georgia*? Is it possible to accept Justice Wilson's identification of the sovereign and still find that States have immunity to suit in actions by individuals seeking money damages? Why or why not?

CHAPTER 5

THE ELECTION OF 1800 AND THE TRANSFORMATION OF THE JUDICIARY

When President Washington retired after two terms, John Adams was elected President and Thomas Jefferson was elected Vice President. The political differences between Adams (and Alexander Hamilton) and the Federalist Party, on the one hand, and Jefferson (and James Madison) and the Republican Party, on the other hand, continued to grow throughout the term of President Adams. In the election of 1800, the parties clashed. The Federalist Party had held the Presidency and majorities in both houses of Congress since 1789. As a result, most federal officers, including judges, were loyal Federalists.

In the fall of 1800, both Thomas Jefferson and Aaron Burr received more votes for President than any Federalist candidate. Republican candidates were elected to a majority of the seats in the Senate and House of Representatives.

Between the time the election results became known and the time the new Congress and President were to be sworn into office, President Adams and the Federalist-controlled majority took several key actions.

There was a vacancy in the position of Chief Justice of the United States. On January 20, 1801, President Adams nominated, and the Federalist Senate confirmed, Secretary of State John Marshall to fill the vacancy.

Congress expanded (and in one key respect contracted) the size of the judiciary in the Federal Judiciary Act of 1801. The bill passed the House on January 20 and the Senate on February 7, 1801. President Adams signed the law on February 13 and filled all the positions for the first four circuits on February 20, 1801. President Adams nominated, and the Federalist Senate confirmed, judges to the newly created offices. The new judges were Federalists.

On February 27, 1801, President Adams signed into law a provision that established offices to help govern the District of Columbia to which the seat of government had been recently transferred.* President Adams nominated, and the Federalist Senate confirmed, persons to these offices, a majority of whom were Federalists. After filling judgeships created by the statute, on March 2 and 3, the Senate approved nominations to the posts of marshals and justices of the peace.

On March 3, the terms of the new President and Members of Congress took effect.

As one might imagine, transitions in the Presidency and in control of Congress rendered many of these measures controversial *both* at the time of the actions and once the Jeffersonians were in power. But although President Jefferson and his political party controlled the executive and legislative branches of the government, the federal judiciary remained almost completely in the hands of Federalist appointees. That circumstance presented one of the first opportunities to test constitutional provisions regarding the structure and power of the judiciary.

---

* The Senate passed the bill on February 5 and the House passed the bill on February 24.

Exercise 11(A):

Consider the Federal Judiciary Act of 1801 and the Act establishing a court system for the District of Columbia. Did either of those statutes raise any constitutional (as distinguished from political) issues? Did the provisions for appointment and removal of judges and other officers comply with the Constitution? If so, once individuals were nominated for the positions newly created by these statutes, confirmed by vote of the Senate, and commissioned by the President and Secretary of State, what options remained President Jefferson and the Republican Congress to remove those "midnight appointees"?

Specifically, consider:

(1)   How did the Federal Judiciary Act of 1801 change the staffing of the circuit courts from the Federal Judiciary Act of 1789? How did the Federal Judiciary Act of 1802 address that issue?

(2)   How did the Federal Judiciary Act of 1801 change the staffing of the U.S. Supreme Court? Why would Congress do so less than one month after filling a vacancy on the Court?

(3)   If President Adams appointed one or more judges to positions created by the 1801 Act, with the advice and consent of the U.S. Senate, could newly-elected President Jefferson remove such a judge from office?

(4)   Could the newly-elected Jeffersonian Congress remove such a judge from office by any means other than impeachment?

(5)   After the enactment of the 1802 Act, what happened to a judge appointed to a position under the 1801 Act?

THE FEDERAL JUDICIARY ACT OF 1801

An Act to provide for the more convenient organization of the Courts of the United States.

Section 1.   *Be it enacted by the Senate and House of Representatives of the United States of America in Congress assembled,* That from and after the next session of the Supreme Court of the United States, the said court shall be holden by the justices thereof, or any four of them, at the city of Washington, and shall have two sessions in each and every year thereafter, to commence on the first Monday of June and December respectively . . . .

. . . .

Section 3.   *And be it further enacted,* That from and after the next vacancy that shall happen in the said court, it shall consist of five justices only; that is to say, of one chief justice, and four associate justices.

Section 4.   *And be it further enacted,* That for the better establishment of the circuit courts of the United States, the said states shall be, and hereby are divided into districts, in manner following . . . .

. . . .

Section 6.   *And be it further enacted,* That the said districts shall be classed into six circuits in manner following; that is to say: The first circuit shall consist of the districts of Maine, New Hampshire, Massachusetts, and Rhode Island; the second, of the districts of Connecticut, Vermont, Albany and New York; the third, of the districts of [New] Jersey, the Eastern and Western districts of Pennsylvania, and

Delaware; the fourth, of the districts of Maryland, and the Eastern and Western districts of Virginia; the fifth, of the districts of North Carolina, South Carolina, and Georgia; and the sixth, of the districts of East Tennessee, West Tennessee, Kentucky, and Ohio.

Section 7. *And be it further enacted,* That there shall be in each of the aforesaid circuits, except the sixth circuit, three judges of the United States, to be called circuit judges . . .; and that there shall be a circuit court of the United States, in and for each of the aforesaid circuits, to be composed of the circuit judges within the five first circuits respectively . . . .

. . . .

Section 10. *And be it further enacted,* That the circuit courts shall have, and hereby are, invested with, all the powers heretofore granted by law to the circuit courts of the United States, unless otherwise provided by this act.

Section 11. *And be it further enacted,* That the said circuit courts respectively shall have cognizance of all crimes and offences cognizable under the authority of the United States, and committed within their respective districts, or upon the high seas; and also of all cases in law or equity, arising under the constitution and laws of the United States, and treaties made, or which shall be made, under their authority; and also of all actions, or suits of a civil nature, at common law, or in equity, where the United States shall be plaintiffs or complainants . . .; and also of all actions, or suits, matters or things cognizable by the judicial authority of the United States, under and by virtue of the constitution thereof, where the matter in dispute shall amount to four hundred dollars, and where original jurisdiction is not given by the constitution of the United States to the supreme court thereof, or exclusive jurisdiction by law to the district courts of the United States . . . .

Section 12. *And be it further enacted,* That the said circuit courts respectively shall have cognizance concurrently with the district courts, of all cases which shall arise, within their respective circuits, under the act to establish an uniform system of bankruptcy throughout the United States . . . .

Section 13. *And be it further enacted,* That where any action or suit shall be, or shall have been commenced, in any state court within the United States, against an alien, or by a citizen or citizens of the state in which such suit or action shall be, or shall have been commenced against a citizen or citizens of another state, and the matter in dispute . . . shall exceed the sum or value of four hundred dollars, exclusive of costs, . . .; or where any suit or action shall have been, or shall be commenced in any such court, against any person or persons, in any cases arising under the constitution or laws of the United States, or treaties made or to be made under their authority; then, and in any of the said cases, it shall be lawful for the defendant or defendants . . . to file in such court a petition for the removal of such suit, action, writ of error, or writ of review, to the next circuit court of the United States . . . .

. . . .

Section 17. *And be it further enacted,* That the trials of all issues of fact, before any of the circuit courts hereby established, except in cases of equity, and admiralty and maritime jurisdiction, shall be by jury.

. . . .

Section 20. *And be it further enacted,* That all actions, suits, process, pleadings, and other proceedings of what nature or kind soever, depending or existing in any of the present circuit courts of the United States, or in any of the present district courts of the United States, acting as circuit courts, shall be, and hereby are, continued over to the circuit courts established by this act . . .; and shall there be equally regular and effectual, and shall be proceeded in, in the same manner as they could have been, if this act had not been made.

Section 21. *And be it further enacted,* That for the better dispatch of the business of the district courts of the United States, in the district of [New] Jersey, Maryland, Virginia, and North Carolina, additional district courts shall be established therein, in the manner following . . . .

. . . .

Section 26. *And be it further enacted,* That the several circuit courts hereby established shall have power to appoint clerks for their respective courts. . . .

Section 27. *And be it further enacted,* That the circuit courts of the United States, heretofore established, shall cease and be abolished . . . .

. . . .

Section 33. *And be it further enacted,* That from all final judgments or decrees, in any of the district courts of the United States, an appeal, where the matter in dispute, exclusive of costs, shall exceed the sum or value of fifty dollars, shall be allowed to the circuit court . . .; and that from all final judgments or decrees in any circuit court, in any cases of equity, of admiralty and maritime jurisdiction, and of prize or no prize, an appeal, where the matter in dispute, exclusive of costs, shall exceed the sum or value of two thousand dollars, shall be allowed to the supreme court of the United States . . .; and that such appeals shall be subject to the same rules, regulations and restrictions, as are prescribed by law in case of writs of error

. . . .

Section 34. *And be it further enacted,* That all final judgments in civil actions at common law, in any of the circuit courts hereby established, . . . and all final judgments in any of the district courts of the United States may, where the matter in dispute, exclusive of costs, shall exceed the sum or value of two thousand dollars, be re-examined and reversed or affirmed, in the supreme court of the United States, by writ of error . . . .

. . . .

Approved: February 13, 1801 — 2 Stat. 89

JUDICIARY ACT FOR THE DISTRICT OF COLUMBIA

Section 1. *Be it enacted by the Senate and House of Representatives of the United States of America in Congress, assembled,* . . . .

Section 2. *And be it further enacted,* That the said district of Columbia shall be formed into two counties . . . .

Section 3. *Be it further enacted,* That there shall be a court in said district, which shall be called the circuit court of the district of Columbia; and the said court and the judges thereof shall have all the powers by law vested in the circuit courts and the judges of the circuit courts of the United States. Said court shall consist of one chief judge and two assistant judges resident within said district, to hold their respective offices during good behaviour; any two of whom shall constitute a quorum . . . .

. . . .

Section 5. *Be it further enacted,* That said court shall have cognizance of all crimes and offences committed within said district, and of all cases in law and equity between parties, both or either of which shall be resident or be found within said district, and also of all actions or suits of a civil nature at common law or in equity, in which the United States shall be plaintiffs or complainants; and of all seizures on land or water, and all penalties and forfeitures made, arising or accruing under the laws of the United States.

. . . .

Section 7. *Be it further enacted,* That there shall be a marshal for the said district

. . . .

Section 8. *Be it further enacted,* That any final judgment, order or decree in said circuit court, wherein the matter in dispute, exclusive of costs, shall exceed the value of one hundred dollars, may be re-examined and reversed or affirmed in the supreme court of the United States, by writ of error or appeal . . . .

Section 9. *Be it further enacted,* That there shall be appointed an attorney of the United States for said district . . . .

. . . .

Section 11. *Be it further enacted,* That there shall be appointed in and for each of the said counties, such number of discreet persons to be justices of the peace, as the President of the United States shall from time to time think expedient, to continue in office five years; and such justices . . . shall, in all matters, civil and criminal, and in whatever relates to the conservation of the peace, have all the powers vested in . . . justices of the peace, as individual magistrates, by the laws herein before continued in force in those parts of said district, for which they shall have been respectively appointed; and they shall have cognizance in personal demands to the value of twenty dollars, exclusive of costs . . . .

Section 12. *And be it further enacted,* That there shall be appointed in and for each of the said counties, a register of wills, and a judge to be called the judge of the orphans' court . . . and appeals from the said courts shall be to the circuit court of said district, who shall therein have all the powers of the chancellor of [Maryland].

. . . .

Approved: February 27, 1801 — 2 Stat. 103

THE FEDERAL JUDICIARY ACT OF 1802

An Act to repeal certain acts respecting the organization of the Courts of the United States; and for other purposes.

Section 1. *Be it enacted by the Senate and House of Representatives of the United States of America in Congress assembled,* That the act of Congress passed on the thirteenth day of February one thousand eight hundred and one, entitled "An act to provide for the more convenient organization of the courts of the United States," from and after the first day of July next, shall be, and is hereby repealed.

Section 2. *And be it further enacted,* That the act passed on the third day of March, [1801], entitled "An act for altering the times and places of holding certain courts therein mentioned and for other purposes," from and after the said first day of July next, shall be, and is hereby repealed.

Section 3. *And be it further enacted,* That all the acts, and parts of acts, which were in force before the passage of the aforesaid two acts, and which by the same were either amended, explained, altered, or repealed, shall be, and hereby are, after the said first day of July next, revived, and in as full and complete force and operation, as if the said two acts had never been made.

Section 4. *And be it further enacted,* That all actions, suits, process, pleadings, and other proceedings, of what nature or kind soever, depending or existing in any of the circuit courts of the United States, or in any of the district courts of the

United States, acting as circuit courts, or in any of the additional district courts, which were established by the aforesaid act of Congress, passed on the thirteenth day of February, [1801], shall be, and hereby are, from and after the said first day of July next, continued over to the circuit courts, and to the district courts, and to the district courts acting as circuit courts respectively, which shall be first thereafter holden in and for the respective circuits and districts, which are revived and established by this act, and to be proceeded in, in the same manner as they would have been, had they originated prior to the passage of the said act, passed on the thirteenth day of February, [1801].

Section 5. *And be it further enacted,* That all writs and process, which have issued, or may issue before the said first day of July next, returnable to the circuit courts, or to any district court acting as a circuit court, or any additional district court established by the aforesaid act passed the thirteenth day of February, [1801], shall be returned to the next circuit court, or district court, or district court acting as a circuit court, re-established by this act: and shall be proceeded on therein, in the same manner as they could, had they been originally returnable to the circuit courts, and district courts acting as circuit courts, hereby revived and established.

Approved: March 8, 1802 — 2 Stat. 132

When the 1802 Act passed Congress, a Federalist Party newspaper published the following account of the matter.

The Washington Federalist (March 3, 1802)

The fatal Bill has passed; Our Constitution is no more. . . .

When all the speeches on the federal side shall be published, we dare assert that there will not be a single candid intelligent mind that will not be convinced both of the inexpedience and unconstitutionality of the bill. . . .

Added to the others, there is one violation of the Constitution "open, gross, palatable." The Constitution says the salaries of no judge shall be DIMINISHED while in office. By this bill the judges of Kentucky and Tennessee are curtailed in their salaries FIVE HUNDRED DOLLARS each.

The judges will continue to hold their courts as if the bill had not passed. 'Tis their solemn duty to do it; their country, all that is dear and valuable, call on them to do it. By the judges this bill will be declared null and void . . . .

. . . .

Should Mr. Breckenridge now bring forward a resolution to repeal the law establishing the Supreme Court of the United States, we should only consider it a part of the system intended to be pursued. . . . They can then repeal the law establishing that Court, having caution not to have the *repeal* operate till the *new law* commences then the old judges cease of course of the old law, the executive appoints new judges for the new law; [and] still they will comply with the Constitution which says there shall be one supreme court. To make it quite nothing, they'll perhaps have but one judge. Such is democracy.

The Reaction of the Federal Judiciary

The prediction that the judiciary would disregard the federal Judiciary Act of 1802 was no wild speculation. Chief Justice John Marshall privately assured leading Federalists in Congress that the Supreme Court would oppose the measure. He then communicated with the other members of the Supreme Court to ascertain whether there was agreement to refuse to ride circuit, leaving the judges appointed under the federal Judiciary Act of 1801 to continue to hold sessions. Even after Justice Bushrod Washington refused to join in a strike, Marshall continued to press the idea until May 1802 when Justice William Paterson also rejected a strike.[1]

Shortly after passage of the federal Judiciary Act of 1802, a formal petition was presented to Congress from the displaced Circuit Judges requesting the identification of their duties and provision for their compensation. Congress neither specified any duties left to the Circuit Judges nor provided for payment of their salaries.

Richard Bassett, who had been appointed as a Circuit Judge under the federal Judiciary Act of 1801, published a lengthy public protest that called for the Supreme Court to refuse to ride circuit.

> [W]hat I contend for is this; that a *law* which abolished the *courts,* and *all the judicial powers* of one set of judges *lawfully appointed,* and transfers to new courts, and to other judges the same judicial powers, leaving the first without *any official* rights, or provision for their salaries, is unconstitutional and void. *Such* a law or laws carry on the *face* of them indubitable signs and evidence of a *design* in the legislature to take away from the first judges their offices, and are therefore manifestly contrary to the letter and spirit of the constitution.
>
> *Such* an act made and operating against the words, the true intent, and obvious policy of the *Constitution,* is not to *prevail.*
>
> The judges, to whom the same office, in *effect,* is transferred, will not *accept the legislative commission,* nor, by executing the act, participate in the overthrow of the Constitution. . . .
>
> . . . .
>
> The *judges* designated to execute the repealing act of the 8th of March, 1802, or in other terms, the judges called upon to *assist* and *sanction* the usurpation and illegality, if such is the opinion they entertain of those acts must necessarily refuse to participate or aid in their design and consequences.

When the Justices resumed riding circuit they were confronted by prominent Federalist lawyers who, in the role as counsel for private litigants, challenged the jurisdiction of the courts. If the federal Judiciary Act of 1802 was unconstitutional, they reasoned, the proper tribunals to hear their cases were the Circuit Courts established by the federal Judiciary Act of 1801 and staffed with a distinct set of judges.

Objections were raised by counsel in cases before the First, Second, and Third Circuits. In each instance, however, the Justices apparently convinced counsel to withdraw the objection so as to avoid a controversial ruling. In the Fourth Circuit, Charles Lee — who had served as Attorney General to President Adams — objected to the court's jurisdiction. Chief Justice Marshall addressed the objection on the merits and thereby provided a foundation for the matter to be brought before the U.S. Supreme Court on appellate review.[2]

---

[1] For a book-length examination of the matters discussed throughout this Chapter, see BRUCE ACKERMAN, THE FAILURE OF THE FOUNDING FATHERS: JEFFERSON, MARSHALL, AND THE RISE OF PRESIDENTIAL DEMOCRACY (2005). For the events described in this paragraph, *see id.* at 157–172.

[2] *See id.* at 173–176.

STUART v. LAIRD
5 U.S. 299 (1803)

[At the December 1802 sitting of the circuit court in Richmond, Virginia, John Laird sought a ruling on a matter that had been initiated before a circuit court that had been created under the federal Judiciary Act of 1801. The representatives of the estate of Hugh Stuart contended that the court lacked subject matter jurisdiction because the repeal of the federal Judiciary Act of 1801 was unconstitutional.

On March 2, 1802, Chief Justice John Marshall, sitting as a circuit justice, held that the repeal was constitutional and that the court had subject matter jurisdiction to rule on the merits of Laird's motion. Representatives of Stuart's estate sought review by the Supreme Court. Charles Lee, who had served as Attorney General to President Adams, argued for the unconstitutionality of the 1802 Act. He urged that the circuit court created by the federal Judiciary Act of 1801 continued to exist (because the federal Judiciary Act of 1802 was unconstitutional) and only that court properly had jurisdiction to proceed on the case initiated there.

[Lee conceded: "If the acts of 8th March and 29th April, 1802, are constitutional, then it is admitted there is no error in the judgment; because in that case, the courts ceased to exist, the judges were constitutionally removed, and the transfer from the one court to the other was legal." Lee argued that the federal Judiciary Act of 1802 was unconstitutional because it removed circuit judges despite the lack of impeachable bases, stripped the circuit court judges "of all power and jurisdiction", imposed new duties on Justices of the Supreme Court and did so without separate appointment and commission as judges of the circuit courts, and required the Justices of the Supreme Court to exercise trial jurisdiction on circuit in matters where Article III confined the Court to appellate jurisdiction.]

JUSTICE PATTERSON delivered the Opinion of the Court.[*]

Two reasons have been assigned by counsel for reversing the judgment . . . . 1. That as the bond was given for delivery of property levied on by virtue of an execution issuing out of, and returnable to a court for the fourth circuit, no other court could legally proceed upon the said bond. This is true, if there be no [statutory] provision to direct and authorize such proceeding. Congress ha[s] constitutional authority to establish from time to time such inferior tribunals as they may think proper; and to transfer a cause from one such tribunal to another. In this last particular, there are no words in the constitution to prohibit or restrain the exercise of legislative power.

The present is a case of this kind. It is nothing more than the removal of the suit brought by Stuart against Laird from the court of the fourth circuit [under the 1801 Act] to the court of the fifth circuit [under the 1802 Act], which is authorized to proceed upon and carry it into full effect. This is apparent from the ninth section of the act entitled, "an act to amend the judicial system of the United States," passed the 29th of April, 1802. The forthcoming bond is an appendage to the cause, or rather a component part of the proceedings.

2d. Another reason for the reversal is, that the judges of the supreme court have no right to sit as circuit judges, not being appointed as such, or in other words, that they ought to have distinct commissions for that purpose. To this objection, which

---

[*] Chief Justice Marshall did not participate in the decision, having ruled on the case at the circuit court level. Justice Cushing was absent due to ill health.

is of recent date, it is sufficient to observe, that practice and acquiescence under it for a period of several years, commencing with the organization of the judicial system, affords an irresistible answer, and has indeed fixed the construction. It is a contemporary interpretation of the most forcible nature. This practical exposition is too strong and obstinate to be shaken or controlled. Of course, the question is at rest, and ought not now to be disturbed.

Judgment affirmed.

Exercise 11(B):

What is the consequence of the Court's holding in *Stuart v. Laird*? What is the scope of the precedent it established?

Could Congress in 1802 have similarly repealed the Act creating the offices for the District of Columbia? If it had, would the judges, justices of the peace, and other officers appointed under that Act have had a constitutional claim to remain in office?

Could Congress today repeal statutory authorization for the U.S. Courts of Appeals and U.S. District Courts? If so, could it replace them with a set of new "Appellate Courts of the United States" and "Trial Courts of the United States" thereby permitting the current President and Senate to effectively replace all sitting federal judges without impeachment proceedings?

The Aftermath

Early commentary was hostile to the ruling in *Stuart v. Laird*. Justice Joseph Story observed that "(so far as it is a precedent) . . . notwithstanding the constitutional tenure of office of the judges of the inferior courts is during good behavior, Congress may, at any time, by a mere act of legislation, deprive them of their offices at pleasure, and with it take away their whole title to their salaries. How this can be reconciled with the terms, or the intent of the Constitution, is more, than any ingenuity of argument has ever, as yet, been able to demonstrate." 2 JOSEPH STORY, COMMENTARIES ON THE CONSTITUTION § 1633, at 415 (2d ed. 1851). The federal Judiciary Act of 1802 "may be asserted, without fear of contradiction, to have been against the opinion of a great majority of all the ablest lawyers at the time; and probably now, when the passions of the day have subsided, few lawyers will be found to maintain the constitutionality of the Act." *Id.* at 415 n.5.

In 1863, Congress again abolished courts on which judges were actively serving with tenure during good behavior. Again, the effect (and purpose) was to oust sitting judges. Congress simply provided for replacement courts with a new name to which new judges were appointed. *See* An Act to Reorganize the Courts in the District of Columbia, 12 Stat. 762 (1863). The judges of the new courts had the same tenure as the judges of the old courts. *Id.* § 1. The jurisdiction of the new courts was the same as the old. *Id.* § 3. The time and place of court sessions was the same. *Id.* § 4. Appellate review by the U.S. Supreme Court was on the same terms. *Id.* § 11. Appellate review of justices of the peace by one of the new courts was on the same basis as the review by the old court. *Id.* § 12. All proceedings in the old courts were transferred to the new courts. *Id.* § 13. And all laws applicable to the old courts were made applicable to the new courts. *Id.* § 16. Nonetheless, a completely different set of judges served on the new courts while the judges of the old courts were purged from office.

Unlike the federal Judiciary Act of 1802, which could claim to save money by abolishing unneeded positions, the 1863 Act would seem to lack even a pretext. In fact, the entire measure was in response to concerns that at the height of the Civil War, a Confederate sympathizer was serving in the Union's capital as a judge with tenure during good behavior. *See* JEFFREY BRANDON MORRIS, CALMLY TO POISE THE SCALES OF JUSTICE: A HISTORY OF THE COURTS OF THE DISTRICT OF COLUMBIA CIRCUIT 35–36 (2001).

Does the 1863 episode illustrate that Justice Story was too hasty in his evaluation of the precedential value of *Stuart v. Laird*?

Despite the partisan uproar regarding the federal Judiciary Act of 1802 and the anticipated challenge to its constitutionality, *Stuart v. Laird* is overshadowed by a case decided one week earlier. The effective purge of Article III judges sanctioned by the Supreme Court drew most of the attention at the time, while a small case involving a lowly justice of the peace seemed relatively unimportant.

As Bruce Ackerman observes: "If we look at what the Marshall Court did, and not merely what it said, it is wrong to treat *Marbury* as the main event and *Stuart* as an historical curiosity. *Marbury* is better viewed as a footnote to *Stuart*." BRUCE ACKERMAN, THE FAILURE OF THE FOUNDING FATHERS: JEFFERSON, MARSHALL, AND THE RISE OF PRESIDENTIAL DEMOCRACY 9 (2005).

MARBURY v. MADISON
5 U.S. 137 (1803)

CHIEF JUSTICE MARSHALL delivered the unanimous Opinion of the Court.

At the last term . . . a rule was granted in this case, requiring the secretary of state to show cause why a mandamus should not issue, directing him to deliver to William Marbury his commission as a justice of the peace for the county of Washington, in the district of Columbia.

No cause has been shown, and the present motion is for a mandamus. The peculiar delicacy of this case, the novelty of some of its circumstances, and the real difficulty attending the points which occur in it, require a complete exposition of the principles, on which the opinion to be given by the court, is founded.

. . . .

[I]

[First, has] the applicant a right to the commission he demands?

His right originates in an act of congress passed in February 1801, concerning the district of Columbia.

. . . .

It appears, from the affidavits, that in compliance with this law, a commission for William Marbury as a justice of peace for the county of Washington, was signed by John Adams, then president of the United States; after which the seal of the United States was affixed to it; but the commission has never reached the person for whom it was made out.

In order to determine whether he is entitled to this commission, it becomes necessary to enquire whether he has been appointed to the office. For if he has been appointed, the law continues him in office for five years, and he is entitled to . . . those evidences of office . . . .

[The Court then reviewed the provisions of the Constitution addressing the appointment of officers and preparation of commissions.]

Although that clause of the constitution which requires the President to commission all the officers of the United States, may never have been applied to officers appointed otherwise than by himself, yet it would be difficult to deny the legislative power to apply it to such cases. . . .

. . . [I]f an appointment was to be evidenced by any public act, other than the commission, the performance of such public act would create the officer; and if he was not removable at the will of the President, would either give him a right to his commission, or enable him to perform the duties without it.

. . . .

This is an appointment made by the President, by and with the advice and consent of the senate, and is evidenced by no act but the commission itself. In such a case therefore the commission and the appointment seem inseparable; it being almost impossible to shew an appointment otherwise than by proving existence of a commission; still the commission is not necessarily the appointment; though it is conclusive evidence of it.

. . . .

Some point of time must be taken when the power of the executive over an officer, not removable at will, must cease. That point of time must be when the constitutional power of appointment has been exercised. And this power has been exercised when the last act, required from the person possessing the power, has been performed. This last act is the signature of the commission. That idea seems to have prevailed with the legislature, when the act passed, converting the department of foreign affairs into the department of state. By that act it is enacted, that the secretary of state shall keep the seal of the United States, "and shall make out and record, and shall affix the said seal to all civil commissions to officers of the United States, to be appointed by the President:" "Provided that the said seal shall not be affixed to any commission, before the same shall have been signed by the President of the United States . . . ."

. . . .

The commission being signed, the subsequent duty of the secretary of state is prescribed by law, and not to be guided by the will of the President. He is to affix the seal of the United States to the commission, and is to record it.

. . . .

. . . [I]t has been conjectured that the commission may have been assimilated to a deed, to the validity of which, delivery is essential.

This idea is founded on the supposition that the commission is not merely *evidence* of an appointment, but is itself the actual appointment; a supposition by no means unquestionable. . . .

The appointment being, under the constitution, to be made by the President *personally*, the delivery of the deed of appointment, if necessary to its completion, must be made by the President also. . . . If then the act of delivery be necessary to give validity to the commission, it has been delivered when executed and given to the secretary for the purpose of being sealed, recorded, and transmitted to the party.

. . . .

It has also occurred as possible, and barely possible, that the transmission of the commission, and the acceptance thereof, might be deemed necessary to complete the right of the plaintiff.

The transmission of the commission, is a practice directed by convenience, but not by law. It cannot therefore be necessary to constitute the appointment which must precede it, and which is the mere act of the President. . . .

It may have some tendency to elucidate this point, to enquire, whether the possession of the original commission be indispensably necessary to authorize a person, appointed to any office, to perform the duties of that office. . . . I presume that it could not be doubted, but that a copy from the record of the office of secretary of state, would be, to every intent and purpose, equal to the original. . . .

In the case of commissions, the law orders the secretary of state to record them. . . .

. . . .

If the transmission of a commission be not considered as necessary to give validity to an appointment; still less is its acceptance. The appointment is the sole act of the President; the acceptance is the sole act of the officer, and is, in plain common sense, posterior to the appointment. As he may resign, so may he refuse to accept: but neither the one, nor the other, is capable of rendering the appointment a non-entity.

. . . .

It is therefore decidedly the opinion of the court, that when a commission has been signed by the President, the appointment is made; and that the commission is complete, when the seal of the United States has been affixed to it by the Secretary of state.

Where an officer is removable at the will of the executive, the circumstance which completes his appointment is of no concern; because the act is at any time revocable; and the commission may be arrested, if still in the office. . . .

. . . .

Mr. Marbury, then, since his commission was signed by the President, and sealed by the secretary of state, was appointed; and as the law creating the office, gave the officer a right to hold for five years, independent of the executive, the appointment was not revocable; but vested in the officer legal rights, which are protected by the laws of this country.

To withhold his commission, therefore, is an act deemed by the court not warranted by law, but violative of a vested legal right.

. . . .

[II]

[Second, if] he has a right, and that right has been violated, do the laws of this country afford him a remedy?

. . . .

The government of the United States has been emphatically termed a government of laws, and not of men. It will certainly cease to deserve this high appellation, if the laws furnish no remedy for the violation of a vested legal right.

. . . .

It behooves us then to enquire whether there be in its composition any ingredient which shall exempt it from legal investigation, or exclude the injured party from legal redress. . . .

. . . .

Is it in the nature of the transaction? Is the act of delivering or withholding a commission to be considered as a mere political act, belonging to the executive department alone, for the performance of which, entire confidence is placed by our constitution in the supreme executive; and for any misconduct respecting which, the injured individual has no remedy?

That there may be such cases is not to be questioned; but that every act of duty, to be performed in any of the great departments of government, constitutes such a case, is not to be admitted.

By the act concerning invalids, passed in June, 1794, the secretary of war is ordered to place on the pension list, all persons whose names are contained in a report previously made by him to congress. If he should refuse to do so, would the wounded veteran be without remedy? Is it to be contended that where the law in precise terms, directs the performance of an act, in which an individual is interested, the law is incapable of securing obedience to its mandate? Is it on account of the character of the person against whom the complaint is made? Is it to be contended that the heads of departments are not amenable to the laws of their country?

Whatever the practice on particular occasions may be, the theory of this principle will certainly never be maintained. No act of the legislature confers so extraordinary a privilege, nor can it derive countenance from the doctrines of the common law. . . .

. . . .

It follows then that the question, whether the legality of an act of the head of a department be examinable in a court of justice or not, must always depend on the nature of that act.

If some acts be examinable, and others not, there must be some rule of law to guide the court in the exercise of its jurisdiction.

. . . .

By the constitution of the United States, the President is invested with certain important political powers, in the exercise of which he is to use his own discretion, and is accountable only to his country in his political character, and to his own conscience. To aid him in the performance of these duties, he is authorized to appoint certain officers, who act by his authority and in conformity with his orders.

In such cases, their acts are his acts; and whatever opinion may be entertained of the manner in which executive discretion may be used, still there exists, and can exist, no power to control that discretion. The subjects are political. They respect the nation, not individual rights, and being entrusted to the executive, the decision of the executive is conclusive. The application of this remark will be perceived by adverting to the act of congress for establishing the department of foreign affairs. This officer, as his duties were prescribed by that act, is to conform precisely to the will of the President. He is the mere organ by whom that will is communicated. The acts of such an officer, as an officer, can never be examinable by the courts.

But the legislature proceeds to impose on that officer other duties; when he is directed peremptorily to perform certain acts; when the rights of individuals are dependent on the performance of those acts; he is so far the officer of the law; is amenable to the laws for his conduct; and cannot at his discretion sport away the vested rights of others.

The conclusion from this reasoning is, that where the heads of departments are the political or confidential agents of the executive, merely to execute the will of the President, or rather to act in cases in which the executive possesses a constitutional or legal discretion, nothing can be more perfectly clear than that their acts are only politically examinable. But where a specific duty is assigned by law, and individual rights depend upon the performance of that duty, it seems equally clear that the individual who considers himself injured, has a right to resort to the laws of his country for a remedy.

. . . .

The power of nominating to the senate, and the power of appointing the person nominated, are political powers, to be exercised by the President according to his own discretion. When he has made an appointment, he has exercised his whole power . . . . [I]f the officer is not removable at the will of the President; the rights he has acquired are protected by the law, and are not resumable by the President. . . .

The question whether a right has vested or not, is, in its nature, judicial, and must be tried by the judicial authority. . . .

So, if he conceives that, by virtue of his appointment, he has a legal right, either to the commission which has been made out for him, or to a copy of that commission, it is equally a question examinable in a court . . . .

. . . .

. . . [B]y signing the commission of Mr. Marbury, the president of the United States appointed him justice of the peace . . .; and that the seal of the United States, affixed thereto by the secretary of state, is conclusive of the verity of the signature, and of the completion of the appointment; and that the appointment conferred on him a legal right to the office for the space of five years.

. . . [H]aving this legal title to the office, he has a consequent right to the commission; a refusal to deliver which, is a plain violation of that right, for which the laws of his country afford him a remedy.

[III]

. . . [Third, is Marbury] entitled to the remedy for which he applies[?] This depends on, . . . the nature of the writ applied for, and . . . [t]he power of this court.

[A]

. . . .

Blackstone . . . defines a mandamus to be, "a command issuing in the king's name from the court of a king's bench, and directed to any person, corporation, or inferior court of judicature within the king's dominions, requiring them to do some particular thing therein specified, which appertains to their office and duty, and which the court of king's bench has previously determined, or at least supposes, to be consonant to right and justice."

Lord Mansfield . . . states with much precision and explicitness the cases in which this writ may be used.

"Whenever," says that very able judge, "there is a right to execute an office . . . and a person is kept out of possession, or dispossessed of such right, and has no other specific legal remedy, this court ought to assist by mandamus . . . ." In this same case he says, "this writ ought to be used upon all occasions where the law has established no specific remedy, and where in justice and good government there ought to be one."

. . . .

This writ, if awarded, would be directed to an officer of government, and its mandate to him would be, to use the words of Blackstone, "to do a particular thing therein specified, which appertains to his office . . . ."

These circumstances certainly concur in this case.

Still, to render the mandamus a proper remedy, the officer to whom it is to be directed, must be one to whom, on legal principles, such a writ may be directed; and the person applying for it must be without any other specific and legal remedy.

[1]

. . . The intimate political relation, subsisting between the president of the United States and the heads of departments, necessarily renders any legal investigation of the acts of one of those high officers peculiarly irksome, as well as delicate; and excites some hesitation with respect to the propriety of entering into such investigation. . . .

. . . The province of the court is, solely, to decide on the rights of individuals, not to enquire how the executive, or executive officers, perform duties in which they have a discretion. Questions, in their nature political, or which are, by the constitution and laws, submitted to the executive, can never be made in this court.

. . . .

If one of the heads of departments commits any illegal act, under color of his office, by which an individual sustains an injury, it cannot be pretended that his office alone exempts him from being sued in the ordinary mode of proceeding, and being compelled to obey the judgment of the law. . . .

It is not by the office of the person to whom the writ is directed, but the nature of the thing to be done that the propriety or impropriety of issuing a mandamus, is to be determined. . . .

. . . .

It must be well recollected that in 1792, an act passed, directing the secretary [of] war to place on the pension list such disabled officers and soldiers as should be reported to him, by the circuit courts, which act, so far as the duty was imposed on the courts, was deemed unconstitutional; but some of the judges, thinking that the law might be executed by them in the character of commissioners, proceeded to act and to report in that character.

This law being deemed unconstitutional at the circuits, was repealed, and a different system was established; but the question whether those persons, who had been reported by the judges, as commissioners, were entitled, in consequence of that report, to be placed on the pension list, was a legal question, properly determinable in the courts, although the act of placing such persons on the list was to be performed by the head of a department.

That this question might be properly settled, congress passed an act in February, 1793, making it the duty of the secretary of war, in conjunction with the attorney general, to take such measures, as might be necessary to obtain an adjudication of the supreme court of the United States on the validity of any such rights, claimed under the act aforesaid.

After the passage of this act, a mandamus was moved for, to be directed to the secretary of war, commanding him to place on the pension list, a person stating himself to be on the report of the judges.

There is, therefore, much reason to believe, that this mode of trying the legal right of the complainant, was deemed by the head of a department, and by the highest law officer of the United States, the most proper which could be selected for the purpose.

When the subject was brought before the court the decision was, not that a mandamus would not lie to the head of a department, directing him to perform an act, enjoined by law, in the performance of which an individual has a vested interest; but that a mandamus ought not to issue in that case — the decision necessarily to be made if the report of the commissioners did not confer on the applicant a legal right.

The judgment in that case, is understood to have decided the merits of all claims of that description, and the persons on the report of the commissioners found it necessary to pursue the mode prescribed by the law subsequent to that which had been deemed unconstitutional, in order to place themselves on the pension list.

The doctrine, therefore, now advanced, is by no means a novel one.

It is true that the mandamus, now moved for, is not for the performance of an act expressly enjoined by statute.

It is to deliver a commission; on which subject the acts of Congress are silent. This difference is not considered as affecting the case. It has already been stated that the applicant has, to that commission, a vested legal right, of which the executive cannot deprive him. He has been appointed to an office, from which he is not removable, at the will of the executive . . . .

It was at first doubted whether the action of *detinue* was not a specific legal remedy for the commission which has been withheld from Mr. Marbury; in which case a mandamus would be improper. But this doubt has yielded to the consideration that the judgment in *detinue* is for the thing itself, *or* its value. The value of a public office not to be sold, is incapable of being ascertained; and the applicant has a right to the office itself, or to nothing. He will obtain the office by obtaining the commission, or a copy of it from the record.

This, then, is a plain case for a mandamus, either to deliver the commission, or a copy of it from the record . . . .

[2]

[It remains to be determined whether the writ of mandamus] can issue from this court.

[a]

The [Federal Judiciary Act of 1789, section 13,] authorizes the supreme court "to issue writs of mandamus, in cases warranted by the principles and usages of law, to any courts appointed, or persons holding office, under authority of the United States."

The secretary of state, being a person holding an office under the authority of the United States, is precisely within the letter of the description; and if this court is not authorized to issue a writ of mandamus to such an officer, it must be because the law is unconstitutional, and therefore absolutely incapable of conferring the authority, and assigning the duties which its words purport to confer and assign.

[b]

The constitution vests the whole judicial power of the United States in one supreme court, and such inferior courts as congress shall, from time to time, ordain and establish. This power is expressly extended to all cases arising under the laws of the United States; and consequently, in some form, may be exercised over the present case; because the right claimed is given by a law of the United States.

In the distribution of this power it is declared that "the supreme court shall have original jurisdiction in all cases affecting ambassadors, other public ministers and consuls, and those in which a state shall be a party. In all other cases, the supreme court shall have appellate jurisdiction."

It has been insisted, at the bar, that as the original grant of jurisdiction, to the supreme and inferior courts, is general, and the clause, assigning original jurisdiction to the supreme court, contains no negative or restrictive words; the power remains to the legislature, to assign original jurisdiction to that court in other cases than those specified in the article which has been recited; provided those cases belong to the judicial power of the United States.

If it had been intended to leave it in the discretion of the legislature to apportion the judicial power between the supreme and inferior courts according to the will of that body, it would certainly have been useless to have proceeded further than to have defined the judicial power, and the tribunals in which it should be vested. The subsequent part of the section is mere surplusage, is entirely without meaning, if such is to be the construction. If congress remains at liberty to give this court appellate jurisdiction, where the constitution has declared their jurisdiction shall be original; and original jurisdiction where the constitution has declared it shall be appellate; the distribution of jurisdiction, made in the constitution, is form without substance.

Affirmative words are often, in their operation, negative of other objects than those affirmed; and in this case, a negative or exclusive sense must be given to them or they have no operation at all.

It cannot be presumed that any clause in the constitution is intended to be without effect; and therefore such a construction is inadmissible, unless the words require it.

If the solicitude of the convention, respecting our peace with foreign powers, induced a provision that the supreme court should take original jurisdiction in cases which might be supposed to affect them; yet the clause would have proceeded no further than to provide for such cases, if no further restriction on the powers of congress had been intended. That they should have appellate jurisdiction in all other cases, with such exceptions as congress might make, is no restriction; unless the words be deemed exclusive of original jurisdiction.

. . . [T]he plain import of the words seems to be, that in one class of cases its jurisdiction is original, and not appellate; in the other it is appellate, and not original. If any other construction would render the clause inoperative, that is an additional reason for rejecting such other construction, and for adhering to their obvious meaning.

To enable this court then to issue a mandamus, it must be shown to be an exercise of appellate jurisdiction, or to be necessary to enable them to exercise appellate jurisdiction.

It has been stated at the bar that the appellate jurisdiction may be exercised in a variety of forms, and that if it be the will of the legislature that a mandamus should be used for that purpose, that will must be obeyed. This is true, yet the jurisdiction must be appellate, not original.

It is the essential criterion of appellate jurisdiction, that it revises and corrects the proceedings in a cause already instituted, and does not create that cause. . . .

[T]o issue such a writ to an officer for the delivery of a paper, is in effect the same as to sustain an original action for that paper, and therefore seems not to belong to appellate, but to original jurisdiction. Neither is it necessary in such a case as this, to enable the court to exercise its appellate jurisdiction.

The authority, therefore, given to the supreme court, by the act establishing the judicial courts of the United States, to issue writs of mandamus to public officers, appears not to be warranted by the constitution; and it becomes necessary to enquire whether a jurisdiction, so conferred, can be exercised.

[c]

The question, whether an act, repugnant to the constitution, can become the law of the land, is a question deeply interesting to the United States; but, happily, not of an intricacy proportioned to its interest. It seems only necessary to recognize certain principles, supposed to have been long and well established, to decide it.

[i]

That the people have an original right to establish, for their future government, such principles as, in their opinion, shall most conduce to their own happiness, is the basis, on which the whole American fabric has been erected. The exercise of this original right is a very great exertion; nor can it, nor ought it to be frequently repeated. The principles, therefore, so established, are deemed fundamental. And as the authority, from which they proceed, is supreme, can seldom act, they are designed to be permanent.

This original and supreme will organizes the government, and assigns, to different departments, their respective powers. It may either stop here; or establish certain limits not to be transcended by those departments.

The government of the United States is of the latter description. The powers of the legislature are defined, and limited; and that those limits may not be mistaken, or forgotten, the constitution is written. To what purpose are powers limited, and to what purpose is that limitation committed to writing, if the limits may, at any time, be passed by those intended to be restrained? The distinction, between a government with limited and unlimited powers, is abolished, if those limits do not confine the persons on whom they are imposed, and if acts prohibited and acts allowed, are of equal obligation. It is a proposition too plain to be contested, that the constitution controls any legislative act repugnant to it; or, that the legislature may alter the constitution by an ordinary act.

Between these alternatives there is no middle ground. The constitution is either a superior, paramount law, unchangeable by ordinary means, or it is on a level with ordinary legislative acts, and like other acts, is alterable when the legislature shall please to alter it.

If the former part of the alternative be true, then a legislative act contrary to the constitution is not law: if the latter part be true, then written constitutions are absurd attempts, on the part of the people, to limit a power, in its own nature illimitable.

Certainly all those who have formed written constitutions contemplate them as forming the fundamental and paramount law of the nation, and consequently the theory of every such government must be, that an act of the legislature, repugnant to the constitution, is void.

This theory is essentially attached to a written constitution, and is consequently to be considered, by this court, as one of the fundamental principles of our society. It is not therefore to be lost sight of in the further consideration of this subject.

If an act of the legislature, repugnant to the constitution, is void, does it, notwithstanding its invalidity, bind the courts, and oblige them to give it effect? Or, in other words, though it be not law, does it constitute a rule as operative as if it was a law? This would be to overthrow in fact what was established in theory; and would seem, at first view, an absurdity too gross to be insisted on. . . .

It is emphatically the province and duty of the judicial department to say what the law is. Those who apply the rule to particular cases, must of necessity expound and interpret that rule. If two laws conflict with each other, the courts must decide on the operation of each.

So, if a law be in opposition to the constitution; if both the law and the constitution apply to a particular case, so that the court must either decide that case conformably to the law, disregarding the constitution; or conformably to the constitution, disregarding the law; the court must determine which of these conflicting rules governs the case. This is the very essence of judicial duty.

If then courts are to regard the constitution; and the constitution is superior to any ordinary act of the legislature; the constitution, and not such ordinary act, must govern the case to which they both apply.

Those then who controvert the principle that the constitution is to be considered, in court, as a paramount law, are reduced to the necessity of maintaining that courts must close their eyes on the constitution, and see only the law.

This doctrine would subvert the very foundation of all written constitutions. It would declare that an act, which, according to the principles and theory of our government, is entirely void; is yet, in practice, completely obligatory. It would declare, that if the legislature shall do what is expressly forbidden, such act, notwithstanding the express prohibition, is in reality effectual. It would be giving to the legislature a practical and real omnipotence, with the same breath which professes to restrict their powers within narrow limits. It is prescribing limits, and declaring that those limits may be passed at pleasure.

That it thus reduces to nothing what we have deemed the greatest improvement on political institutions — a written constitution — would of itself be sufficient, in America, where written constitutions have been viewed with so much reverence, for rejecting the construction. But the peculiar expressions of the constitution of the United States furnish additional arguments in favor of its rejection.

[ii]

The judicial power of the United States is extended to all cases arising under the constitution.

Could it be the intention of those who gave this power, to say that, in using it, the constitution should not be looked into? That a case arising under the constitution should be decided without examining the instrument under which it arises?

This is too extravagant to be maintained.

In some cases then, the constitution must be looked into by the judges. And if they can open it at all, what part of it are they forbidden to read, or to obey?

There are many other parts of the constitution which serve to illustrate this subject.

It is declared that "no tax or duty shall be laid on articles exported from any state." Suppose a duty on the export of cotton, of tobacco, or of flour; and a suit instituted to recover it. Ought judgment to be rendered in such a case? Ought the judges to close their eyes on the constitution, and only see the law?

The constitution declares that "no bill of attainder or *ex post facto* law shall be passed."

If, however, such a bill should be passed and a person should be prosecuted under it; must the court condemn to death those victims whom the constitution endeavors to preserve?

"No person," says the constitution, "shall be convicted of treason unless on the testimony of two witnesses to the same overt act, or on confession in open court."

Here the language of the constitution is addressed especially to the courts. It prescribes, directly for them, a rule of evidence not to be departed from. If the legislature should change that rule, and declare *one* witness, or a confession *out of court*, sufficient for conviction, must the constitutional principle yield to the legislative act?

From these, and many other selections which might be made, it is apparent, that the framers of the constitution contemplated that instrument, as a rule for the government of *courts*, as well as of the legislature.

[iii]

Why otherwise does it direct the judges to take an oath to support it? This oath certainly applies, in an especial manner, to their conduct in their official character. How immoral to impose on them, if they were to be used as the instruments, and the knowing instruments, for violating what they swear to support?

The oath of office, too, imposed by the legislature, is completely demonstrative of the legislative opinion on this subject. It is in these words, "I do solemnly swear that I will administer justice without respect to persons, and do equal right to the poor and to the rich; and that I will faithfully and impartially discharge all the duties incumbent on me as according to the best of my abilities and understanding, agreeably to *the constitution*, and laws of the United States."

Why does a judge swear to discharge his duties agreeably to the constitution of the United States, if that constitution forms no rule for his government if it is closed upon him, and cannot be inspected by him?

If such be the real state of things, this is worse than solemn mockery. To prescribe, or take this oath, becomes equally a crime.

[iv]

It is also not entirely unworthy of observation, that in declaring what shall be the *supreme* law of the land, the *constitution* itself is first mentioned; and not the laws of the United States generally, but those only which shall be made in *pursuance* of the constitution, have that rank.

Thus, the particular phraseology of the constitution of the United States confirms and strengthens the principle, supposed to be essential to all written constitutions, that a law repugnant to the constitution is void; and that *courts*, as well as other departments, are bound by that instrument.

The rule must be discharged.

Exercise 12:

Consider the following questions in relation to the Court's decision in *Marbury v. Madison*:

(1)   With less than a week remaining in its existence, on Friday, February 27, 1801, the "lame duck" Federalist Congress enacted legislation authorizing the appointment of various officers to assist in governing the District of Columbia, including justices of the peace who were to be appointed for terms of five years. Up until that point, all federal officers (other than judgeships granted life tenure by Article III of the Constitution) served at the pleasure of the President and were removable at will. What argument is there that the President has constitutional authority to remove officers at will (and, concomitantly, that Congress may not limit that power)? What argument is there that Congress could limit the power of the President to remove *these* officers even if it lacked the power to limit the President's removal of some other non-judicial officers, such as the Secretary of State? If Congress could not limit the President's power to remove the justice of the peace from office at will, does that affect the Court's analysis of this case?

(2)   Only three days before he was to leave office, on Saturday, February 28, 1801, the "lame duck" Federalist President, John Adams, nominated individuals to all offices created under the Act he signed the previous day. His nominations included 42 prospective justices of the peace. (Recall that President Adams may have been delayed in assembling his list of nominees by having to relieve President-elect Jefferson of the burden of filling the judgeships and other offices created under the Federal Judiciary Act of 1801, as well as the task — too daunting for a new administration — of finding a suitable Chief Justice of the United States). On Tuesday, March 3, the Senate confirmed all the nominees. (The Senate was unavoidably delayed in taking more prompt action upon the nominees because it was not finished confirming the new judges under the Federal Judiciary Act of 1801 until Monday, March 2, 1801.) After Senate confirmation of the justices of the peace, President Adams allegedly signed commissions for the officers. If President Adams had failed to sign the commissions before leaving office, would a confirmed nominee — like William Marbury — have had a right to the office? Recall, in that regard, the statutory provisions regarding the commissioning of officers in Chapter 2.

(3)   Because William Marbury never received his commission before Jefferson was inaugurated on Wednesday, March 4, 1801, he lacked personal knowledge that it had ever been signed (or, for that matter, sealed by the Secretary of State). How did the Court know whether the Commission was ever signed (and sealed)?

(4)   Assuming the commission was signed, recorded, and sealed, who was responsible for delivering the commission to Marbury? (*Hint*: Who was Secretary of State to President Adams?) Why is James Madison the named party?

(5)   If President Adams changed his mind after signing the commission for Marbury, could he have directed his Secretary of State to destroy the commission rather than to seal it? Why or why not?

(6)   Assuming Marbury had a vested legal right to his office, could he have sued the United States for the payment of any salary associated with the office? Why or why not? (If he could not do so, does that render the government of the United States one of men and not of laws? Or, does the Constitution recognize that there are some governmental wrongs that the judiciary is not necessarily authorized to address?)

(7)   Assuming Marbury had a vested legal right to his office, could he have instituted an action in the Circuit Court for the District of Columbia (created by the very same statute that created the justice of the peace office) for a writ of mandamus commanding the delivery of his commission? Why or why not?

(8)   Did Section 13 of the Federal Judiciary Act of 1789 (in Chapter 2) purport to confer jurisdiction on the Supreme Court to consider Marbury's request for a writ of mandamus as an original matter? Is there any reasonable basis for construing the reference to mandamus as applicable only when the Supreme Court was exercising appellate jurisdiction? Is there any reasonable basis for construing the reference to mandamus as providing only a remedy available to the Court in such cases properly within the Court's jurisdiction? If the Court declined jurisdiction based on a construction of the statute, would the outcome of the case have remained the same?

(9)   What is the import of the Article III text defining certain cases as within the original jurisdiction of the Supreme Court? Did the Framers mean that at least these cases should be heard initially by the Supreme Court but that Congress could give the Supreme Court trial-court jurisdiction over other matters within the federal judicial power by making "such Exceptions" to the Court's "appellate Jurisdiction"? (Note that such an interpretation would prevent Congress from prohibiting the Court from exercising appellate review over some matters within the scope of Article III while still giving some meaning to the exceptions language.) Or, were the Framers establishing a "default" rule to ensure certain matters would be heard initially in the Supreme Court at least until Congress made provision for inferior federal courts and a comprehensive allocation of jurisdiction? (Note that such an interpretation would permit Congress today to authorize suits against Ambassadors, for example, to be brought before the Supreme Court only upon appellate review. Would that flexibility be preferable to having the Court conduct jury trials today?) If instead of either of those interpretations, the original jurisdiction of the Supreme Court described in Article III is the fixed maximum of such jurisdiction, what purpose is served by that view? Why would the Framers have designed such a system?

(10)   Upon which principles of textual analysis, if any, did the Court rely in answering the preceding question? Upon which historical sources, if any, did the Court rely to support its interpretation? Does the Court's method of analysis withstand scrutiny?

(11)   The Court asserted that judicial review logically and invariably follows from the premise of a written constitution. Is that true? Or, does a written constitution serve some other purpose? (Review your answer to that question in *Exercise 3*.)

(12)   How broad a power of judicial review did the Court claim in *Marbury*? What did the Court mean by: "It is emphatically the province and duty of the judicial department to say what the law is." Does that statement broaden or narrow the claimed scope of judicial review?

(13)   The Court also based judicial review on the oath taken by judges. Does the existence of the oath support the Court's argument?

(14)   The Court also based judicial review on the fact that the Constitution declares as supreme law only such legislation "which shall be made in Pursuance" of the Constitution. Does that observation require judicial review?

(15)   In *Cohens v. Virginia* (in Chapter 4), the Court emphasized the respect it accorded to a contemporaneous interpretation of the Constitution by the First

Congress as reflected in Section 25 of the Federal Judiciary Act of 1789 when the validity of that provision was challenged. Could the same Court (speaking through the same Chief Justice) fairly rely on that basis after the decision in *Marbury*? Or, was *Cohens* correct and the Court was too quick to disregard the views of Congress in *Marbury*?

(16) By the time the Court decided *Marbury,* existing Supreme Court precedents included the decisions regarding the Hayburn and Todd applications for Revolutionary War pensions (in Chapter 3) and *Calder v. Bull* (in Chapter 3). Did *Marbury* extend judicial review beyond those precedents? If so, how?

(17) What is the holding of *Marbury*?

(18) If the Circuit Court for the District of Columbia would have had jurisdiction if Marbury initially presented his case there (*see* Question 7 *supra*), would that forum have remained available to Marbury after the Supreme Court's decision or did the Supreme Court identify a pertinent obstacle to Marbury's relief in that court?

(19) In *Stuart v. Laird,* a week after *Marbury,* the same Court held that judges appointed under the Federal Judiciary Act of 1801 who had received signed and sealed commissions and who had started to serve in office could be denied their posts despite the Article III guarantee of life tenure to judges. Why did Marbury have a superior right to relief than one of those judges? Would then-former President Adams and the former-Federalist Senate have preferred to preserve the offices at issue in *Stuart* or in *Marbury*? Which case would have been of greater concern to President Jefferson and the new Congress? Can the two cases be harmonized?

(20) If, after the Supreme Court decision in his case, Marbury could have brought an action in the Circuit Court for the District of Columbia (*see* Question 18 *supra*) and if once the case was filed — but before it was decided — the Jeffersonian Congress repealed that portion of the February 27, 1801 Act creating the office of justice of the peace, how should the Circuit Court have ruled on the petition for a writ of mandamus?

A Side Note on the "First Party System"

While the focus of this Volume is the federal judicial power, the clash between the party of Adams (and Hamilton) and the party of Jefferson (and Madison) produced other lasting changes to the constitutional structure as well, including the last constitutional amendment prior to the Civil War.

Article II, Section 1 of the Constitution of 1789 specified the manner of selecting the President and Vice President. As originally structured, the candidate with a majority of votes in the Electoral College would become President and the candidate with the next largest number of votes would become Vice President. The rise of rival political parties meant that the leading candidates of different parties might well finish first and second. That is exactly what happened in 1796 when President Washington declined to seek a third term.

Vice President John Adams (of Massachusetts) finished with a majority of Electoral College votes. He had the support of the Federalist party which also supported Thomas Pinckney (of South Carolina), whom Federalists expected would serve as Vice President if Adams prevailed. Thomas Jefferson (of Virginia) had the support of the opposing Republican party which also supported Aaron Burr (of New York), whom Republicans expected would serve as Vice President if Jefferson prevailed. To accomplish the informal arrangement of running mates, each party would arrange to have *one* Elector cast his first vote for the party's first choice and cast the second vote for some third person, thereby assuring that Adams or Jefferson would finish a vote ahead of Pinckney or Burr. The informal arrangement failed. Within the Federalist party, Alexander Hamilton worked behind the scenes to secure strong support for Pinckney (even to the extent, some believed, of hoping he would receive more votes than Adams). The results of the election of 1796 demonstrated that the informal arrangements of each party were inadequate. Adams narrowly finished first, with 71 votes to 68 for Jefferson. The second man of each party received considerably fewer votes than those at the head of the parties. Pinckney received 59 votes and Burr received only 30.

President Adams excluded Jefferson from cabinet meetings and other business of the Executive Branch. Vice President Jefferson meanwhile headed opposition to the Administration from within. If elections continued to produce such results, that may have been enough to suggest a change to the manner of selecting the President and Vice President. But an even larger problem soon presented itself.

In the election of 1800, the Federalists determined to cast votes for President Adams (of Massachusetts) and for Charles Cotesworth Pinckney (of South Carolina, brother of Thomas Pinckney), whom they expected would serve as Vice President if Adams prevailed. Meanwhile, the Republicans again determined to cast votes for Vice President Jefferson (of Virginia) and for Aaron Burr (of New York). Once again, the informal arrangement failed.

On the Republican side, both Jefferson and Burr finished with 73 votes in the Electoral College. (Adams and Pinckney received 65 and 63 votes, respectively.) The lame duck House of Representatives dominated by Federalists was thereby empowered to determine whether Jefferson or Burr would be President. There were numerous opportunities for intrigue (including some suggestion that they might perpetuate the deadlock and select a Federalist to fill the vacancy),[1] as the deadlock lasted until the thirty-sixth ballot in the House, on February 17, 1801.

For a recent, detailed examination of the contest, see JOHN FERLING, ADAMS V. JEFFERSON: THE TUMULTUOUS ELECTION OF 1800 (2004), or SUSAN DUNN, JEFFERSON'S SECOND REVOLUTION: THE ELECTION CRISIS OF 1800 AND THE TRIUMPH OF REPUBLICANISM (2004).

The Twelfth Amendment was proposed and ratified before the expiration of President Jefferson's first term. That Amendment ensured that a President would serve with a Vice President who had appeared on the ballot with him, rather than a member of an opposing party. In addition, the Twelfth Amendment ensured that there would be no confusion about which of the candidates on the ballot would be President and which would be Vice President. The Twelfth Amendment thus "neatly operated to transform the executive into a reliable instrument of party rule."[2] That is, a single political party won the prize of the Presidency including successorship in the event of unanticipated death or disability.

---

[1] Professor Bruce Ackerman suggests that John Marshall was the likely candidate for interim President as the senior officer in the Executive Branch (Secretary of State) *and* senior officer in the Judicial Branch (Chief Justice of the Supreme Court). *See* BRUCE ACKERMAN, THE FAILURE OF THE FOUNDING FATHERS: JEFFERSON, MARSHALL, AND THE RISE OF PRESIDENTIAL DEMOCRACY 34–54, 80–82, 85–86 (2005). Ackerman also argues that Marshall himself was behind anonymous publications laying the groundwork for such a solution. *See id.* at 45–54.

[2] *See* Bruce Ackerman, *supra* note 1, at 205.

CHAPTER 6
REFINING THE SCOPE OF THE JUDICIAL POWER

The early cases in the previous chapters addressed many important questions regarding the structure of the judiciary and its appropriate powers under the Constitution. In reviewing the material in this Chapter, consider to what extent more-recent cases depart from those decisions. In doing so, consider what weight should be accorded to earlier judicial determinations of the Constitution. Stated otherwise, what weight should be given to *stare decisis* relative to arguments based upon the structure of government established by the Constitution, the text of the Constitution, the original shared understanding of the Constitution, and tradition of long-standing that has not necessarily received judicial consideration.

The materials in this Chapter address the following distinct topics: (a) the extent to which judicial determinations are subject to revision or reopening by other branches (Exercise 13 and accompanying materials); (b) the "justiciability doctrines" of standing, mootness, and ripeness (Exercise 14 and accompanying materials); (c) standards of review applied by the federal judiciary on constitutional questions (Exercise 15 and accompanying materials); (d) principles of judicial self-restraint in addressing constitutional issues (Exercise 16 and accompanying materials); (e) the role of *stare decisis* in constitutional interpretation (Exercise 17 and accompanying materials); (f) the "political question" doctrine (Exercise 18 and accompanying materials); and (g) adjudication by non-Article III tribunals.

A. Revision and Reopening of Judicial Determinations

MILLER v. FRENCH
530 U.S. 327 (2000)

JUSTICE O'CONNOR delivered the opinion of the Court.

The Prison Litigation Reform Act of 1995 (PLRA) establishes standards for the entry and termination of prospective relief in civil actions challenging prison conditions. If prospective relief under an existing injunction does not satisfy these standards, a defendant or intervener is entitled to "immediate termination" of that relief. And under the PLRA's "automatic stay" provision, a motion to terminate prospective relief "shall operate as a stay" of that relief during the period beginning 30 days after the filing of the motion (extendable to up to 90 days for "good cause") and ending when the court rules on the motion. The superintendent of Indiana's Pendleton Correctional Facility, which is currently operating under an ongoing injunction to remedy violations of the Eighth Amendment regarding conditions of confinement, filed a motion to terminate prospective relief under the PLRA. Respondent prisoners moved to enjoin the operation of the automatic stay provision of § 3626(e)(2), arguing that it is unconstitutional. The District Court enjoined the stay, and the Court of Appeals for the Seventh Circuit affirmed. We must decide whether a district court may enjoin the operation of the PLRA's automatic stay provision and, if not, whether that provision violates separation of powers principles.

I

A

. . . .

B

In 1996, Congress enacted the PLRA. . . . [Under that Act,] a court "shall not grant or approve any prospective relief unless the court finds that such relief is narrowly drawn, extends no further than necessary to correct the violation of the Federal right, and is the least intrusive means necessary to correct the violations of the Federal right." 18 U.S.C. § 3626(a)(1)(A). The same criteria apply to existing injunctions, and a defendant or intervenor may move to terminate prospective relief that does not meet this standard. *See* § 3626(b)(2). . . . The PLRA also requires courts to rule "promptly" on motions to terminate prospective relief, with mandamus available to remedy a court's failure to do so. § 3626(e)(1).

Finally, the provision at issue here, § 3626(e)(2), dictates that, in certain circumstances, prospective relief shall be stayed pending resolution of a motion to terminate. . . .

C

. . . .

The Court of Appeals for the Seventh Circuit . . . conclud[ed] that although § 3626(e)(2) precluded courts from exercising their equitable powers to enjoin operation of the automatic stay, the statute, so construed, was unconstitutional on separation of powers grounds. . . . [T]he court characterized § 3626(e)(2) as "a self-executing legislative determination that a specific decree of a federal court . . . must be set aside at least for a period of time." As such, it concluded that § 3626(e)(2) directly suspends a court order in violation of the separation of powers doctrine under *Plaut v. Spendthrift Farm, Inc.*, 514 U.S. 211 (1995), and mandates a particular rule of decision, at least during the pendency of the § 3626(b)(2) termination motion, contrary to *United States v. Klein*, 80 U.S. 128 (1872). . . .

. . . .

II

. . . .

. . . Like the Court of Appeals, we find that § 3626(e)(2) is unambiguous . . . . Any construction that preserved courts' equitable discretion to enjoin the automatic stay would effectively convert the PLRA's mandatory stay into a discretionary one. Because this would be plainly contrary to Congress's intent in enacting the stay provisions, we must confront the constitutional issue.

III

The Constitution enumerates and separates the powers of the three branches of government in Articles I, II, and III, and it is this "very structure" of the Constitution that exemplifies the concept of separation of powers. *INS v. Chadha*, 462 U.S. 919, 946 (1983). While the boundaries between the three branches are not " 'hermetically' sealed," *see id.* at 951, the Constitution prohibits one branch from encroaching on the central prerogatives of another. The powers of the Judicial Branch are set forth in Article III, § 1 . . . . As we explained in *Plaut v. Spendthrift Farm, Inc.,* 514 U.S. at 218–19, Article III "gives the Federal Judiciary the power, not merely to rule on cases, but to *decide* them, subject to review only by superior courts in the Article III hierarchy."

Respondent prisoners contend that § 3626(e)(2) encroaches on the central prerogatives of the Judiciary and thereby violates the separation of powers doctrine. It does this, the prisoners assert, by legislatively suspending a final judgment of an Article III court in violation of *Plaut* and *Hayburn's Case,* 2 U.S. 408 (1792). According to the prisoners, the remedial order governing living conditions at the Pendleton Correctional Facility is a final judgment of an Article III court, and § 3626(e)(2) constitutes an impermissible usurpation of judicial power because it commands the district court to suspend prospective relief under that order, albeit temporarily. An analysis of the principles underlying *Hayburn's Case* and *Plaut,* as well as an examination of § 3626(e)(2)'s interaction with the other provisions of § 3626, makes clear that § 3626(e)(2) does not offend these separation of powers principles.

Hayburn's Case arose out of a 1792 statute that authorized pensions for veterans of the Revolutionary War. The statute provided that the circuit courts were to review the applications and determine the appropriate amount of the pension, but that the Secretary of War had the discretion either to adopt or reject the courts' findings. 2 U.S. at 409–10. Although this Court did not reach the constitutional issue in *Hayburn's Case,* the statements of five Justices, acting as circuit judges, were reported, and we have since recognized that the case "stands for the principle that Congress cannot vest review of the decisions of Article III courts in officials of the Executive Branch." *Plaut,* 514 U.S. at 218. As we recognized in *Plaut,* such an effort by a coequal branch to "annul a final judgment" is " 'an assumption of Judicial power' and therefore forbidden." *Id.* at 224.

Unlike the situation in *Hayburn's Case,* § 3626(e)(2) does not involve the direct review of a judicial decision by officials of the Legislative or Executive branches. Nonetheless, the prisoners suggest that § 3626(e)(2) falls within *Hayburn's* prohibition against an indirect legislative "suspension" or reopening of a final judgment, such as that addressed in *Plaut.* In *Plaut,* we held that a federal statute that required federal courts to reopen final judgments that had been entered before the statute's enactment was unconstitutional on separation of powers grounds. 514 U.S. at 211. The plaintiffs had brought a civil securities fraud action seeking money damages. *Id.* at 213. While that action was pending, we ruled in *Lampf, Pleva, Lipkind, Prupis & Petigrow v. Gilbertson,* 501 U.S. 350 (1991), that such suits must be commenced within one year after the discovery of the facts constituting the violation and within three years after such violation. In light of this intervening decision, the *Plaut* plaintiffs' suit was untimely, and the District Court accordingly dismissed the action as time barred. 514 U.S. at 214. After the judgment dismissing the case had become final, Congress enacted a statute providing for the reinstatement of those actions, including the *Plaut* plaintiffs', that had been dismissed under *Lampf* but that would have been timely under the previously applicable statute of limitations. 514 U.S. at 215.

We concluded that this retroactive command that federal courts reopen final judgments exceeded Congress' authority. *Id.* at 218–19. The decision of an inferior court within the Article III hierarchy is not the final word of the department (unless the time for appeal has expired), and "[i]t is the obligation of the last court in the hierarchy that rules on the case to give effect to Congress's latest enactment, even when that has the effect of overturning the judgment of an inferior court, since each court, at every level, must 'decide according to existing laws.' " *Id.* at 227 (quoting *United States v. Schooner Peggy*, 5 U.S. 103, 109 (1801)). But once a judicial decision achieves finality, it "becomes the last word of the judicial department." 514 U.S. at 227. And because Article III "gives the Federal Judiciary the power, not merely to rule on cases, but to *decide* them, subject to review only by superior courts in the Article III hierarchy," *id.* at 218–19, the "judicial Power is one to render dispositive judgments," and Congress cannot retroactively command Article III courts to reopen final judgments, *id.* at 219.

Plaut, however, was careful to distinguish the situation before the Court in that case — legislation that attempted to reopen the dismissal of a suit seeking money damages — from legislation that "altered the prospective effect of injunctions entered by article III courts." 514 U.S. at 232. . . . Prospective relief under a continuing, executory decree remains subject to alteration due to changes in the underlying law. *Cf. Landgraf v. USI Film Products*, 511 U.S. 244, 273 (1994) ("When the intervening statute authorizes or affects the propriety of prospective relief, application of the new provision is not retroactive"). This conclusion follows from our decisions in *Pennsylvania v. Wheeling & Belmont Bridge Co.*, 54 U.S. 518 (1852) (*Wheeling Bridge I*), and *Pennsylvania v. Wheeling & Belmont Bridge Co.*, 59 U.S. 421 (1856) (*Wheeling Bridge II*).

In *Wheeling Bridge I*, we held that a bridge across the Ohio River, because it was too low, unlawfully "obstruct[ed] the navigation of the Ohio," and ordered that the bridge be raised or permanently removed. 54 U.S. at 578. Shortly thereafter, Congress enacted legislation declaring the bridge to be a "lawful structur[e]," establishing the bridge as a " 'post-road for the passage of the mails of the United States,' " and declaring that the Wheeling and Belmont Bridge Company was authorized to maintain the bridge at its then-current site and elevation. *Wheeling Bridge II*, 59 U.S. at 429. After the bridge was destroyed in a storm, Pennsylvania sued to enjoin the bridge's reconstruction, arguing that the statute legalizing the bridge was unconstitutional because it effectively annulled the Court's decision in *Wheeling Bridge I*. We rejected that argument, concluding that the decree in *Wheeling Bridge I* provided for ongoing relief by "directing the abatement of the obstruction" which enjoined the defendants from any continuance or reconstruction of the obstruction. Because the intervening statute altered the underlying law such that the bridge was no longer an unlawful obstruction, we held that it was "quite plain the decree of the court cannot be enforced." *Wheeling Bridge II*, 59 U.S. at 431–32. The Court explained that had *Wheeling Bridge I* awarded money damages in an action at law, then that judgment would be final, and Congress' later action could not have affected plaintiff's right to those damages. *See* 59 U.S. at 431. But because the decree entered in *Wheeling Bridge I* provided for prospective relief — a continuing injunction against the continuation or reconstruction of the bridge — the ongoing validity of the injunctive relief depended on "whether or not [the bridge] interferes with the right of navigation." 59 U.S. at 431. When Congress altered the underlying law such that the bridge was no longer an unlawful obstruction, the injunction against the maintenance of the bridge was not enforceable. *See id.* at 432.

Applied here, the principles of *Wheeling Bridge II* demonstrate that the automatic stay of § 3626(e)(2) does not unconstitutionally "suspend" or reopen a judgment of an Article III court. Section 3626(e)(2) does not by itself "tell judges when, how, or what to do." Instead, § 3626(e)(2) merely reflects the change implemented by § 3626(b), which does the "heavy lifting" in the statutory scheme by establishing new standards for prospective relief. . . . The PLRA's automatic stay provision assists in the enforcement of §§ 3626(b)(2) and (3) by requiring the court to stay any prospective relief that, due to the change in the underlying standard, is no longer enforceable, *i.e.*, prospective relief that is not supported by the findings specified in §§ 3626(b)(2) and (3).

By establishing new standards for the enforcement of prospective relief in § 3626(b), Congress has altered the relevant underlying law. The PLRA has restricted courts' authority to issue and enforce prospective relief concerning prison conditions, requiring that such relief be supported by findings and precisely tailored to what is needed to remedy the violation of a federal right. We note that the constitutionality of § 3626(b) is not challenged here; we assume, without deciding, that the new standards it pronounces are effective. As *Plaut* and *Wheeling Bridge I* instruct, when Congress changes the law underlying a judgment awarding prospective relief, that relief is no longer enforceable to the extent that it is inconsistent with the new law. Although the remedial injunction here is a "final judgment" for purposes of appeal, it is not the "last word of the judicial department." *Plaut*, 514 U.S. at 227. The provision of prospective relief is subject to the continuing supervisory jurisdiction of the court, and therefore may be altered according to subsequent changes in the law. *See Rufo v. Inmates of Suffolk County Jail*, 502 U.S. 367, 388 (1992). Prospective relief must be "modified if, as it later turns out, one or more of the obligations placed upon the parties has become impermissible under federal law." *Id.; see also Railway Employees v. Wright*, 364 U.S. 642, 646–47 (1961) (a court has the authority to alter the prospective effect of an injunction to reflect a change in circumstances, whether of law or fact, that has occurred since the injunction was entered).

The entry of the automatic stay under § 3626(e)(2) helps to implement the change in the law caused by §§ 3626(b)(2) and (3). If the prospective relief under the existing decree is not supported by the findings required under § 3626(b)(2), and the court has not made the findings required by § 3626(b)(3), then prospective relief is no longer enforceable and must be stayed. The entry of the stay does not reopen or "suspend" the previous judgment, nor does it divest the court of authority to decide the merits of the termination motion. Rather, the stay merely reflects the changed legal circumstances — that prospective relief under the existing decree is no longer enforceable, and remains unenforceable unless and until the court makes the findings required by § 3626(b)(3).

For the same reasons, § 3626(e)(2) does not violate the separation of powers principle articulated in *United States v. Klein*, 80 U.S. 128 (1872). In that case, Klein, the executor of the estate of a Confederate sympathizer, sought to recover the value of property seized by the United States during the Civil War, which by statute was recoverable if Klein could demonstrate that the decedent had not given aid or comfort to the rebellion. *Id.* at 131. In *United States v. Padelford*, 76 U.S. 531, 542–43 (1870), we held that a Presidential pardon satisfied the burden of proving that no such aid or comfort had been given. While Klein's case was pending, Congress enacted a statute providing that a pardon would instead be taken as proof that the pardoned individual had in fact aided the enemy, and if the claimant offered proof of a pardon the court must dismiss the case for lack of jurisdiction. *Klein*, 80 U.S. at 133–34. We concluded that the statute was unconstitutional because it purported to "prescribe rules of decision to the Judicial Department of the government in cases pending before it." *Id.* at 146.

Here, the prisoners argue that Congress has similarly prescribed a rule of decision because, for the period of time until the district court makes a final decision on the merits of the motion to terminate prospective relief, § 3626(e)(2) mandates a particular outcome: the termination of prospective relief. As we noted in *Plaut*, however, "[w]hatever the precise scope of *Klein*, . . . later decisions have made it clear that its prohibition does not take hold when Congress 'amend[s] applicable law.' " 514 U.S. at 218. The prisoners concede this point but contend that, because § 3626(e)(2) does not itself amend the legal standard, *Klein* is still applicable. As we have explained, however, § 3626(e)(2) must be read not in isolation, but in the context of § 3626 as a whole. . . . Rather than prescribing a rule of decision, § 3626(e)(2) simply imposes the consequences of the court's application of the new legal standard.

Finally, the prisoners assert that, even if § 3626(e)(2) does not fall within the recognized prohibitions of *Hayburn's Case, Plaut,* or *Klein,* it still offends the principles of separation of powers because it places a deadline on judicial decisionmaking, thereby interfering with core judicial functions. Congress' imposition of a time limit in § 3626(e)(2), however, does not in itself offend the structural concerns underlying the Constitution's separation of powers. For example, if the PLRA granted courts 10 years to determine whether they could make the required findings, then certainly the PLRA would raise no apprehensions that Congress had encroached on the core function of the Judiciary to decide "cases and controversies properly before them." *United States v. Raines*, 362 U.S. 17, 20 (1960). Respondents' concern with the time limit, then, must be its relative brevity. But whether the time is so short that it deprives litigants of a meaningful opportunity to be heard is a due process question, an issue that is not before us. . . .

In contrast to due process, which principally serves to protect the personal rights of litigants to a full and fair hearing, separation of powers principles are primarily addressed to the structural concerns of protecting the role of the independent Judiciary within the constitutional design. In this action, we have no occasion to decide whether there could be a time constraint on judicial action that was so severe that it implicated these structural separation of powers concerns. The PLRA does not deprive courts of their adjudicatory role, but merely provides a new legal standard for relief and encourages courts to apply that standard promptly.

. . . [W]e conclude that this provision does not violate separation of powers principles. Accordingly, the judgment of the Court of Appeals for the Seventh Circuit is reversed, and the action is remanded for further proceedings consistent with this opinion.

JUSTICE SOUTER, with whom JUSTICE GINSBERG joins, concurring in part and dissenting in part.

[Justices Souter and Ginsberg joined in the Court's opinion except for its discussion of whether the time limit contained within the statute raises a separation of powers concern.]

JUSTICE BREYER, with whom JUSTICE STEVENS joins, dissenting.

[Justices Breyer and Stevens would have interpreted the statute differently so as to avoid constitutional issues.]

Exercise 13:

Consider the following matters in connection with *Miller v. French:*

(1)   What does the Court view as the critical defect at issue in the cases regarding the statutory mechanism for administering pensions for disabled veterans of the Revolutionary War? Compare your answers in *Exercise 6* to the Court's discussion in this case.

(2)   If Congress may not "review" the judgment of an Article III court, may Congress require such courts to reconsider their judgments and/or permit parties to seek reconsideration? For example, if a federal court awarded a plaintiff $2,500,000 in damages, and Congress subsequently enacted a law requiring more stringent appellate review of awards in excess of $1,000,000, would the statute apply to the previous award? Does the answer to that question depend upon whether appellate review was still pending at the time of the enactment? Why?

(3)   How, if at all, would the answer to the preceding question vary if the court had issued an injunction imposing compliance costs on the defendant of $2,500,000 and Congress subsequently enacted a law requiring more stringent appellate review of injunctions with compliance costs in excess of $1,000,000? Does the answer to that question depend upon whether appellate review was still pending at the time of the enactment? Why?

(4)   If Congress may change existing law and that law would be applicable to cases not yet finally adjudicated, what was the problem in *United States v. Klein*?

B.   Justiciability Doctrines

FRIENDS OF EARTH, INC. v.
LAIDLAW ENVIRONMENTAL SERVICES (TOC), INC.
528 U.S. 167 (2000)

JUSTICE GINSBURG delivered the opinion of the Court.

[Under the federal Clean Water Act (CWA) the Environmental Protection Agency (EPA) or authorized States issue permits that impose limitations on the discharge of pollutants. The CWA authorizes any "citizen" to bring suit to enforce permit limitations. The Act further defines a citizen as "a person or persons having an interest which is or may be adversely affected." The Act limits the citizen-suit provisions by requiring the prospective plaintiff to provide sixty days advance notice to the alleged violator, the EPA, and the pertinent State. In an earlier case, the Supreme Court had explained that the purpose of such notice was to permit the regulated party to bring itself into compliance with the CWA and thus obviate the need for a lawsuit. Based on that rationale, the Court had previously determined that if violations of the Act ceased before the complaint was filed, the plaintiff lacked statutory standing to proceed. In addition, the Act also bars citizen suits if the EPA or the State has already commenced and is "diligently prosecuting" an enforcement action.

Laidlaw acquired a waste-water treatment facility in South Carolina and was issued a permit by the South Carolina Department of Health and Environmental Control (DHEC). Laidlaw's discharges repeatedly exceeded the limits set by the permit.

On April 10, 1992, the prospective plaintiffs (FOE) notified Laidlaw of their intention to file a citizen suit after the expiration of the requisite 60-day notice period. Laidlaw's attorney then contacted the DHEC and asked it to sue the company. DHEC agreed, and Laidlaw's attorney wrote the complaint and paid the filing fee. On the last day of the notice period, DHEC and Laidlaw reached a settlement agreement which required Laidlaw to pay a civil penalty of $100,000 and to make "every effort" to comply with the permit obligations.

Two months later, FOE filed this action alleging noncompliance with the permit and seeking declaratory and injunctive relief and an award of civil penalties. Laidlaw moved for summary judgment on the ground that FOE had failed to present evidence demonstrating injury in fact, and therefore lacked Article III standing to bring the lawsuit. The District Court denied Laidlaw's motion, finding — albeit "by the very slimmest of margins" — that FOE had standing to bring suit.

Laidlaw also sought to have FOE's suit dismissed on grounds that, under the Act, it was barred by the DHEC action and settlement. The District Court rejected that argument because the suit was not "diligently prosecuted," as evidenced by the fact Laidlaw's attorney drew up the complaint and paid the filing fee. Moreover, the record indicated that even after FOE filed suit, Laidlaw violated the provisions of the discharge permit without facing further enforcement proceedings.]

On January 22, 1997, the District Court issued its judgment. It found that Laidlaw had gained a total economic benefit of $1,092,581 as a result of its extended period of noncompliance with the mercury discharge limit in its permit. The court concluded, however, that a civil penalty of $405,800 was adequate in light of the guiding factors listed in [the CWA]. In particular, the District Court stated that the lesser penalty was appropriate taking into account the judgment's "total deterrent effect." In reaching this determination, the court "considered that Laidlaw will be required to reimburse plaintiffs for a significant amount of legal fees." The court declined to grant FOE's request for injunctive relief, stating that an injunction was inappropriate because "Laidlaw has been in substantial compliance with all parameters in its NPDES permit since at least August 1992."

[FOE appealed, claiming the sum of the penalty was inadequate. Laidlaw cross-appealed the District Court's determination that FOE had standing to bring suit.]

. . . The Court of Appeals assumed without deciding that FOE initially had standing to bring the action, but went on to hold that the case had become moot. The appellate court stated first, that the elements of Article III standing — injury, causation, and redressability — must persist at every stage of review, or else the action becomes moot. Citing our decision in *Steel Co. v. Citizens for Better Environment*, 523 U.S. 83 (1998), the Court of Appeals reasoned that the case had become moot because "the only remedy currently available to [FOE] — civil penalties payable to the government — would not redress any injury [FOE has] suffered." The court therefore vacated the District Court's order and remanded with instructions to dismiss the action.

[After the appellate decision but before the grant of certiorari, Laidlaw informed the Court that it had closed the facility in question and permanently ceased discharge from that plant.]

II

A

The Constitution's case-or-controversy limitation on federal judicial authority, Art. III, § 2, underpins both our standing and mootness jurisprudence, but the two inquires differ in respects critical to the proper resolution of this case, so we address them separately. Because the Court of Appeals was persuaded that the case had become moot and so held, it simply assumed without deciding that FOE had initial standing. But because we hold that the Court of Appeals erred in declaring the case moot, we have an obligation to assure ourselves that FOE had Article III standing at the outset of the litigation. We therefore address the question of standing before turning to mootness.

In *Lujan v. Defenders of Wildlife*, 504 U.S. 555, 560–61 (1992), we held that, to satisfy Article III's standing requirements, a plaintiff must show (1) it has suffered an "injury in fact" that is (a) concrete and particularized and (b) actual or imminent, not conjectural or hypothetical; (2) the injury is fairly traceable to the challenged action of the defendant; and (3) it is likely, as opposed to merely speculative, that the injury will be redressed by a favorable decision. An association has standing to bring suit on behalf of its members when its members would otherwise have standing to sue in their own right, the interests at stake are germane to the organization's purpose, and neither the claim asserted nor the relief requested requires the participation of individual members in the lawsuit. *Hunt v. Washington State Apple Advertising Comm'n*, 432 U.S. 333, 343 (1977).

Laidlaw contends first that FOE lacked standing from the outset even to seek injunctive relief, because the plaintiff organization failed to show that any of their members had sustained or faced the threat of any "injury in fact" from Laidlaw's activities. In support of this contention Laidlaw points to the District Court's finding, made in the course of setting the penalty amount, that there had been "no demonstrated proof of harm to the environment" from Laidlaw's mercury discharge violations.

The relevant showing for purposes of Article III standing, however, is not injury to the environment but injury to the plaintiff. To insist upon the former rather than the latter as part of the standing inquiry (as the dissent in essence does) is to raise the standing hurdle higher than the necessary showing for success on the merits in an action alleging noncompliance with an NPDES permit. Focusing properly on injury to the plaintiff, the District Court found that FOE had demonstrated sufficient injury to establish standing. For example, FOE member Kenneth Lee Curtis averred in affidavits that he lived a half-mile from Laidlaw's facility; that he occasionally drove over the North Tyger River, and that it looked and smelled polluted; and that he would like to fish, camp, swim, and picnic in and near the river between 3 and 15 miles downstream from the facility, as he did when he was a teenager, but would not do so because he was concerned that the water was polluted by Laidlaw's discharges. . . .

Other members presented evidence to similar effect. . . .

These sworn statements, as the District Court determined, adequately documented injury in fact. We have held that environmental plaintiffs adequately allege injury in fact when they aver that they use the affected area and are persons "for whom the aesthetic and recreational values of the area will be lessened" by the challenged activity. *Sierra Club v. Morton*, 405 U.S. 727, 735 (1972).

Our decision in *Lujan v. National Wildlife Federation*, 497 U.S. 871 (1990), is not to the contrary. In that case an environmental organization assailed the Bureau of Land Management's "land withdrawal review program," a program covering millions of acres, alleging that the program illegally opened up public lands to mining activities. The defendants moved for summary judgment, challenging the plaintiff organization's standing to initiate the action . . . . We held that the plaintiff could not survive the summary judgment motion merely by offering "averments which state only that one of [the organization's] members uses unspecified portions of an immense tract of territory, on some portions of which mining activities have occurred or probably will occur by virtue of the governmental action." *Id.* at 889.

In contrast, the affidavits and testimony presented by FOE in this case assert that Laidlaw's discharges, and the affiant members' reasonable concerns about the effects of those discharges, directly affected those affiants' recreational, aesthetic, and economic interests. These submissions present dispositively more than the mere "general averments" and "conclusory allegations" found inadequate in *National Wildlife Federation*. Nor can the affiants' conditional statements — that they would use the nearby North Tyger River for recreation if Laidlaw were not discharging pollutants into it — be equated with the speculative " 'some day' intentions" to visit endangered species halfway around the world that we held insufficient to show injury in fact in *Defenders of Wildlife*. 504 U.S. at 564.

Los Angeles v. Lyons, 461 U.S. 95 (1983), relied on by the dissent, does not weigh against standing in this case. In *Lyons*, we held that a plaintiff lacked standing to seek an injunction against the enforcement of a police choke-hold policy because he could not credibly allege that he faced a realistic threat from the policy. *Id.* at 107 n.7. In the footnote from *Lyons* cited by the dissent, we noted that "[t]he reasonableness of Lyons' fear is dependent upon the likelihood of a recurrence of the allegedly unlawful conduct," and that his "subjective apprehensions" that such a recurrence would even *take place* were not enough to support standing. *Id.* at 108 n.8. Here, in contrast, it is undisputed that Laidlaw's unlawful conduct — discharging pollutants in excess of permit limits — was occurring at the time the complaint was filed. Under *Lyons*, then, the only "subjective" issue here is "[t]he reasonableness of [the] fear" that led the affiants to respond to that concededly ongoing conduct by refraining from use of the North Tyger River and surrounding areas. Unlike the dissent, we see nothing "improbable" about the proposition that a company's continuous and pervasive illegal discharges of pollutants into a river would cause nearby residents to curtail their recreational use of that waterway and would subject them to other economic and aesthetic harms. . . .

Laidlaw argues next that even if FOE had standing to seek injunctive relief, it lacked standing to seek civil penalties. Here the asserted defect is not injury but redressability. Civil penalties offer no redress to private plaintiffs, Laidlaw argues, because they are paid to the Government, and therefore a citizen plaintiff can never have standing to seek them.

Laidlaw is right to insist that a plaintiff must demonstrate standing separately for each form of relief sought. But it is wrong to maintain that citizen plaintiffs facing ongoing violations never have standing to seek civil penalties.

We have recognized on numerous occasions that "all civil penalties have some deterrent effect." *Hudson v. United States*, 522 U.S. 93, 102 (1997). More specifically, Congress has found that civil penalties in Clean Water Act cases do more than promote immediate compliance by limiting the defendant's economic incentive to delay its attainment of permit limits; they also deter future violations. This congressional determination warrants judicial attention and respect. "The legislative history of the Act reveals that Congress wanted the district court to consider the need for retribution and deterrence, in addition to restitution, when it imposed civil penalties. . . . [The district court may] seek to deter future violation by basing the penalty on its economic impact." *Tull v. United States*, 481 U.S. 412, 422–23 (1987).

It can scarcely be doubted that, for a plaintiff who is injured or faces the threat of future injury due to illegal conduct ongoing at the time of the suit, a sanction that effectively abates that conduct and prevents its recurrence provides a form of redress. Civil penalties can fit that description. To the extent that they encourage defendants to discontinue current violations and deter them from committing future ones, they afford redress to citizen plaintiffs who are injured or threatened with injury as a consequence of ongoing unlawful conduct.

The dissent argues that it is the *availability* rather than the *imposition* of civil penalties that deters any particular polluter from continuing to pollute. This argument misses the mark in two ways. First, it overlooks the interdependence of the availability and the imposition; a threat has no deterrent value unless it is credible that it will be carried out. Second, it is reasonable for Congress to conclude that an actual award of civil penalties does in fact bring with it a significant quantum of deterrence over and above what is achieved by the mere prospect of such penalties. A would-be polluter may or may not be dissuaded by the existence of a remedy on the books, but a defendant once hit in its pocketbook will surely think twice before polluting again.

We recognize that there may be a point at which the deterrent effect of a claim for civil penalties becomes so insubstantial or so remote that it cannot support citizen standing. The fact that this vanishing point is not easy to ascertain does not detract from the deterrent power of such penalties in the ordinary case. . . . In this case we need not explore the outer limits of the principle that civil penalties provide sufficient deterrence to support redressability. . . .

Laidlaw contends that the reasoning of our decision in *Steel Co.* directs the conclusion that citizen plaintiffs have no standing to seek civil penalties under the Act. We disagree. *Steel Co.* established that citizen suitors lack standing to seek civil penalties for violations that have abated by the time of suit. 523 U.S. at 106–07. We specifically noted in that case that there was no allegation in the complaint of any continuing or imminent violation, and that no basis for such an allegation appeared to exist. *Id.* at 108. In short, *Steel Co.* held that private plaintiffs, unlike the Federal Government, may not sue to assess penalties for wholly past violations, but our decision in that case did not reach the issue of standing to seek penalties for violations that are ongoing at the time of the complaint and that could continue into the future if undeterred.

B

Satisfied that FOE had standing under Article III to bring this action, we turn to the question of mootness.

The only conceivable basis for a finding of mootness in this case is Laidlaw's voluntary conduct — either its achievement by August 1992 of substantial compliance with its NPDES permit or its more recent shutdown of the Roebuck facility. It is well settled that "a defendant's voluntary cessation of a challenged practice does not deprive a federal court of its power to determine the legality of the practice." *City of Mesquite v. Aladdin's Castle, Inc.*, 455 U.S. 283, 289 (1982). "[I]f it did, the courts would be compelled to leave '[t]he defendant . . . free to return to his old ways.'" *Id.* at 289 n.10. In accordance with this principle, the standard we have announced for determining whether a case has been mooted by the defendant's voluntary conduct is stringent: "A case might become moot if subsequent events made it absolutely clear that the allegedly wrongful behavior could not reasonably be expected to recur." *United States v. Concentrated Phosphate Export Assn., Inc.*, 393 U.S. 199, 203 (1968). The "heavy burden of persua[ding]" the court that the challenged conduct cannot reasonably be expected to start up again lies with the party asserting mootness. *Id.*

The Court of Appeals justified its mootness disposition by reference to *Steel Co.*, which held citizen plaintiffs lack standing to seek civil penalties for wholly past violations. In relying on *Steel Co.*, the Court of Appeals confused mootness with standing. The confusion is understandable, given this Court's repeated statements that the doctrine of mootness can be described as "the doctrine of standing set in a time frame: The requisite personal interest that must exist at the commencement of the litigation (standing) must continue throughout its existence (mootness)." *Arizonans for Official English v. Arizona*, 520 U.S. 43, 68 n.22 (1997) (quoting *United States Parole Comm'n v. Geraghty*, 445 U.S. 388, 397 (1980)).

Careful reflection on the long-recognized exceptions to mootness, however, reveals that the description of mootness as "standing set in a time frame" is not comprehensive. As just noted, a defendant claiming that its voluntary compliance moots a case bears the formidable burden of showing that it is absolutely clear the allegedly wrongful behavior could not reasonably be expected to recur. *Concentrated Phosphate Export Assn.*, 393 U.S. at 203. By contrast, in a lawsuit brought to force compliance, it is the plaintiff's burden to establish standing by demonstrating that, if unchecked by the litigation, the defendant's allegedly wrongful behavior will likely occur or continue, and that the "threatened injury [is] certainly impending." *Whitmore v. Arkansas*, 495 U.S. 149, 158 (1990). Thus, in *Lyons*, as already noted, we held that a plaintiff lacked initial standing to seek an injunction against the enforcement of a police chokehold policy because he could not credibly allege that he faced a realistic threat arising from the policy. 461 U.S. at 105–10. Elsewhere in the opinion, however, we noted that a citywide moratorium on police chokeholds — an action that surely diminished the already slim likelihood that any particular individual would be choked by the police — would not have mooted an otherwise valid claim for injunctive relief, because the moratorium by its terms was not permanent. *Id.* at 101. The plain lesson of these cases is that there are circumstances in which the prospect that a defendant will engage in (or resume) harmful conduct may be too speculative to overcome mootness.

Furthermore, if mootness were simply "standing set in a time frame," the exception to mootness that arises when the defendant's allegedly unlawful activity is "capable of repetition, yet evading review," could not exist. When, for example, a mentally disabled patient files a lawsuit challenging her confinement in a segregated institution, her postcomplaint transfer to a community-based program will not moot the action, *Olmstead v. L.C.*, 527 U.S. 581, 594 n.6 (1999), despite the fact that she would have lacked initial standing had she filed the complaint after the transfer. Standing admits of no similar exception; if a plaintiff lacks standing at the time the action commences, the fact that the dispute is capable of repetition yet evading review will not entitle the complaint to a federal judicial forum. *See Steel Co.*, 523 U.S. at 109.

. . . .

Standing doctrine functions to ensure, among other things, that the scarce resources of the federal courts are devoted to those disputes in which the parties have a concrete stake. In contrast, by the time mootness is an issue, the case has been brought and litigated, often (as here) for years. To abandon the case at an advanced stage may prove more wasteful than frugal. This argument from sunk cost does not licence courts to retain jurisdiction over cases in which one or both of the parties plainly lack a continuing interest, as when the parties have settled or a plaintiff pursuing a nonsurviving claim has died.

In its brief, Laidlaw appears to argue that, regardless of the effect of Laidlaw's compliance, FOE doomed its own civil penalty claim to mootness by failing to appeal the District Court's denial of injunctive relief. This argument misconceives the statutory scheme. Under § 1365(a), the district court has discretion to determine which form of relief is best suited, in the particular case, to abate current violations and deter future ones. "[A] federal judge sitting as chancellor is not mechanically obligated to grant an injunction for every violation of law." *Weinberger v. Romero-Barcelo*, 456 U.S. 305, 313 (1982). Denial of injunctive relief does not necessarily mean that the district court has concluded there is no prospect of future violations for civil penalties to deter. Indeed, it meant no such thing in this case. The District Court denied injunctive relief, but expressly based its award of civil penalties on the need for deterrence. As the dissent notes, federal courts should aim to ensure " 'the framing of relief no broader than required by the precise facts.' " *Schlesinger v. Reservists Comm. to Stop the War*, 418 U.S. 208, 222 (1974). In accordance with this aim, a district court in a Clean Water Act citizen suit properly may conclude that an injunction would be an excessively intrusive remedy, because it could entail continuing superintendence of the permit holder's activities by a federal court — a process burdensome to court and permit holder alike.

Laidlaw also asserts . . . that the closure of its Roebuck facility, which took place after the Court of Appeals issued its decision, mooted the case. The facility closure, like Laidlaw's earlier achievement of substantial compliance with its permit requirements, might moot the case, but — we once more reiterate — only if one or the other of these events made it absolutely clear that Laidlaw's permit violations could not reasonably be expected to recur. *Concentrated Phosphate Export Assn.*, 393 U.S. at 203. The effect of both Laidlaw's compliance and the facility closure on the prospect of future violations is a disputed factual matter. . . . These issues have not been aired in the lower courts; they remain open for consideration on remand.

. . . .

For the reasons stated, the judgment of the United States Court of Appeals for the Fourth Circuit is reversed, and the case is remanded for further proceedings consistent with this opinion.

Justice Stevens, concurring.

Although the Court has identified a sufficient reason for rejecting the Court of Appeals' mootness determination, it is important also to note that the case would not be moot even if it were absolutely clear that respondent had gone out of business and posed no threat of future permit violations. The District Court entered a valid judgment requiring respondents to pay a civil penalty of $405,800 to the United States. No postjudgment conduct of respondent could retroactively invalidate that judgment. A record of voluntary postjudgment compliance that would justify a decision that injunctive relief is unnecessary, or even a decision that any claim for injunctive relief is now moot, would not warrant vacation of the valid money judgment.

. . . .

Justice Kennedy, concurring.

[Omitted.]

Justice Scalia, with whom Justice Thomas joins, dissenting.

The Court begins its analysis by finding injury in fact on the basis of vague affidavits that are undermined by the District Court's express finding that Laidlaw's discharges caused no demonstrable harm to the environment. It then proceeds to marry private wrong with public remedy in a union that violates traditional principles of federal standing — thereby permitting law enforcement to be placed in the hands of private individuals. Finally, the Court suggests that to avoid mootness one needs even less of a stake in the outcome than the Court's watered-down requirements for initial standing. I dissent from all of this.

I

Plaintiffs, as the parties invoking federal jurisdiction, have the burden of proof and persuasion as to the existence of standing. *Lujan v. Defenders of Wildlife*, 504 U.S. 555, 561 (1992) (hereinafter *Lujan*). The plaintiffs in this case fell far short of carrying their burden of demonstrating injury in fact. The Court cites affiants' testimony asserting that their enjoyment of the North Tyger River has been diminished due to "concern" that the water was polluted, and that they "believed" that Laidlaw's mercury exceedances had reduced the value of their homes. These averments alone cannot carry the plaintiffs' burden of demonstrating that they have suffered a "concrete and particularized" injury. *Lujan*, 504 U.S. at 560. General allegations of injury may suffice at the pleading stage, but at summary judgment plaintiffs must set forth "specific facts" to support their claims. *Id.* at 561. And where, as here, the case has proceeded to judgment, those specified facts must be "supported adequately by the evidence adduced at trial." *Id.* (quoting *Gladstone, Realtors v. Village of Bellwood*, 441 U.S. 91, 115 n.31 (1979)). In this case, the affidavits themselves are woefully short on "specific facts," and the vague allegations of injury they do make are undermined by the evidence adduced at trial.

Typically, an environmental plaintiff claiming injury due to discharges in violation of the Clean Water Act argues that the discharges harm the environment, and that the harm to the environment injures him. This route to injury is barred in the present case, however, since the District Court concluded after considering all the evidence that there had been "no demonstrated proof of harm to the environment," that the "permit violations at issue in this citizen suit did not result in any health risk or environmental harm," that "[a]ll available data . . . fail to show that Laidlaw's *actual* discharges have resulted in harm to the North Tyger River," and that "the overall quality of the river exceeds levels necessary to support . . . recreation in and on the water."

The Court finds these conclusions unproblematic for standing, because "[t]he relevant showing for purposes of Article III standing . . . is not injury to the environment but injury to the plaintiff." This statement is correct, as far as it goes. We have certainly held that a demonstration of harm to the environment is not *enough* to satisfy the injury-in-fact requirement unless the plaintiff can demonstrate how he personally was harmed. *E.g., Lujan*, 504 U.S. at 563. In the normal course, however, a lack of demonstrable harm to the environment will translate, as it plainly does here, into a lack of demonstrable harm to citizen plaintiffs. While it is perhaps possible that a plaintiff could be harmed even though the environment was not, such a plaintiff would have the burden of articulating and demonstrating the nature of that injury. Ongoing "concerns" about the environment are not enough, for "[i]t is the *reality* of the threat of repeated injury that is relevant to the standing inquiry, not the plaintiff's subjective apprehensions." *Los Angeles v. Lyons*, 461 U.S. 95, 107 n.8 (1983). At the very least, in the present case, one would expect to see evidence supporting the affidavits' bald assertions regarding decreasing recreational usage and declining home values, as well as evidence for the improbable proposition that Laidlaw's violations, even though harmless to the environment, are somehow responsible for these effects. Plaintiffs here have made no attempt at such a showing, but rely entirely upon unsupported and unexplained affidavit allegations of "concern."

Indeed, every one of the affiants deposed by Laidlaw cast into doubt the (in any event inadequate) proposition that subjective "concerns" actually affected their conduct. . . .

The Court is correct that the District Court explicitly found standing — albeit "by the slimmest of margins," and as "an awfully close call." That cautious finding, however, was made in 1993, long before the court's 1997 conclusion that Laidlaw's discharges did not harm the environment. As we have previously recognized, an initial conclusion that plaintiffs have standing is subject to reexamination, particularly if later evidence proves inconsistent with that conclusion. *Gladstone*, 441 U.S. at 115 & n.31. Laidlaw challenged the existence of injury in fact on appeal to the Fourth Circuit, but that court did not reach the question. Thus no lower court has reviewed the injury-in-fact issue in light of the extensive studies that led the District Court to conclude that the environment was not harmed by Laidlaw's discharges.

Inexplicably, the Court is untroubled by this, but proceeds to find injury in fact in the most casual fashion, as though it is merely confirming a careful analysis made below. . . . By accepting plaintiffs' vague, contradictory, and unsubstantiated allegations of "concern" about the environment as adequate to prove injury in fact, and accepting them even in the face of a finding that the environment was not demonstrably harmed, the Court makes the injury-in-fact requirement a sham. If there are permit violations, and a member of a plaintiff environmental organization lives near the offending plant, it would be difficult not to satisfy today's lenient standard.

II

The Court's treatment of the redressability requirement . . . is equally cavalier. . . . [T]he remedy petitioners seek is neither recompense for their injuries nor an injunction against future violations. Instead, the remedy is a statutorily specified "penalty" for past violations, payable entirely to the United States Treasury. Only last Term, we held that such penalties do not redress any injury a citizen plaintiff has suffered from past violations. *Steel Co. v. Citizens for Better Environment*, 523 U.S. 83, 106–07 (1998). The Court nonetheless finds the redressability requirement satisfied here, distinguishing *Steel Co.* on the ground that in this case petitioners allege ongoing violations; payment of the penalties, it says, will remedy petitioners' injury by deterring future violations by Laidlaw. It holds that a penalty payable to the public "remedies" a threatened private harm, and suffices to sustain a private suit.

That holding has no precedent in our jurisprudence, and takes this Court beyond the "cases and controversies" that Article III of the Constitution has entrusted to its resolution. Even if it were appropriate, moreover, to allow Article III's remediation requirement to be satisfied by the indirect private consequences of a public penalty, those consequences are entirely too speculative in the present case. The new standing law that the Court makes — like all expansions of standing beyond the traditional constitutional limits — has grave implications for democratic governance. I shall discuss these three points in turn.

A

. . . [In *Linda R.S. v. Richard D.*, 410 U.S. 614 (1973), there] was no "logical nexus" between nonenforcement of the statute and Linda R.S.'s failure to receive support payments because "[t]he prospect that prosecution will . . . result in payment of support" was "speculative," *id.* at 618, — that is to say, it was uncertain whether the relief would prevent the injury. Of course precisely the same situation exists here. The principle that "in American jurisprudence . . . a private citizen lacks a judicially cognizable interest in the prosecution or nonprosecution of another," *id.* at 619, applies no less to prosecution for civil penalties payable to the State than to prosecution for criminal penalties owing to the State.

The Court's opinion reads as though the only purpose and effect of the redressability requirement is to assure that the plaintiffs receive *some* of the benefit of the relief that a court orders. That is not so. If it were, a federal tort plaintiff fearing repetition of the injury could ask for tort damages to be paid not only to himself but to other victims as well, on the theory that those damages would have at least some deterrent effect beneficial to him. Such a suit is preposterous because the "remediation" that is the traditional business of Anglo-American courts is relief specifically tailored to the plaintiff's injury, and not *any* sort of relief that has some incidental benefit to the plaintiff. Just as a "generalized grievance" that affects the entire citizenry cannot satisfy the injury-in-fact requirement even though it aggrieves the plaintiff along with everyone else, so also a generalized remedy that deters all future unlawful activity against all persons cannot satisfy the remediation requirement, even though it deters (among other things) repetition of this particular unlawful activity against these particular plaintiffs.

. . . The sort of scattershot redress approved today makes nonsense of our statements in *Schlesinger v. Reservists Comm. to Stop the War*, 418 U.S. 208, 222 (1974), that the requirement of injury in fact "insures the framing of relief no broader than required by the precise facts." A claim of particularized future injury has today been made the vehicle for pursuing generalized penalties for past violations, and a threshold showing of injury in fact has become a lever that will move the world.

B

. . . .

The Court recognizes, of course, that to satisfy Article III, it must be "likely," as opposed to "merely speculative," that a favorable decision will redress plaintiffs' injury. *Lujan*, 504 U.S. at 561. Further, the Court recognizes that not *all* deterrent effects of *all* civil penalties will meet this standard — though it declines to "explore the outer limits" of adequate deterrence. It concludes, however, that in the present case "the civil penalties sought by FOE carried with them a deterrent effect" that satisfied the "likely [rather than] speculative" standard. *Id.* There is little in the Court's opinion to explain why it believes this is so.

The Court cites the District Court's conclusion that the penalties imposed, along with anticipated fee awards, provided "adequate deterrence." There is absolutely no reason to believe, however, that this meant "deterrence adequate to prevent an injury to these plaintiffs that would otherwise occur." The statute does not even *mention* deterrence in general (much less deterrence of future harm to the particular plaintiff) as one of the elements that the court should consider in fixing the amount of the penalty. (That element can come in, if at all, under the last, residual category of "such other matters as justice may require." 33 U.S.C. § 1319(d).) . . . Indeed, neither the District Court's final opinion (which contains the "adequate deterrence" statement) nor its earlier opinion dealing with the preliminary question whether South Carolina's previous lawsuit against Laidlaw constituted "diligent prosecution" that would bar citizen suit, displayed *any* *awareness* that deterrence of *future injury to the plaintiffs* was necessary to support standing.

. . . .

The Court points out that we have previously said " 'all civil penalties have some deterrent effect.' " That is unquestionably true: As a general matter, polluters as a class are deterred from violating discharge limits by the *availability* of civil penalties. However, none of the cases the Court cites focused on the deterrent effect of a single *imposition* of penalties on a particular lawbreaker. Even less did they focus on the question whether that particularized deterrent effect (if any) was enough to redress the injury of a citizen plaintiff in the sense required by Article III. They all involved penalties pursued by the government, not by citizens.

If the Court had undertaken the necessary inquiry into whether significant deterrence of the plaintiffs' feared injury was "likely," it would have had to reason something like this: Strictly speaking, no polluter is deterred by a penalty for past pollution; he is deterred by the *fear* of a penalty for *future* pollution. That fear will be virtually nonexistent if the prospective polluter knows that all the emissions violators are given a free pass; it will be substantial under an emissions program such as the federal scheme here, which is regularly and notoriously enforced; it will be even higher when a prospective polluter subject to such a regularly enforced program has, as here, been the object of public charges of pollution and a suit for injunction; and it will surely be near the top of the graph when, as here, the prospective polluter has already been subjected to *state* penalties for the past pollution. The deterrence on which the plaintiffs must rely for standing in the present case is the marginal increase in Laidlaw's fear of future penalties that will be achieved by adding federal penalties for Laidlaw's past conduct.

. . . .

In sum, if this case is, as the Court suggests, within the central core of "deterrence" standing, it is impossible to imagine what the "outer limits" could possibly be. The Court's expressed reluctance to define those "outer limits" serves only to disguise the fact that it has promulgated a revolutionary new doctrine of standing that will permit the entire body of public civil penalties to be handed over to enforcement by private interests.

C

Article II of the Constitution commits it to the President to "take Care that the Laws be faithfully executed," Art. II, § 3, and provides specific methods by which all persons exercising significant executive power are to be appointed, Art. II, § 2. . . . Article III, no less than Article II, has consequences for the structure of our government, *see Schlesinger*, 418 U.S. at 222, and it is worth noting the changes in that structure which today's decision allows.

By permitting citizens to pursue civil penalties payable to the Federal Treasury, the Act does not provide a mechanism for individual relief in any traditional sense, but turns over to private citizens the function of enforcing the law. . . . And once the target is chosen, the suit goes forward without meaningful public control. . . .

. . . Elected officials are entirely deprived of their discretion to decide that a given violation should not be the object of suit at all, or that the enforcement decision should be postponed. . . .

III

Finally, I offer a few comments regarding the Court's discussion of whether FOE's claims became moot by reason of Laidlaw's substantial compliance with the permit limits. I do not disagree with the conclusion that the Court reaches. Assuming that the plaintiffs had standing to pursue civil penalties in the first instance (which they did not), their claim might well not have been mooted by Laidlaw's voluntary compliance with the permit, and leaving this fact-intensive question open for consideration on remand, as the Court does seems sensible. In reaching this disposition, however, the Court engages in a troubling discussion of the purported distinctions between the doctrines of standing and mootness. I am frankly puzzled as to why this discussion appears at all. Laidlaw's claimed compliance is squarely within the bounds of our "voluntary cessation" doctrine, which is the basis for the remand. There is no reason to engage in an interesting academic excursus upon the differences between mootness and standing in order to invoke this obviously applicable rule.

. . . We have repeatedly recognized that what is required for litigation to continue is essentially identical to what is required for litigation to begin: There must be a justiciable case or controversy as required by Article III. "Simply stated, a case is moot when the issues presented are no longer 'live' or the parties lack a legally cognizable interest in the outcome." *Powell v. McCormack*, 395 U.S. 486, 496 (1969). A court may not proceed to hear an action if, subsequent to its initiation, the dispute loses "its character as a present live controversy of the kind that must exist if [the court is] to avoid advisory opinions on abstract propositions of law." *Hall v. Beals*, 396 U.S. 45, 48 (1969) (*per curiam*). Because the requirement of a continuing case or controversy derives from the Constitution, *Liner v. Jafco, Inc.*, 375 U.S. 301, 306 n.3 (1964), it may not be ignored when inconvenient, *United States v. Alaska S.S. Co.*, 253 U.S. 113, 116 (1920), or, as the Court suggests, to save "sunk costs."

. . . .

By uncritically accepting vague claims of injury, the Court has turned the Article III requirement of injury in fact into a "mere pleading requirement," *Lujan*, 504 U.S. at 561; and by approving the novel theory that public penalties can redress anticipated private wrongs, it has come close to "mak[ing] the redressability requirement vanish." *Steel Co.*, 523 U.S. at 107. The undesirable and unconstitutional consequence of today's decision is to place the immense power of suing to enforce the public laws in private hands. I respectfully dissent.

Exercise 14(A):

Consider the following questions in connection with *Laidlaw*:

(1)   Is "standing" a requirement of Article III or does it have some other basis?

(2)   What are the required elements to establish standing? Which of those elements are at issue in *Laidlaw*? What are the arguments for and against finding each of those elements satisfied in this case?

(3)   How does "mootness" differ from standing? What are the two exceptions to the usual mootness requirement that are identified in the opinions?

(4)   Are there additional jurisdictional problems with the litigation at issue in *Laidlaw*?

(5)   How do these doctrines compare with the scope of the judicial power described by Brutus and Hamilton (in Chapter 2)?

(6)   Are these doctrines consistent with the views Chief Justice Jay expressed in his letter to President Washington (in Chapter 3)? Are they consistent with views

expressed in the early cases, including the cases relating to the Revolutionary War pensions (in Chapter 3)?

A Note on Taxpayer Standing

In *Hein v. Freedom From Religion Foundation, Inc.*, ___ U.S. ___, 127 S. Ct. 2553 (2007), the Court addressed a challenge to conferences and speeches held as part of the President's Faith-Based and Community Initiatives program. The Court determined that the plaintiffs lacked standing. A plurality of the Court explained:

> It has long been established . . . that the payment of taxes is generally not enough to establish standing to challenge an action taken by the Federal Government. In light of the size of the federal budget, it is a complete fiction to argue that an unconstitutional federal expenditure causes an individual federal taxpayer any measurable economic harm. And if every federal taxpayer could sue to challenge any Government expenditure, the federal courts would cease to function as courts of law and would be cast in the role of general complaint bureaus.

> In *Flast v. Cohen*, 392 U.S. 83 (1968), we recognized a narrow exception to the general rule against federal taxpayer standing. Under *Flast*, a plaintiff asserting an Establishment Clause claim has standing to challenge a law authorizing the use of federal funds in a way that allegedly violates the Establishment Clause. In the present case, Congress did not specifically authorize the use of federal funds to pay for the conferences or speeches that the plaintiffs challenged. Instead, the conferences and speeches were paid for out of general Executive Branch appropriations. The Court of Appeals, however, held that the plaintiffs have standing as taxpayers because the conferences were paid for with money appropriated by Congress.

> The question that is presented here is whether this broad reading of *Flast* is correct. We hold that it is not. We therefor reverse the decision of the Court of Appeals.

Only Chief Justice Roberts and Justice Kennedy joined in that opinion by Justice Alito. They further explained that "in the four decades since its creation, the *Flast* exception has been largely confined to its facts" with the Court declining to extend it either to alleged violations of any constitutional provision other than the Establishment Clause or to alleged Establishment Clause violations "that do not implicate Congress' taxing and spending powers." On the basis of *stare decisis*, the plurality declined to extend *Flast* to the limits of its logic.

Justice Scalia, in an opinion joined by Justice Thomas, concurred in the judgment and called for the outright overruling of *Flast* on the basis that "*Flast* is wholly irreconcilable with the Article III restrictions on federal-court jurisdiction that th[e] Court has repeatedly confirmed are embodied in the doctrine of standing." Justice Scalia asserted that *Flast* failed to distinguish contrary prior precedent, that the exception it created disrupted the broader standing doctrine, that the Court had "offer[ed] no intellectual justification" for the boundaries of the exception, and that in subsequent cases the Court had criticized *Flast* for "fail[ing] to recognize the vital separation-of-powers aspect of Article III standing."

Justice Souter dissented in an opinion joined by Justices Stevens, Ginsburg, and Breyer. Justice Souter criticized the plurality for distinguishing *Flast* without a "basis for this distinction in either logic or precedent." As he viewed the case, the plainitiffs sought "not to 'extend' *Flast*, but merely to apply it." The dissent further asserted that the distinction relied upon by the plurality had been rejected by the Court in an earlier case.

NATIONAL PARK HOSPITALITY ASSOCIATION v.
DEPARTMENT OF THE INTERIOR
538 U.S. 803 (2003)

JUSTICE THOMAS delivered the opinion of the Court.

[The Contract Disputes Act ("CDA"), 41 U.S.C. § 601 *et seq.*, establishes a mechanism for the resolution of disputes arising out of certain contracts with the federal government. The CDA mechanism requires disputes to be submitted to an agency's contracting officer and permits that officer's decision to be reviewed by various administrative and judicial tribunals.

[Under congressional authorization, the National Park Service ("NPS") promotes and regulates the use of national parks. Congress further authorized NPS to "grant privileges, leases, and permits for the use of land for the accommodation of visitors." NPS entered into national parks concession contracts.

[Congress also authorized NPS to promulgate regulations, including a new program for comprehensive concession management program for national parks. NPS issued a regulation that expressly declared its concession contracts "are not contracts" within the meaning of the CDA. *See* 36 C.F.R. § 51.3 (2002). A trade association of parties to NPS concession contracts brought suit in federal court asserting a facial challenge to the NPS regulation.]

. . . .

. . . We granted certiorari to consider whether the CDA applies to contracts between NPS and concessioners in the national parks. 537 U.S. 1018 (2002). Because petitioner has brought a facial challenge to the regulation and is not litigating any concrete dispute with NPS, we asked the parties to provide supplemental briefing on whether the case is ripe for judicial action.

III

Ripeness is a justiciability doctrine designed "to prevent the courts, through avoidance of premature adjudication, from entangling themselves in abstract disagreements over administrative policies, and also to protect the agencies from judicial interference until an administrative decision has been formalized and its effects felt in a concrete way by the challenging parties." *Abbott Laboratories v. Gardner*, 387 U.S. 136, 148–49 (1967); *accord Ohio Forestry Assn., Inc. v. Sierra Club*, 523 U.S. 726, 732–33 (1998). The ripeness doctrine is "drawn both from Article III limitations on judicial power and from prudential reasons for refusing to exercise jurisdiction," *Reno v. Catholic Social Services, Inc.*, 509 U.S. 43, 57 n.18 (1993) (citations omitted), but, even in a case raising only prudential concerns, the question of ripeness may be considered on a court's own motion. *Id.*

Determining whether administrative action is ripe for judicial review requires us to evaluate (1) the fitness of the issues for judicial decision and (2) the hardship to the parties of withholding court consideration. *Abbott Laboratories*, 387 U.S. at 149. "Absent [a statutory provision providing for immediate judicial review], a regulation is not ordinarily considered the type of agency action 'ripe' for judicial review under the [Administrative Procedure Act (APA)] until the scope of the controversy has been reduced to more manageable proportions, and its factual components fleshed out, by some concrete action applying the regulation to the claimant's situation in a fashion that harms or threatens to harm him. (The major exception, of course, is a substantive rule which as a practical matter requires the plaintiff to adjust his conduct immediately . . . .)" *Lujan v. National Wildlife Federation*, 497 U.S. 871, 891 (1990). Under the facts now before us, we conclude this case is not ripe.

[A]

We turn first to the hardship inquiry. The federal respondents concede . . . NPS has no delegated rulemaking authority under the CDA . . . .

. . . [W]e consider § 51.3 to be nothing more than a "general statemen[t] of policy" designed to inform the public of NPS' views on the proper application of the CDA.

Viewed in this light, § 51.3 does not create "adverse effects of a strictly legal kind," which we have previously required for a showing of hardship. *Ohio Forestry Assn., Inc.*, 523 U.S. at 733. Just like the Forest Service plan at issue in *Ohio Forestry*, § 51.3 "do[es] not command anyone to do anything or to refrain from doing anything; [it] do[es] not grant, withhold, or modify any formal legal license, power, or authority; [it] do[es] not subject anyone to any civil or criminal liability; [and it] create[s] no legal rights or obligations." *Id.*

Moreover, § 51.3 does not affect a concessioner's primary conduct. *Toilet Goods Ass'n, Inc. v. Gardner*, 387 U.S. 158, 164 (1967); *Ohio Forestry Ass'n*, 523 U.S. at 733–34. Unlike the regulation at issue in *Abbott Laboratories*, which required drug manufacturers to change the labels, advertisements, and promotional materials they used in marketing prescription drugs on pain of criminal and civil penalties, *see* 387 U.S. at 152–53, the regulation here leaves a concessioner free to conduct its business as it sees fit. *See also Gardner v. Toilet Goods Ass'n, Inc.*, 387 U.S. 167, 171 (1967) (regulations governing conditions for use of color additives in foods, drugs, and cosmetics were "self-executing" and had "an immediate and substantial impact upon the respondents").

We have previously found that challenges to regulations similar to § 51.3 were not ripe for lack of a showing of hardship. In *Toilet Goods Assn.*, for example, the Food and Drug Administration (FDA) issued a regulation requiring producers of color additives to provide FDA employees with access to all manufacturing facilities, processes, and formulae. 387 U.S. at 161–62. We concluded the case was not ripe for judicial review because the impact of the regulation could not "be said to be felt immediately by those subject to it in conducting their day-to-day affairs" and "no irremediabl[y] adverse consequences flow[ed] from requiring a later challenge." *Id.* at 164. Indeed, the FDA regulation was more onerous than § 51.3 because failure to comply with it resulted in the suspension of the producer's certification and, consequently, could affect production. *See id.* at 165 & n.2. Here, by contrast, concessioners suffer no practical harm as a result of § 51.3. All the regulation does is announce the position NPS will take with respect to disputes arising out of concession contracts. While it informs the public of NPS' view that concessioners are not entitled to take advantage of the provisions of the CDA, nothing in the regulation prevents concessioners from following the procedures set forth in the CDA once a dispute over a concession contract actually arises. And it appears that, notwithstanding § 51.3, the [Department of Interior's Board of Contract Appeals] has been quite willing to apply the CDA to certain concession contracts. . . .

Petitioner contends that delaying judicial resolution of this issue will result in real harm because the applicability *vel non* of the CDA is one of the factors a concessioner takes into account when preparing its bid for NPS concession contracts. Petitioner's argument appears to be that mere uncertainty as to the validity of a legal rule constitutes a hardship for purposes of the ripeness analysis. We are not persuaded. If we were to follow petitioner's logic, courts would soon be overwhelmed with requests for what essentially would be advisory opinions because most business transactions could be priced more accurately if even a small portion of existing legal uncertainties were resolved. In short, petitioner has failed to demonstrate that deferring judicial review will result in real hardship.

[B]

We consider next whether the issue in this case is fit for review. Although the question presented here is "a purely legal one" and § 51.3 constitutes "final agency action" within the meaning of [the APA], *Abbott Laboratories,* 387 U.S. at 149, we nevertheless believe that further factual development would "significantly advance our ability to deal with the legal issues presented," *Duke Power Co. v. Carolina Environmental Study Group, Inc.,* 438 U.S. 59, 82 (1978); *accord Ohio Forestry Assn., Inc.,* 523 U.S. at 736–37. While the federal respondents generally argue that NPS was correct to conclude that the CDA does not cover concession contracts, they acknowledge that certain types of concession contracts might come under the broad language of the CDA. Similarly, while petitioner and respondent Xanterra Parks & Resorts, LLC, present a facial challenge to § 51.3, both rely on specific characteristics of certain types of concession contracts to support their positions. In light of the foregoing, we conclude that judicial resolution of the question presented here should await a concrete dispute about a particular concession contract.

. . . .

For the reasons stated above, we vacate the judgment of the Court of Appeals insofar as it addressed the validity of § 51.3 and remand the case with instructions to dismiss the case with respect to this issue.

It is so ordered.

JUSTICE STEVENS, concurring in the judgment.

Petitioner seeks this Court's resolution of the straightforward legal question whether the Contract Disputes Act of 1978 (CDA) applies to concession contracts with the National Park Service. Though this question is one that would otherwise be appropriate for this Court to decide, in my view petitioner has not satisfied the threshold requirement of alleging sufficient injury to invoke federal-court jurisdiction. If such allegations of injury were present, however, this case would not raise any of the concerns that the ripeness doctrine was designed to avoid.

I

The CDA provides certain significant protections for private parties contracting with federal agencies. It authorizes *de novo* review of a contractor's disputed decision, payment of prejudgment interest if a dispute with the agency is resolved in the contractor's favor, and expedited procedures for resolving minor disputes. The value to contractors of these protections have not been quantified in this case, but the protections are unquestionably significant.

Ever since the enactment of the CDA in 1978, the National Park Service has insisted that the statute does not apply to contracts with concessionaires who operate restaurants, lodges, and gift shops in the national parks. In its view, the statute applies to Government contracts involving the procurement of goods or services that the Government agrees to pay for, not to licenses issued by the Government to concessionaires who sell goods and services to the public. After the enactment of the National Parks Omnibus Management Act of 1998, 16 U.S.C. §§ 5951–5966, the Park Service issued a regulation restating that position. 36 C.F.R. § 51.3 (2002). There is nothing tentative or inconclusive about the agency's position. The promulgation of the regulation indicated that the agency had determined that a clear statement of its interpretation of the CDA would be useful to potential concessionaires bidding for future contracts. Under the Park Service's view, nearly 600 concession contracts in 131 national parks fall outside of the CDA.

Petitioner is a trade association whose members are parties to such contracts and periodically enter into negotiations for future contracts. They are undisputedly interested in knowing whether disputes that are sure to arise under some of those contracts will be resolved pursuant to the CDA procedures or the less favorable procedures that will apply if the Park Service regulation is valid.

II

In our leading case discussing the "ripeness doctrine" we explained that the question whether a controversy is "ripe" for judicial resolution has a "twofold aspect, requiring us to evaluate both the fitness of the issues for judicial decision and the hardship to the parties of withholding court consideration." *Abbott Laboratories v. Gardner*, 387 U.S. 136, 148–49 (1967). Both aspects of the inquiry involve the exercise of judgment, rather than the application of a black-letter rule.

The first aspect is the more important and it is satisfied in this case. The CDA applies to any express or implied contract for the procurement of property, services, or construction. 41 U.S.C. § 602(a). In the view of the Park Service, a procurement contract is one that obligates the Government to pay for goods and services that it receives, whereas concession contracts authorize third parties to provide services to park area visitors. Petitioner, on the other hand, argues that the contracts provide for the performance of services that discharge a public duty even though the Government does not pay the concessionaires. Whichever view may better reflect the intent of the Congress that enacted the CDA, it is perfectly clear that this question of statutory interpretation is as "fit" for judicial decision today as it will ever be. Even if there may be a few marginal cases in which the applicability of the CDA may depend on unique facts, the regulation's blanket exclusion of concession contracts is either a correct or an incorrect interpretation of the statute. The issue has been fully briefed and argued and, in my judgment, is ripe for decision.

The second aspect of the ripeness inquiry is less clear and less important. If there were reason to believe that further development of the facts would clarify the legal question, or that the agency's view was tentative or apt to be modified, only a strong showing of hardship to the parties would justify a prompt decision. In this case, it is probably correct that the hardship associated with a delayed decision is minimal. On the other hand, as the Park Service's decision to promulgate the regulation demonstrates, eliminating the present uncertainty about the applicable dispute resolution procedures will provide a benefit for all interested parties. If petitioner had alleged sufficient injury arising from the Park Service's position, I would favor the exercise of our discretion to consider the case ripe for decision. Because such an allegation of injury is absent, however, petitioner does not have standing to have this claim adjudicated.

. . . .

Neither in its complaint in the District Court, nor in its briefing or argument before this Court, has petitioner identified a specific incident in which the Park Service's regulation caused a concessionaire to refuse to bid on a contract, to modify its bid, or to suffer any other specific injury. Rather, petitioner has focused entirely on the importance of knowing whether the Park Service's position is valid. While it is no doubt important for petitioner and its members to know as much as possible about the future of their business transactions, importance does not necessarily establish injury. Though some of petitioner's members may well have suffered some sort of injury from the Park Service's regulation, neither the allegations of the complaint nor the evidence in the record identifies any specific injury that would be redressed by a favorable decision on the merits of the case. Accordingly, petitioner has no standing to pursue its claim.

For this reason, I concur in the Court's judgment.

JUSTICE BREYER, with whom JUSTICE O'CONNOR joins, dissenting.

Like the majority, I believe that petitioner National Park Hospitality Association has standing here to pursue its legal claim . . . . But, unlike the majority, I believe that the question is ripe for our consideration.

. . . .

. . . [T]he challenged Park Service interpretation causes a present injury. If the CDA does not apply to concession contract disagreements, as the Park Service regulation declares, then some of petitioner's members must plan now for higher contract implementation costs. Given the agency's regulation, bidders will likely be forced to pay more to obtain, or to retain, a concession contract than they believe the contract is worth. That is what petitioner argues. Certain general allegations in the underlying complaints support this claim. And several uncontested circumstances indicate that such allegations are likely to prove true.

. . . .

Given this threat of immediate concrete harm (primarily in the form of increased bidding costs), this case is also ripe for judicial review. As Justice Stevens explains . . . the case now presents a legal issue — the applicability of the CDA to concession contracts — that is fit for judicial determination. That issue is a purely legal one, demanding for its resolution only use of ordinary judicial interpretive techniques. The relevant administrative action, i.e., the agency's definition of "concession contract" under the National Parks Omnibus Management Act of 1998, 16 U.S.C. §§ 5951–5966, has been "formalized," Abbott Laboratories v. Gardner, 387 U.S. 136, 148 (1967). It is embodied in an interpretive regulation. . . . The Park Service's interpretation is definite and conclusive, not tentative or likely to change . . . .

The only open question concerns the nature of the harm that refusing judicial review at this time will cause petitioner's members. See Abbott Laboratories, 387 U.S. at 149. The fact that concessioners can raise the legal question at a later time, after a specific contractual dispute arises, militates against finding this case ripe. So too does a precedential concern: Will present review set a precedent that leads to premature challenges in other cases where agency interpretations may be less formal, less final, or less well suited to immediate judicial determination?

But the fact of immediate and particularized (and not totally reparable) injury during the bidding process offsets the first of these considerations. [Congressional policy reflected in a different statute that is not directly applicable to these disputes offsets the second of these considerations.].

In sum, given this congressional policy, the concrete nature of the injury asserted by petitioner, and the final nature of the agency action at issue, I see no good reason to postpone review. I would find the issue ripe for this Court's consideration. And I would affirm the decision of the Court of Appeals on the merits, primarily for the reasons set forth in its opinion as supplemented here by the Government.

Exercise 14(B):

Consider these additional questions in regard to justiciability doctrines:

(1)   Are there cases other than challenges to congressional spending that allegedly violates the Establishment Clause where a taxpayer has standing in federal court?

(2)   What purposes are served by the "ripeness" doctrine? Are those the same purposes served by the standing and mootness doctrines?

(3)   Outside of the context of actions of federal administrative agencies, when are ripeness problems likely to arise?

C. Standards of Review

In *Marbury v. Madison,* the Supreme Court reaffirmed its previous assertions of the power to review the constitutionality of federal legislation. The Court did not again wield that power to declare an Act of Congress unconstitutional until the infamous case of *Dred Scott v. Sandford,* 60 U.S. 393 (1856).

Determining that the judiciary may review the constitutionality of legislation raises more questions than it answers. *See* Lee J. Strang, *The Clash of Rival and Incompatible Philosophical Traditions in Constitutional Interpretation: Originalism and the Aristotelian Tradition,* 2 GEO. J.L. & PUB. POL'Y 523, 562–97 (2004) (reviewing the numerous attempts by scholars to justify constitutional judicial review).

Exercise 15(A):

Consider the problems posed by judicial review in a democracy. How can one reconcile the practice with democratic rule?

Specifically, consider:

(1)   How severe a conflict is required before a court is justified in declaring legislation unconstitutional? How was that matter described in the ratification debates (in Chapter 2)? How was that matter described in *Marbury* and the earlier cases discussing judicial review (in Chapters 3 and 5)?

(2)   Does the federal judiciary claim a *superior* right to interpret the Constitution or does it merely maintain that, as a coordinate branch of government, it has an *equal* right to consider matters?

(3)   To the extent *Marbury* involved a matter of particular concern to the judiciary (that is, the scope of its jurisdiction) are there other matters of greater concern to other branches where the judiciary should decline to engage in judicial review?

(4)   What degree of deference, if any, should the judiciary afford to the interpretations of other branches of the central government or the States? Is there any basis to vary the level of deference with respect to different constitutional provisions?

(5) To the extent the judiciary is viewed as having a superior right to interpret the Constitution, what, if anything, limits potential abuse of that power? What checks were identified in the ratification debates (in Chapter 2)?

FIELD v. CLARK
143 U.S. 649 (1892)

JUSTICE HARLAN delivered the Opinion of the Court.

. . . .

The contention of the appellants is that this enrolled act, in the custody of the secretary of state, and appearing, upon its face, to have become a law in the mode prescribed by the constitution, is to be deemed an absolute nullity, in all its parts, because — such is the allegation — it is shown by the congressional records of proceedings, reports of committees of each house, reports of the committees of conference, and other papers printed by authority of congress, . . . that a section of the bill, as it finally passed, was not in the bill authenticated by the signatures of the presiding officers of the respective houses of congress, and approved by the president. . . .

The argument, in behalf of the appellants, is that a bill, signed by the speaker of the house of representatives and by the president of the senate, presented to and approved by the president of the United States, and delivered by the latter to the secretary of state, as an act passed by congress, does not become a law of the United States if it had not in fact been passed by congress. In view of the express requirements of the constitution, the correctness of this general principle cannot be doubted. . . .

But this concession of the correctness of the general principle for which the appellants contend does not determine the precise question before the court; for it remains to inquire as to the nature of the evidence upon which a court may act when the issue is made as to whether a bill . . . asserted to have become a law, was or was not passed by congress. This question is now presented for the first time in this court. . . . We recognize, on one hand, the duty of this court, from the performance of which it may not shrink, to give full effect to the provisions of the constitution relating to the enactment of laws that are to operate wherever the authority and jurisdiction of the United States extend. On the other hand, we cannot be unmindful of the consequences that must result if this court should feel obligated, in fidelity to the constitution, to declare that an enrolled bill, on which depend public and private interests of vast magnitude, and which has been authenticated by the signatures of the presiding officers of the two houses of congress, and by the approval of the president, and been deposited in the public archives, as an act of congress, was not in fact passed by the house of representatives and the senate, and therefore did not become a law.

The clause of the constitution upon which the appellants rest their contention that the act in question was never passed by congress is the one declaring that "each house shall keep a journal of its proceedings, and from time to time publish the same. . . ." Art. I, § 5. It was assumed in argument that the object of this clause was to make the journal the best, if not conclusive, evidence upon the issue as to whether a bill was, in fact, passed by the two houses of congress. But the words used do not require such interpretation. On the contrary, as Mr. Justice Story has well said, "the object of the whole clause is to insure publicity to the proceedings of the legislature, and a correspondent responsibility of the members to their constituents. . . ."

. . . [W]hether bills, orders, resolutions, reports, and amendments shall be entered at large on the journal, or only referred to and designated by their titles or by numbers, — these and like matters were left to the discretion of the respective houses of congress. Nor does any clause of that instrument, either expressly or by necessary implication, prescribe the mode in which the fact of the original passage of a bill by the house of representatives and the senate shall be authenticated, or preclude congress from adopting any mode to that end which its wisdom suggests. . . .

The signing by the speaker of the house of representatives, and by the president of the senate, in open session, of an enrolled bill, is an official attestation by the two houses of such bill as one that has passed congress. It is a declaration by the two houses, through their presiding officers, to the president, that a bill, thus attested, has received, in due form, the sanction of the legislative branch of the government, and that it is delivered to him in obedience to the constitutional requirement that all bills which pass congress shall be presented to him. And when a bill, thus attested, receives his approval, and is deposited in the public archives, its authentication as a bill that has passed congress should be deemed complete and unimpeachable. . . . The respect due to coequal and independent departments requires the judicial department to act upon that assurance, and to accept, as having passed congress, all bills authenticated in the manner stated; leaving the courts to determine, when the question properly arises, whether the act so authenticated, is in conformity with the constitution.

It is admitted that an enrolled act, thus authenticated, is sufficient evidence of itself — nothing to the contrary appearing upon its face — that it passed congress. But the contention is that it cannot be regarded as a law of the United States if the journal of either house fails to show that it passed in the precise form in which it was signed by the presiding officers of the two houses, and approved by the president. It is said that, under any other view, it becomes possible for the speaker of the house of representatives and the president of the senate to impose upon the people as a law a bill that was never passed by congress. But this possibility is too remote to be seriously considered in the present inquiry. It suggests a deliberate conspiracy to which the presiding officers, the committees on enrolled bills, and the clerks of the two houses must necessarily be parties, all acting with a common purpose to defeat an expression of the popular will in the mode prescribed by the constitution. Judicial action, based on such a suggestion, is forbidden by the respect due a co-ordinate branch of the government. . . .

. . . .

The case of *Gardner v. Collector*, 73 U.S. 499, 511 (1867), was relied on in argument as supporting the contention of the appellants. The question there was as to the time when an act of congress took effect; the doubt, upon that point, arising from the fact that the month and day, but not the year, of the approval of the act by the president appeared upon the enrolled act in the custody of the department of state. This omission, it was held, could be supplied in support of the act from the legislative journals. It was said by the court:

> We are of opinion, therefore, on principle as well as authority, that whenever a question arises in a court of law of the existence of a statute, or of the time when a statute took effect, or of the precise terms of a statute, the judges who are called upon to decide it have a right to resort to any source of information which in its nature is capable of conveying to the judicial mind a clear and satisfactory answer to such question; always seeking first for that which in its nature is most appropriate, unless the positive law has enacted a different rule.

There was no question in that case as to the existence or terms of a statute, and the point in judgment was that the time when an admitted statute took effect, not appearing from the enrolled act, could be shown by the legislative journals. It is scarcely necessary to say that that case does not meet the question here presented.

Nor do the cases of *South Ottawa v. Perkins,* 94 U.S. 260 (1876); *Walnut v. Wade,* 103 U.S. 683 (1880); and *Post v. Supervisors,* 105 U.S. 667 (1881), — proceed upon any ground inconsistent with the views we have expressed. In each of those cases it was held that the question whether a seeming act of the legislature became a law, in accordance with the constitution, was a judicial one, to be decided by the courts and judges, and not a question of fact to be tried by a jury . . . .

. . . .

We are of opinion, for the reasons stated, that it is not competent for the appellants to show, from the journals of either house, from the reports of committees, or from other documents printed by authority of congress, that the enrolled bill, designated "H.R. 9416," as finally passed, contained a section that does not appear in the enrolled act in the custody of the state department.

[A discussion of two additional grounds for challenging the statute are omitted.]

Justice Lamar, with whom Justice Fuller joined, dissenting.

[The dissent was exclusively on other bases than excerpted above.]

Exercise 15(B):

What are the implications of *Field v. Clark* for the doctrine of judicial review? Specifically, consider:

(1)   To what extent, if any, does this case support a different scope of review than *Marbury v. Madison* and the pre-*Marbury* precedents?

(2)   What textual analysis, if any, supports any assertions of limited judicial authority in *Field v. Clark*?

(3)   What historical analysis (whether based upon ratification materials or tradition), if any, supports any assertions of limited judicial authority in this case?

(4)   From a separation of powers perspective, what form of judicial review is more intrusive upon the legislative power: review of procedural regularity of legislation (like that at issue in *Field v. Clark*) or review of substantive compliance of legislation with the Constitution (like that at issue in *Marbury v. Madison* and *Cohens v. Virginia*)? Which of these forms of judicial review provides the greater opportunity for Congress to promulgate its public policy choices?

(5)   The Court refused to consider "a deliberate conspiracy" to produce fraudulent legislation despite an offer of evidence to demonstrate a discrepancy based upon the records maintained by Congress itself. Are the events suggested in this case any more "remote" than the allegations of William Marbury?

COOPER v. AARON
358 U.S. 1 (1958)

Chief Justice Warren and Justices Black, Frankfurter, Douglas, Burton, Clark, Harlan, Brennan, and Whittaker delivered the Opinion of the Court.

As this case reaches us it raises questions of the highest importance to the maintenance of our federal system of government. It necessarily involves a claim by the Governor and Legislature of a State that there is no duty on state officials to obey federal court orders resting on this Court's considered interpretation of the United States Constitution. Specifically it involves actions by the Governor and Legislature of Arkansas upon the premise that they are not bound by our holding in *Brown v. Board of Education*, 347 U.S. 483 (1954). . . .

. . . .

. . . [W]e should answer the premise of the actions of the Governor and Legislature that they are not bound by our holding in the *Brown* case. It is necessary only to recall some basic constitutional propositions which are settled doctrine.

Article VI of the Constitution makes the Constitution the "supreme Law of the Land." In 1803, Chief Justice Marshall, speaking for a unanimous Court, referring to the Constitution as "the fundamental and paramount law of the nation," declared in the notable case of *Marbury v. Madison,* that "It is emphatically the province and duty of the judicial department to say what the law is." This decision declared the basic principle that the federal judiciary is supreme in the exposition of the law of the Constitution, and that principle has ever since been respected by this Court and the Country as a permanent and indispensable feature of our constitutional system. It follows that the interpretation of the Fourteenth Amendment enunciated by this Court in the *Brown* case is the supreme law of the land, and Art. VI of the Constitution makes it of binding effect on the States "any Thing in the Constitution or Laws of any State to the Contrary notwithstanding." . . .

. . . .

No state legislator or executive or judicial officer can war against the Constitution without violating his undertaking to support it. Chief Justice Marshall spoke for a unanimous Court in saying that: "If the legislatures of the several states may, at will, annul the judgments of the courts of the United States, and destroy the rights acquired under those judgments, the constitution itself becomes a solemn mockery. . . ." *United States v. Peters*, 9 U.S. 115, 136 (1809). A Governor who asserts a power to nullify a federal court order is similarly restrained. . . .

. . . The principles announced in [*Brown*] and the obedience of the States to them, according to the command of the Constitution, are indispensable for the protection of the freedoms guaranteed by our fundamental charter for all of us. Our constitutional ideal of equal justice under law is thus made a living truth.

JUSTICE FRANKFURTER, concurring.

While unreservedly participating with my brethren in our joint opinion, I deem it appropriate also to deal individually with the great issue here at stake.

. . . .

We are now asked to hold that the illegal, forcible interference by the State of Arkansas with the continuance of what the Constitution commands, and the consequences in disorder that it entrained, should be recognized as justification for undoing what the School Board had formulated, what the District Court in 1955 had directed to be carried out, and what was in process of obedience. No explanation that may be offered in support of such a request can obscure the inescapable meaning that law should bow to force. To yield such a claim would be to enthrone official lawlessness and lawlessness if not checked is the precursor to anarchy. On the few tragic occasions in the history of the Nation, North and South, when law was forcibly resisted or systematically evaded, it has signalled the breakdown of constitutional processes of government on which ultimately rest the liberties of all. Violent resistance to law cannot be made a legal reason for its suspension without loosening the fabric of our society. . . .

When defiance of law, judicially pronounced, was last sought to be justified before this Court, views were expressed which are now especially relevant:

> The historic phrase 'a government of laws and not of men' epitomizes the distinguishing character of our political society. When John Adams put that phrase into the Massachusetts Declaration of Rights . . . he was not indulging in a rhetorical flourish. He was expressing the aim of those who, with him, framed the Declaration of Independence and founded the Republic. 'A government of laws and not of men' was the rejection in positive terms of rule by fiat, whether by fiat of governmental or private power. Every act of government may be challenged by an appeal to law, as finally pronounced by this Court. Even this Court has the last say only for a time. Being composed of fallible men, it may err. But revision of its errors must be by orderly process of law. The Court may be asked to reconsider its decisions, and this has been done successfully again and again throughout our history. Or, what this Court has deemed its duty to decide may be changed by legislation, as it often has been, and, on occasion, by constitutional amendment.

> But from their own experience and their deep reading in history, the Founders knew that Law alone saves a society from being rent by internecine strife or ruled by mere brute power however disguised. 'Civilization involves subjection of force to reason, and the agency of this subjection is law.' Roscoe Pound, *The Future of Law*, 47 YALE L.J. 1, 13 (1937). The conception of a government of laws dominated the thoughts of those who founded this Nation and designed its Constitution, although they knew as well as the belittlers of the conception that laws have to be made, interpreted and enforced by men. To that end, they set apart a body of men, who were to be the depositories of law, who by their disciplined training and character and by withdrawal from the usual temptations of private interest may reasonably be expected to be 'as free, impartial, and independent as the lot of humanity will admit.' So strong were the framers of the Constitution bent on securing a reign of law that they endowed the judicial office with extraordinary safeguards and prestige. No one, no matter how exalted his public office or how righteous his private motive, can be judge in his own case. That is what courts are for.

United States v. United Mine Workers, 330 U.S. 258, 307–09 (1947) (Frankfurter, J., concurring).

The duty to abstain from resistance to "the supreme Law of the Land," U.S. Const. Art. VI, ¶ 2, as declared by the organ of our Government for ascertaining it, does not require immediate approval of it nor does it deny the right of dissent. Criticism need not be stilled. Active obstruction or defiance is barred. . . . Particularly is this so where the declaration of what "the supreme Law" commands on an underlying moral issue is not the dubious pronouncement of a gravely divided Court but is the unanimous conclusion of a long-matured deliberative process. The Constitution is not the formulation of the merely personal views of the members of this Court, nor can its authority be reduced to the claim that state officials are its controlling interpreters. . . .

. . . .

Lincoln's appeal to "the better angels of our nature" failed to avert a fratricidal war. But the compassionate wisdom of Lincoln's First and Second Inaugurals bequeathed to the Union, cemented with blood, a moral heritage which, when drawn upon in times of stress and strife, is sure to find specific ways and means to surmount difficulties that may appear to be insurmountable.

Exercise 15(C):

In connection with *Cooper v. Aaron*, consider:

(1) To what extent, if any, does this case support a different scope of judicial review than *Marbury v. Madison* and the pre-*Marbury* precedents?

(2) Did *Marbury*, in fact, declare "that the federal judiciary is supreme in the exposition of the law of the Constitution"?

(3) Is this case consistent with *Field v. Clark*?

(4)

What textual analysis, if any, supports any additional assertions of judicial authority in this case?

(5) What historical analysis, if any, supports any additional assertions of judicial authority in this case? Are the assertions in this case consistent with Hamilton's description of the judicial role (in Chapter 2)? Are they consistent with the assertions of Brutus (in Chapter 2)?

(6) Justice Frankfurter asserts: "No one, no matter how exalted his public office or how righteous his private motive, can be judge in his own case." Under that principle, should Chief Justice Marshall have ruled on whether his failure to deliver a commission to William Marbury deprived Marbury of a right to the justice of the peace office?

A Note Regarding Standards of Review

A comparison of *Field v. Clark* with *Cooper v. Aaron* illustrates that even when federal courts exercise the power of judicial review, there are a range of levels of deference to the views of coordinate branches of government. Such differences are not wholly attributable to the distinction between review of actions of the central government and review of actions of the States. Nor are such differences wholly attributable to review under different clauses of the Constitution. Rather, even when reviewing state legislation under the Equal Protection Clause, the Supreme Court has articulated several different standards of judicial review:

In considering whether state legislation violates the Equal Protection Clause of the Fourteenth Amendment, U.S. Const., Amdt. 14, § 1, we apply different levels of scrutiny to different types of classifications. At a minimum, a statutory classification must be rationally related to a legitimate governmental purpose. *San Antonio Independent School Dist. v. Rodriguez*, 411 U.S. 1, 17 (1973); *cf. Lyng v. Automobile Workers*, 485 U.S. 360, 370 (1988). Classifications based on race or national origin, *e.g., Loving v. Virginia*, 388 U.S. 1, 11 (1967), and classifications affecting fundamental rights, *e.g., Harper v. Virginia Bd. of Elections*, 383 U.S. 663, 672 (1966), are given the most exacting scrutiny. Between these extremes of rational basis of review and strict scrutiny lies a level of intermediate scrutiny, which generally has been applied to discriminatory classifications based on sex or illegitimacy. *See, e.g., Mississippi University for Women v. Hogan*, 458 U.S. 718, 723–724 & n.9 (1982); *Mills v. Habluetzel*, 456 U.S. 91, 99 (1982); *Craig v. Boren*, 429 U.S. 190, 197 (1976); *Mathews v. Lucas*, 427 U.S. 495, 505–506 (1976).

To withstand intermediate scrutiny, a statutory classification must be substantially related to an important governmental objective. . . .

Clark v. Jeter, 486 U.S. 456, 461 (1988).

As a consequence, determining that the federal judiciary has the power of judicial review only serves to pose numerous additional questions, including the appropriate level of scrutiny of the challenged action. *See also Madsen v. Women's Health Center, Inc.,* 512 U.S. 753, 790–794 (1994) (Scalia, J., dissenting) (describing the development of a fourth standard — falling between strict scrutiny and intermediate scrutiny — applicable to abortion-related matters); *United States v. Virginia,* 518 U.S. 515, 566–575 (1996) (Scalia, J., dissenting) (describing potential expanded applications of various standards).

D. Judicial Restraint

ASHWANDER v. TENNESSEE VALLEY AUTHORITY
297 U.S. 288 (1936)

[George Ashwander and others sued the Tennessee Valley Authority. Chief Justice Hughes delivered the opinion of the Court affirming the judgment below.]

JUSTICE BRANDEIS, with whom JUSTICES STONE, ROBERTS, and CARDOZO, join, concurring.

"Considerations of propriety, as well as long-established practice, demand that we refrain from passing upon the constitutionality of an act of Congress unless obligated to do so in the proper performance of our judicial function, when the question is raised by a party whose interests entitle him to raise it."

I do not disagree with the conclusions on the constitutional question announced by the Chief Justice; but, in my opinion, the judgment of the Circuit Court of Appeals should be affirmed without passing upon it. . . .

. . . .

. . . The fact that it would be convenient for the parties and the public to have promptly decided whether the legislation assailed is valid, cannot justify a departure from these settled rules of corporate law and established principles of equity practice. On the contrary, the fact that such is the nature of the enquiry proposed should deepen the reluctance of courts to entertain the stockholder's suit. "It must be evident to any one that the power to declare a legislative enactment void is one which the judge, conscious of the fallibility of the human judgment, will shrink from exercising in any case where he can conscientiously and with due regard to duty and official oath decline the responsibility."

The Court has frequently called attention to the "great gravity and delicacy" of its function in passing upon the validity of an act of Congress; and has restricted exercise of this function by rigid insistence that the jurisdiction of federal courts is limited to actual cases and controversies; and that they have no power to give advisory opinions. On this ground it has in recent years ordered the dismissal of several suits challenging the constitutionality of important acts of Congress. . . .

The Court developed, for its own governance in the cases confessedly within its jurisdiction, a series of rules under which it has avoided passing upon a large part of all the constitutional questions pressed upon it for decision. They are:

[First, the] Court will not pass upon the constitutionality of legislation in a friendly, nonadversary, proceeding, declining because to decide such questions "is legitimate only in the last resort, and as a necessity in the determination of real, earnest, and vital controversy between individuals. It never was the thought that, by means of a friendly suit, a party beaten in the legislature could transfer to the courts an inquiry as to the constitutionality of the legislative act."

[Second, the] Court will not "anticipate a question of constitutional law in advance of the necessity of deciding it." "It is not the habit of the court to decide questions of a constitutional nature unless absolutely necessary to a decision of the case."

[Third, the] Court will not "formulate a rule of constitutional law broader than is required by the precise facts to which it is to be applied."

[Fourth, the] Court will not pass upon a constitutional question although properly presented by the record, if there is also present some other ground upon which the case may be disposed of. . . . Thus, if a case can be decided on either of two grounds, one involving a constitutional question, the other a question of statutory construction or general law, the Court will decide only the latter. Appeals from the highest court of a state challenging its decision of a question under the Federal Constitution are frequently dismissed because the judgment can be sustained on an independent state ground.

[Fifth, the] Court will not pass upon the validity of a statute upon complaint of one who fails to show that he is injured by its operation. Among the many applications of this rule, none is more striking than the denial of the right to challenge to one who lacks a personal or property right. Thus, the challenge by a public official interested only in the performance of his official duty will not be entertained. . . .

[Sixth, the] Court will not pass upon the constitutionality of a statute at the instance of one who has availed himself of its benefits.

[Seventh,] "[w]hen the validity of an act of the Congress is drawn in question, and even if a serious doubt of constitutionality is raised, it is a cardinal principle that this Court will first ascertain whether a construction of the statute is fairly possible by which the question may be avoided."

. . . .

Justice Iredell said, as early as 1798, in *Calder v. Bull:* "If any act of congress, or of the legislature of a state, violates those constitutional provisions, it is unquestionably void; though, I admit, that as the authority to declare it void is of a delicate and awful nature, the court will never resort to that authority, but in a clear and urgent case."

Chief Justice Marshall said, in *Dartmouth College v. Woodward:* "On more than one occasion, this court has expressed the cautious circumspection with which it approaches the consideration of such questions; and has declared, that in no doubtful case, would it pronounce a legislative act to be contrary to the constitution."

Justice Washington said, in *Ogden v. Saunders:* "But if I could rest my opinion in favour of the constitutionality of the law on which the question arises, on no other ground than this doubt so felt and acknowledged, that alone, would, in my estimation, be a satisfactory vindication of it. It is but a decent respect due to the wisdom, the integrity and the patriotism of the legislative body, by which any law is passed, to presume in favour of its validity, until its violation of the constitution is proved beyond all reasonable doubt. This has always been the language of this court, when that subject has called for its decision; and I know that it expresses the honest sentiments of each and every member of this bench."

Chief Justice Waite said in the *Sinking-Fund Cases:* "This declaration (that an act of Congress is unconstitutional) should never be made except in a clear case. Every possible presumption is in favor of the validity of a statute, and this continues until the contrary is shown beyond a rational doubt. One branch of government cannot encroach on the domain of another without danger. The safety of our institutions depends in no small degree on a strict observance of this salutary rule."

. . . .

Exercise 16:

Consider the following questions in connection with the view of Justice Brandeis in *Ashwander v. TVA:*

(1)   Under what circumstances has the Supreme Court asserted that, despite jurisdiction, a court should decline to reach the merits of a constitutional issue?

(2)   Do the principles articulated by Justice Brandeis serve to improve the development of constitutional law in a case law system? Or, do one or more of these principles hinder the development of doctrine?

(3)   Justice Brandeis asserted that it is inappropriate for a court to "pass upon the constitutionality of legislation in a friendly, nonadversary proceeding" and that such questions may legitimately be addressed only as a "last resort." Has the Court adhered to that approach in the cases in prior chapters?

(4)   Justice Brandeis asserted that it is inappropriate for a court "to decide questions of a constitutional nature unless absolutely necessary to a decision of the case." In *Marbury,* was it "absolutely necessary" to determine at what point in the appointment process a right to office vests as a matter of constitutional law? Was it "absolutely necessary" to determine whether a writ of mandamus could constitutionally issue to the Secretary of State?

(5)   Justice Brandeis asserted that it is inappropriate for a court to "formulate a rule of constitutional law broader than is required by the precise facts to which it is to be applied." In *Cohens* — a case addressing the problems posed by prior *dicta* — how broad a rule did the facts of the case require? Was it necessary to determine whether the Eleventh Amendment did not apply to cases against an unconsenting State based on "arising under" jurisdiction?

(6)   Justice Brandeis asserted that it is inappropriate for a court to hold a federal statute unconstitutional without first attempting to avoid that question by construing the statute in a manner to render it constitutional. In *Marbury,* was it possible to construe the statutory provision at issue "fairly" and in a way that the constitutional issue could be avoided?

(7)   How, if at all, are the considerations Justice Brandeis identified consistent with the view that the judiciary has an obligation to address any matter within its jurisdiction, as stated in *Cohens v. Virginia?*

(8)   Throughout the remainder of the course, identify cases in which the Court fails to follow the principles summarized by Justice Brandeis.

E. *Stare Decisis*

PLANNED PARENTHOOD OF SOUTHEASTERN PENNSYLVANIA v. CASEY
505 U.S. 833 (1992)

Justice O'Connor, Justice Kennedy and Justice Souter announced the judgment of the Court.

I

Liberty finds no refuge in a jurisprudence of doubt. Yet 19 years after our holding that the Constitution protects a woman's right to terminate her pregnancy in its early stages, *Roe v. Wade*, 410 U.S. 113 (1973), that definition of liberty is still questioned. Joining the respondents as *amicus curiae*, the United States, as it has done in five other cases in the past decade, again asks us to overrule *Roe*. . . .

. . . .

III

A

The obligation to follow precedent begins with necessity, and a contrary necessity marks its outer limit. With Cardozo, we recognize that no judicial system could do society's work if it eyed each issue afresh in every case that raised it. *See* Benjamin Cardozo, The Nature of the Judicial Process 149 (1921). Indeed, the very concept of the rule of law underlying our own Constitution requires such continuity over time that a respect for precedent is, by definition, indispensable. *See* Lewis F. Powell, Jr., *Stare Decisis and Judicial Restraint*, 1991 J. of Sup. Ct. Hist. 13, 16. At the other extreme, a different necessity would make itself felt if a prior judicial ruling should come to be seen so clearly as error that its enforcement was for that very reason doomed.

Even when the decision to overrule a prior case is not, as in the rare, latter instance, virtually foreordained, it is common wisdom that the rule of *stare decisis* is not an "inexorable command," and certainly it is not such in every constitutional case, *see Burnet v. Coronado Oil & Gas Co.*, 285 U.S. 393, 405–411 (1932) (Brandeis, J., dissenting). . . . Rather, when this Court reexamines a prior holding, its judgment is customarily informed by a series of prudential and pragmatic considerations designed to test the consistency of overruling a prior decision with the ideal of the rule of law, and to gauge the respective costs of reaffirming and overruling a prior case. Thus, for example, we may ask whether the rule has proven to be intolerable simply in defying practical workability, *Swift & Co. v. Wickham*, 382 U.S. 111, 116 (1965); whether the rule is subject to a kind of reliance that would lend a special hardship to the consequences of overruling and add inequity to the cost of repudiation, *e.g., United States v. Title Ins. & Trust Co.*, 265 U.S. 472, 486 (1924); whether related principles of law have so far developed as to have left the old rule no more than a remnant of abandoned doctrine, *see Patterson v. McLean Credit Union*, 491 U.S. 164, 173–174 (1989); or whether facts have so changed, or come to be seen so differently, as to have robbed the old rule of significant application or justification, *e.g., Burnet*, 285 U.S. at 412 (Brandeis, J., dissenting).

So in this case we may enquire whether *Roe*'s central rule has been found unworkable; whether the rule's limitation on state power could be removed without serious inequity to those who have relied upon it or significant damage to the stability of the society governed by it; whether the law's growth in the intervening years have left *Roe*'s central rule a doctrinal anachronism discounted by society; and whether *Roe*'s premises of fact have so far changed in the ensuing two decades as to render its central holding somehow irrelevant or unjustifiable in dealing with the issue it addressed.

1

Although *Roe* has engendered opposition, it has in no sense proven "unworkable," *see Garcia v. San Antonio Metropolitan Transit Authority,* 469 U.S. 528, 546 (1985), representing as it does a simple limitation beyond which a state law is unenforceable. While *Roe* has, of course, required judicial assessment of state laws affecting the exercise of the choice guaranteed against government infringement, and although the need for such review will remain as a consequence of today's decision, the required determinations fall within judicial competence.

2

The inquiry into reliance counts the cost of a rule's repudiation as it would fall on those who have relied reasonably on the rule's continued application. Since the classic case for weighing reliance heavily in favor of following the earlier rule occurs in the commercial context, *see Payne v. Tennessee,* 501 U.S. at 828, where advance planning of great precision is most obviously a necessity, it is no cause for surprise that some would find no reliance worthy of consideration in support of *Roe.*

. . . Abortion is customarily chosen as an unplanned response to the consequence of unplanned activity or to the failure of conventional birth control, and except on the assumption that no intercourse would have occurred but for *Roe*'s holding, such behavior may appear to justify no reliance claim. Even if reliance could be claimed on that unrealistic assumption, the argument might run, any reliance interest would be *de minimis.* This argument would be premised on the hypothesis that reproductive planning could take virtually immediate account of any sudden restoration of state authority to ban abortions.

To eliminate the issue of reliance that easily, however, one would need to limit cognizable reliance to specific instances of sexual activity. But to do this would be simply to refuse to face the fact that for two decades of economic and social developments, people have organized intimate relationships and made choices that define their views of themselves and their places in society, in reliance on the availability of abortion in the event that contraception should fail. The ability of women to participate equally in the economic and social life of the Nation has been facilitated by their ability to control their reproductive lives. . . .

3

No evolution of legal principle has left *Roe*'s doctrinal footings weaker than they were in 1973. No development of constitutional law since the case was decided has implicitly or explicitly left *Roe* behind as a mere survivor of obsolete constitutional thinking.

It will be recognized, of course, that *Roe* stands at an intersection of two lines of decisions, but in whichever doctrinal category one reads the case, the result for present purposes will be the same. The *Roe* Court itself placed its holding in the succession of cases most prominently exemplified by *Griswold v. Connecticut,* 381 U.S. 479 (1965). *See Roe,* 410 U.S. at 152–153. When it is so seen, *Roe* is clearly in no jeopardy, since subsequent constitutional developments have neither disturbed, nor do they threaten to diminish, the scope of recognized protection accorded to the liberty relating to intimate relationships, the family, and decisions about whether or not to beget or bear a child. *See, e.g., Carey v. Population Services International,* 431 U.S. 678 (1977); *Moore v. East Cleveland,* 431 U.S. 494 (1977).

Roe, however, may be seen not only as an exemplar of *Griswold* liberty but as a rule (whether or not mistaken) of personal autonomy and bodily integrity, with doctrinal affinity to cases recognizing limits on governmental power to mandate medical treatment or to bar its rejection. If so, our cases since *Roe* accord with *Roe*'s view that a State's interest in the protection of life falls short of justifying any plenary override of individual liberty claims. *Cruzan v. Director, Missouri Dep't of Health,* 497 U.S. 261, 278 (1990) . . . .

Finally, one could classify *Roe* as *sui generis.* If the case is so viewed, then there clearly has been no erosion of its central determination. The original holding resting on the concurrence of seven Members of the Court in 1973 was expressly affirmed by a majority of six in 1983, *see Akron Center for Reproductive Health, Inc.,* 462 U.S. 416 (*Akron I*), and by a majority of five in 1986, *see Thornburgh v. American College of Obstetricians and Gynecologists,* 476 U.S. 747, expressing adherence to the constitutional ruling despite legislative efforts in some States to test its limits. More recently, in *Webster v. Reproductive Health Services,* 492 U.S. 490 (1989), although two of the present authors questioned the trimester framework in a way consistent with our judgment today . . . a majority of the Court either decided to reaffirm or declined to address the constitutional validity of the central holding of *Roe.* . . .

Nor will courts building upon *Roe* be likely to hand down erroneous decisions as a consequence. Even on the assumption that the central holding of *Roe* was in error, that error would go only to the strength of the state interest in fetal protection, not to the recognition afforded by the Constitution to the woman's liberty. The latter aspect of the decision fits comfortably within the framework of the Court's prior decisions, including *Skinner v. Oklahoma ex rel. Williamson,* 316 U.S. 535 (1942); *Griswold,* 381 U.S. 479; *Loving v. Virginia,* 388 U.S. 1 (1967); and *Eisenstadt v. Baird,* 405 U.S. 438 (1972), the holdings of which are "not a series of isolated points," but mark a "rational continuum." . . . As we described in *Carey v. Population Services International,* the liberty which encompasses those decisions

> include "the interest in independence in making certain kinds of important decisions." While the outer limits of this aspect of [protected liberty] have not been marked by the Court, it is clear that among the decisions that an individual may make without unjustified government interference are personal decisions "relating to marriage, procreation, contraception, family relationships, and child rearing and education."

431 U.S. at 684–85.

The soundness of this prong of the *Roe* analysis is apparent from a consideration of the alternative. If indeed the woman's interest in deciding whether to bear and beget a child had not been recognized as in *Roe,* the State might as readily restrict a woman's right to choose to carry a pregnancy to term as to terminate it, to further asserted state interests in population control, or eugenics, for example. Yet *Roe* has been sensibly relied upon to counter any such suggestions. . . . In any event, because *Roe*'s scope is confined by the fact of its concern with postconception potential life, a concern otherwise likely to be implicated only by some forms of contraception protected independently under *Griswold* and later cases, any error in *Roe* is unlikely to have serious ramifications in future cases.

4

We have seen how time has overtaken some of *Roe*'s factual assumptions: advances in maternal health care allow for abortions safe to the mother later in pregnancy than was true in 1973, *see Akron I,* 462 U.S. at 429 n.11, and advances in neonatal care have advanced viability to a point somewhat earlier. *Compare Roe,* 410 U.S. at 160, *with Webster,* 492 U.S. 490, 515–516 (opinion of Rehnquist, C.J.); *see Akron I,* 462 U.S. at 457 & n.5 (O'Connor, J., dissenting). But these facts go only to the scheme of time limits on the realization of competing interests, and the divergences from the factual premises of 1973 have no bearing on the validity of *Roe*'s central holding, that viability marks the earliest point at which the State's interest in fetal life is constitutionally adequate to justify a legislative ban on nontheraputic abortions. . . . Whenever it may occur, the attainment of viability may continue to serve as the critical fact, just as it has done since *Roe* was decided; which is to say that no change in *Roe*'s factual underpinning has left its central holding obsolete, and none supports an argument for overruling it.

5

The sum of the precedential enquiry to this point shows *Roe*'s underpinnings unweakened in any way affecting its central holding. While it has engendered disapproval, it has not been unworkable. An entire generation has come of age free to assume *Roe*'s concept of liberty in defining the capacity of women to act in society, and to make reproductive decisions; no erosion of principle going to liberty or personal autonomy has left *Roe*'s central holding a doctrinal remnant; *Roe* portends no developments at odds with other precedent for the analysis of personal liberty; and no changes of fact have rendered viability more or less appropriate as the point at which the balance of interests tips. Within the bounds of normal *stare decisis* analysis, then, and subject to the considerations on which it customarily turns, the stronger argument is for affirming *Roe*'s central holding, with whatever degree of personal reluctance any of us may have, not for overruling it.

B

In a less significant case, *stare decisis* analysis could, and would, stop at the point we have reached. But the sustained and widespread debate *Roe* has provoked calls for some comparison between that case and others of comparable dimension that have responded to national controversies and taken on the impress of the controversies addressed. Only two such decisional lines from the past century present themselves for examination, and in each instance the result reached by the Court accorded with the principles we apply today.

The first example is that line of cases identified with *Lochner v. New York,* 198 U.S. 45 (1905), which imposed substantive limitations on legislation limiting economic autonomy in favor of health and welfare regulation, adopting, in Justice Holmes's view, the theory of laissez-faire. *Id.* at 75 (dissenting opinion). The *Lochner* decisions were exemplified by *Adkins v. Children's Hospital of District of Columbia,* 261 U.S. 525 (1923), in which this Court held it to be an infringement of constitutionally protected liberty of contract to require the employers of adult women to satisfy minimum wage standards. Fourteen years later, *West Coast Hotel*

Co. v. Parrish, 300 U.S. 379 (1937), signaled the demise of *Lochner* by overruling *Adkins.* In the meantime, the Depression had come and, with it, the lesson that seemed unmistakable to most people by 1937, that the interpretation of contractual freedom protected in *Adkins* rested on fundamentally false factual assumptions about the capacity of a relatively unregulated market to satisfy minimal levels of human welfare. *See West Coast Hotel Co.,* 300 U.S. at 399. As Justice Jackson wrote of the constitutional crisis of 1937 shortly before he came on the bench: "The older world of *laissez-faire* was recognized everywhere outside the Court to be dead." THE STRUGGLE FOR JUDICIAL SUPREMACY 85 (1941). The facts upon which the earlier case had premised a constitutional resolution of social controversy had proven to be untrue, and history's demonstration of their untruth not only justified but required the new choice of constitutional principle that *West Coast Hotel* announced. Of course, it was true that the Court lost something by its misperception, or its lack of prescience, and the Court-packing crisis only magnified the loss; but the clear demonstration that the facts of economic life were different from those previously assumed warranted the repudiation of the old law.

The second comparison that the 20th century invites is with the cases employing the separate-but-equal rule for applying the Fourteenth Amendment's equal protection guarantee. They began with *Plessy v. Ferguson,* 163 U.S. 537 (1896), holding that legislatively mandated racial segregation in public transportation works no denial of equal protection, rejecting the argument that racial separation enforced by the legal machinery of American society treats the black race as inferior. The *Plessy* Court considered "the underlying fallacy of the plaintiff's argument to consist in the assumption that the enforced separation of the two races stamps the colored race with a badge of inferiority. If this be so, it is not by reason of anything found in the act, but solely because the colored race chooses to put that construction upon it." *Id.* at 551. . . . But this understanding of the facts and the rule it was stated to justify were repudiated in *Brown v. Board of Education,* 347 U.S. 483 (1954) (*Brown I*). As one commentator observed, the question before the Court in *Brown* was "whether discrimination inheres in that segregation which is imposed by law in the twentieth century in certain specific states in the American Union. . . ."

The Court in *Brown* addressed these facts of life by observing that whatever may have been the understanding in *Plessy*'s time of the power of segregation to stigmatize those who were segregated with a "badge of inferiority," it was clear by 1954 that legally sanctioned segregation had just such an effect, to the point that racially separate public educational facilities were deemed inherently unequal. 347 U.S. at 494–95.

Society's understanding of the facts upon which a constitutional ruling was sought in 1954 was thus fundamentally different from the basis claimed for the decision in 1896. While we think *Plessy* was wrong the day it was decided, *see Plessy,* 163 U.S. at 552–64 (Harlan, J., dissenting), we must also recognize that the *Plessy* Court's explanation for its decision was so clearly at odds with the facts apparent to the Court in 1954 that the decision to reexamine *Plessy* was on this ground alone not only justified but required.

West Coast Hotel and *Brown* each rested on facts, or an understanding of facts, changed from those which furnished the claimed justifications for the earlier constitutional resolutions. Each case was comprehensible as the Court's response to facts that the country could understand, or had come to understand already, but which the Court of an earlier day, as its own declarations disclosed, had not been able to perceive. . . . In constitutional adjudication as elsewhere in life, changed circumstances may impose new obligations, and the thoughtful part of the Nation could accept each decision to overrule a prior case as a response to the Court's constitutional duty.

Because the cases before us present no such occasion it could be seen as no such response. . . . [T]he Court could not pretend to be reexamining the prior law with any justification beyond a present doctrinal disposition to come out differently from the Court of 1973. To overrule prior law for no other reason than that would run counter to the view repeated in our cases, that a decision to overrule should rest on some special reason over and above the belief that a prior case was wrongly decided. *See, e.g., Mitchell v. W.T. Grant Co.,* 416 U.S. 600, 636 (1974) (Stewart, J., dissenting) ("A basic change in the law upon a ground no firmer than a change in our membership invites the popular misconception that this institution is little different from the two political branches of the Government. No misconception could do more lasting injury to this Court and to the system of law which it is our abiding mission to serve"); *Mapp v. Ohio,* 367 U.S. 643, 677 (1961) (Harlan, J., dissenting).

C

. . . In the present cases . . . as our analysis to this point makes clear, the terrible price would be paid for overruling. Our analysis would not be complete, however, without explaining why overruling *Roe*'s central holding would not only reach an unjustifiable result under principles of *stare decisis,* but would seriously weaken the Court's capacity to exercise the judicial power and to function as the Supreme Court of a Nation dedicated to the rule of law. . . .

The root of American governmental power is revealed most clearly in the instance of the power conferred by the Constitution upon the Judiciary of the United States and specifically upon this Court. As Americans of each succeeding generation are rightly told, the Court cannot buy support for its decisions by spending money and, except to a minor degree, it cannot independently coerce obedience to its decrees. The Court's power lies, rather, in its legitimacy, a product of substance and perception that shows itself in the people's acceptance of the Judiciary as fit to determine what the Nation's law means and to declare what it demands.

The underlying substance of this legitimacy is of course the warrant for the Court's decisions in the Constitution and the lesser sources of legal principle on which the Court draws. That substance is expressed in the Court's opinions, and our contemporary understanding is such that a decision without principled justification would be no judicial act at all. But even when justification is furnished by apposite legal principle, something more is required. Because not every conscientious claim of principled justification will be accepted as such, the justification claimed must be beyond dispute. The Court must take care to speak and act in ways that allow people to accept its decisions on the terms the Court claims for them, as grounded truly in principle, not as compromises with social and political pressures having, as such, no bearing on the principled choices that the Court is obliged to make. Thus, the Court's legitimacy depends on making legally principled decisions under circumstances in which their principled character is sufficiently plausible to be accepted by the Nation.

The need for principled action to be perceived as such is implicated to some degree whenever this, or any other appellate court, overrules a prior case. This is not to say, of course, that this Court cannot give a perfectly satisfactory explanation in most cases. People understand that some of the Constitution's language is hard to fathom and that the Court's Justices are sometimes able to perceive significant facts or to understand principles of law that eluded their predecessors and that justify departures from existing decisions. However upsetting it may be to those most directly affected when one judicially derived rule replaces another, the country can accept some correction of error without necessarily questioning the legitimacy of the Court.

In two circumstances, however, the Court would almost certainly fail to receive the benefit of the doubt in overruling prior cases. There is, first, a point beyond which frequent overruling would overtax the country's belief in the Court's good faith. Despite the variety of reasons that may inform and justify a decision to overrule, we cannot forget that such a decision is usually perceived (and perceived correctly) as, at the least, a statement that a prior decision was wrong. There is a limit to the amount of error that can plausibly be imputed to prior Courts. If that limit should be exceeded, disturbance of prior rulings would be taken as evidence that justifiable reexamination of principle had given way to drives for particular results in the short term. The legitimacy of the Court would fade with the frequency of its vacillation.

The first circumstance can be described as hypothetical; the second is to the point here and now. Where, in the performance of its judicial duties, the Court decides a case in such a way as to resolve the sort of intensely divisive controversy reflected in *Roe* and those rare, comparable cases, its decision has a dimension that the resolution of the normal case does not carry. It is the dimension present whenever the Court's interpretation of the Constitution calls the contending sides of a national controversy to end their national division by accepting a common mandate rooted in the Constitution.

The Court is not asked to do this very often, having thus addressed the Nation only twice in our lifetime, in the decisions of *Brown* and *Roe*. But when the Court does act in this way, its decision requires an equally rare precedential force to counter the inevitable efforts to overturn it and to thwart its implementation. Some of those efforts may be mere unprincipled emotional reactions; others may proceed from principles worthy of profound respect. But whatever the premises of opposition may be, only the most convincing justification under accepted standards of precedent could suffice to demonstrate that a later decision overruling the first was anything but a surrender to political pressure, and an unjustified repudiation of the principle on which the Court staked its authority in the first instance. So to overrule under fire in the absence of the most compelling reason to reexamine a watershed decision would subvert the Court's legitimacy beyond any serious question. Cf. *Brown v. Board of Education*, 349 U.S. 294, 300 (1955) (*Brown II*) ("[I]t should go without saying that the vitality of th[e] constitutional principles [announced in *Brown I*,] cannot be allowed to yield simply because of disagreement with them").

The country's loss of confidence in the Judiciary would be underscored by an equally certain and equally reasonable condemnation for another failing in over-ruling unnecessarily and under pressure. Some cost will be paid by anyone who approves or implements a constitutional decision where it is unpopular, or who refuses to work to undermine the decision or to force its reversal. The price may be criticism or ostracism, or it may be violence. An extra price will be paid by those who themselves disapprove of the decision's results when viewed outside of constitutional terms, but who nevertheless struggle to accept it, because they respect the rule of law. To all those who will be so tested by following, the Court implicitly undertakes to remain steadfast, lest in the end a price be paid for nothing. The promise of constancy, once given, binds its maker for as long as the power to stand by the decision survives and the understanding of the issue has not changed so fundamentally as to render the commitment obsolete. From the obligation of this promise this Court cannot and should not assume any exemption when duty requires it to decide a case in conformance with the Constitution. A willing breach of it would be nothing less than a breach of faith, and no Court that broke its faith with the people could sensibly expect credit for principle in the decision by which it did that.

It is true that diminished legitimacy may be restored, but only slowly. . . . Like the character of an individual, the legitimacy of the Court must be earned over time. So indeed, must be the character of a Nation of people who aspire to live according to the rule of law. . . . If the Court's legitimacy should be undermined, then, so would the country be in its very ability to see itself through its constitutional ideals. The Court's concern with legitimacy is not for the sake of the Court, but for the sake of the Nation to which it is responsible.

The Court's duty in the present cases is clear. In 1973, it confronted the already-divisive issue of governmental power to limit personal choice to undergo abortion, for which it provided a new resolution based on the due process guaranteed by the Fourteenth Amendment. Whether or not a new social consensus is developing on that issue, its divisiveness is no less today than in 1973, and pressure to overrule the decision, like pressure to retain it, has grown only more intense. A decision to overrule *Roe*'s essential holding under the existing circumstances would address error, if error there was, at the cost of both profound and unnecessary damage to the Court's legitimacy, and to the Nation's commitment to the rule of law. It is therefore imperative to adhere to the essence of *Roe*'s original decision, and we do so today.

IV

From what we have said so far it follows that it is a constitutional liberty of the woman to have some freedom to terminate her pregnancy. . . .

. . . .

We conclude the line should be drawn at viability, so that before that time the woman has a right to choose to terminate her pregnancy. We adhere to this principle for two reasons. First, as we have said, is the doctrine of *stare decisis*. Any judicial act of line-drawing may seem somewhat arbitrary, but *Roe* was a reasoned statement elaborated with great care. We have twice reaffirmed it in the face of great opposition. *See Thornburgh v. American College of Obstetricians and Gynecologists*, 476 U.S. at 759; *Akron I*, 462 U.S. at 419–20. Although we must overrule those parts of *Thornburgh* and *Akron I* which, in our view, are inconsistent with *Roe*'s statement that the State has a legitimate interest in promoting the life or potential life of the unborn, the central premise of those cases represents an unbroken commitment by this Court to the essential holding of *Roe*. It is that premise which we reaffirm today.

The second reason is that the concept of viability, as we noted in *Roe*, is the time at which there is a realistic possibility of maintaining and nourishing a life outside the womb, so that the independent existence of the second life can in reason and all fairness be the object of state protection that now overrides the rights of the woman. *See Roe*, 410 U.S. at 163. Consistent with other constitutional norms, legislatures may draw lines which appear arbitrary without the necessity of offering a justification. But courts may not. We must justify the lines we draw. And there is no line other than viability which is more workable. . . .

. . . .

. . . *Roe v. Wade* speaks with clarity in establishing not only the woman's liberty but also the State's "important and legitimate interest in potential life." *Roe*, 410 U.S. at 163. That portion of the decision in *Roe* has been given too little acknowledgment and implementation by the Court in its subsequent cases. Those cases decided that any regulation touching upon the abortion decision must survive strict scrutiny, to be sustained only if drawn in narrow terms to further a compelling state interest. *See, e.g., Akron I*, 462 U.S. at 427. Not all the cases decided under that formulation can be reconciled with the holding in *Roe* itself that the State has legitimate interests in the health of the woman and in protecting the potential life within her. In resolving this tension, we choose to rely upon *Roe*, as against the later cases.

. . . .

We reject the trimester framework, which we do not consider to be part of the essential holding of *Roe*. . . . A logical reading of the central holding in *Roe* itself, and a necessary reconciliation of the liberty of the woman and the interest of the State in promoting prenatal life, require, in our view, that we abandon the trimester framework as a rigid prohibition on all previability regulation aimed at the protection of fetal life. The trimester framework suffers from these basic flaws: in its formulation it misconceives the nature of the pregnant woman's interest; and in practice it undervalues the State's interest in potential life, as recognized in *Roe*.

. . . .

[Discussion of other bases for the decision as well as the concurring and dissenting opinions have been omitted.]

AGOSTINI v. FELTON
521 U.S. 203 (1997)

JUSTICE O'CONNOR delivered the Opinion of the Court.

In *Aguilar v. Felton*, 473 U.S. 402 (1985), this Court held that the Establishment Clause of the First Amendment barred the city of New York from sending public school teachers into parochial schools to provide remedial education to disadvantaged children pursuant to a congressionally mandated program. On remand, the District Court for the Eastern District of New York entered a permanent injunction reflecting our ruling. Twelve years later, petitioners — the parties bound by that injunction — seek relief from its operation. Petitioners maintain that *Aguilar* cannot be squared with our intervening Establishment Clause jurisprudence and ask that we explicitly recognize what our more recent cases already dictate: *Aguilar* is no longer good law. We agree with petitioners that *Aguilar* is not consistent with our subsequent Establishment Clause decisions . . . .

. . . .

The doctrine of *stare decisis* does not preclude us from recognizing the change in our law and overruling *Aguilar* and those portions of *School District of Grand Rapids v. Ball*, 473 U.S. 373 (1985), inconsistent with our more recent decisions. As we have often noted, "[s]tare decisis is not an inexorable command," *Payne v. Tennessee*, 501 U.S. 808, 828 (1991), but instead reflects a policy judgment that "in most matters it is more important that the applicable rule of law be settled than that it be settled right," *Burnet v. Coronado Oil & Gas Co.*, 285 U.S. 393, 406 (1932) (Brandeis, J., dissenting). That policy is at its weakest when we interpret the Constitution because our interpretation can be altered only by constitutional amendment or by overruling our prior decisions. *Seminole Tribe of Florida v.*

Florida, 517 U.S. 44, 63 (1996); *Payne,* 501 U.S. at 828; *St. Joseph Stock Yards Co. v. United States,* 298 U.S. 38 (1936) (Stone & Cardozo, JJ., concurring in result) ("The doctrine of *stare decisis* . . . has only a limited application in the field of constitutional law"). Thus, we have held in several cases that *stare decisis* does not prevent us from overruling a previous decision where there has been a significant change in, or subsequent development of, our constitutional law. *United States v. Gaudin,* 515 U.S. 506, 521 (1995) (*stare decisis* may yield where a prior decision's "underpinnings [have been] eroded, by subsequent decisions of this Court"); *Alabama v. Smith,* 490 U.S. 794, 803 (1989) (noting that a "later development of . . . constitutional law" is a basis for overruling a decision); *Planned Parenthood of Southeastern Pennsylvania v. Casey,* 505 U.S. 833, 857 (1992) (observing that a decision is properly overruled where "development of constitutional law since the case was decided has implicitly or explicitly left [it] behind as a mere survivor of obsolete constitutional thinking"). As discussed above, our Establishment Clause jurisprudence has changed significantly since we decided *Ball* and *Aguilar,* so our decision to overturn those cases rests on far more than "a present doctrinal disposition to come out differently from the Court of [1985]." *Casey,* 505 U.S. at 864. We therefore overrule *Ball* and *Aguilar* to the extent those decisions are inconsistent with our current understanding of the Establishment Clause.

. . . .

We do not acknowledge, and we do not hold, that other courts should conclude our more recent cases have, by implication, overruled an earlier precedent. We reaffirm that "[i]f a precedent of this Court has direct application in a case, yet appears to rest on reasons rejected in some other line of decisions, the Court of Appeals should follow the case which directly controls, leaving to this Court the prerogative of overruling its own decisions." *Rodriguez de Quijas v. Shearson/American Express, Inc.,* 490 U.S. 477, 484 (1989). Adherence to this teaching by the District Court and Court of Appeals in this litigation does not insulate a legal principle on which they relied from our review to determine its continued vitality. The trial court acted within its discretion in entertaining the motion with supporting allegations, but it was also correct to recognize that the motion had to be denied unless and until this Court reinterpreted the binding precedent.

. . . .

JUSTICE SOUTER, with whom JUSTICES STEVENS and GINSBURG join, dissenting.

. . . .

Finally, there is the issue of precedent. *Stare decisis* is no barrier in the Court's eyes because it reads *Aguilar* and *Ball* for exaggerated propositions that *Witters v. Washington Dep't of Services for the Blind,* 474 U.S. 481, 488 (1986), and *Zobrest v. Catalina Foothills School District,* 509 U.S. 1, 13 (1993), are supposed to have limited to the point of abandoned doctrine. . . . The Court's dispensation from *stare decisis* is, accordingly, no more convincing that its reading of those cases. . . .

The continuity of the law, indeed, is matched by the persistence of the facts. . . . That is, the facts became once again what they were once before, as everyone including the Members of this Court knew they would be. No predictions have gone awry as to excuse the litigation from the claim of precedent, *see Burnet v. Coronado Oil & Gas Co.,* 285 U.S. 393, 412 (1932) (Brandeis, J., dissenting), let alone excuse the Court from adhering to its own prior decision in this very litigation.

. . . .

JUSTICE GINSBURG, with whom JUSTICES STEVENS, SOUTER, and BREYER join, dissenting.

The Court today finds a way to rehear a legal question decided in respondents' favor in this very case some 12 years ago. *See Aguilar v. Felton,* 473 U.S. 402 (1985). Subsequent decisions, the majority says, have undermined *Aguilar* and justify our immediate reconsideration. This Court's Rules do not countenance the rehearing here granted. For good reason, a proper application of those Rules and the Federal Rules of Civil Procedure would lead us to defer reconsideration of *Aguilar* until we are presented with the issue in another case.

We have a rule on rehearing, Rule 44, but it provides only for petitions filed within 25 days of the entry of the judgment in question. . . . Petitioners have not been so bold (or so candid) as to style their plea as one for rehearing in this Court, and the Court has not taken up the petition at the instance of Justice Stevens, the only still-sitting Member of the *Aguilar* majority.

. . . .

. . . [T]he Court "see[s] no reason to wait for a 'better vehicle.' " There are such vehicles in motion, and the Court does not say otherwise. . . .

Unlike the majority, I find just cause to await the arrival of . . . another case in which our review appropriately may be sought, before deciding whether *Aguilar* should remain the law of the land. . . .

Exercise 17:

What role does judicial precedent play relative to arguments based on text, structure, history, and tradition? Specifically, consider:

(1) Recall that Hamilton sought to assuage concerns (raised by Brutus and others) that the Constitution vested broad power in an unelected federal judiciary by pointing out that judges would be constrained by a body of precedent. Does *Casey* endorse that view? *See* Lee J. Strang & Bryce G. Poole, *The Historical (In)Accuracy of the Brandeis Dichotomy: An Assessment of the Two-Tiered Standard of Stare Decisis for Supreme Court Precedents,* 86 N.C. L. REV. 969 (2008) (arguing that the Supreme Court erroneously adopted the practice of giving precedents interpreting the Constitution less precedential weight than precedents interpreting statutes). Is the view in expressed in *Casey* consistent with the exercise of judicial power?

(2) What are the four different bases *Casey* recognizes as sufficient to justify a departure from precedent? How do they apply? What are appropriate examples of each?

(3) Is the *Casey* formulation of *stare decisis* consistent with the Court's treatment of prior precedent in *Cohens v. Virginia*?

(4) What, if anything, does *Agostini* add to *Casey* with respect to arguments grounded in judicial precedents?

F. Political Question Doctrine

BAKER v. CARR
369 U.S. 186 (1962)

JUSTICE BRENNAN delivered the opinion of the Court.

This civil action was brought under 42 U.S.C. §§ 1983 and 1988 to redress the alleged deprivation of federal constitutional rights. The complaint, alleging that by means of a 1901 statute of Tennessee apportioning the members of the General Assembly among the State's 95 counties, "these plaintiffs and other similarly situated, are denied the equal protection of the laws accorded them by the Fourteenth Amendment to the Constitution of the United States by virtue of the debasement of their votes," was dismissed . . . . The court held it lacked jurisdiction of the subject matter and also that no claim was stated upon which relief could be granted. . . .

The General Assembly of Tennessee consists of the Senate with 33 members and the House of Representatives with 99 members. . . .

. . . Tennessee's standard for allocating legislative representation among her counties is the total number of qualified voters resident in the respective counties, subject only to minor qualifications. Decennial reapportionment in compliance with the [State's] constitutional scheme was effected by the General Assembly each decade from 1871 to 1901. . . . In 1901 the General Assembly abandoned separate enumeration in favor of reliance upon the Federal Census and passed the Apportionment Act here in controversy. In the more than 60 years since that action, all proposals in both Houses of the General Assembly for reapportionment have failed to pass.

Between 1901 and 1961, Tennessee has experienced substantial growth and redistribution of her population. . . . The relative standings of the counties in terms of qualified voters have changed significantly. It is primarily the continued application of the 1901 Apportionment Act to this shifted and enlarged voting population which gives rise to the present controversy.

. . . It is further alleged that "because of the population changes since 1900, and the failure of the Legislature to reapportion itself since 1901," the 1901 statute became "unconstitutional and obsolete." Appellants also argue that, because of the composition of the legislature effected by the 1901 Apportionment Act, redress in the form of a state constitutional amendment to change the entire mechanism for reapportioning, or any other change short of that, is difficult or impossible. . . . They seek a declaration that the 1901 statute is unconstitutional and an injunction restraining the appellees from acting to conduct any further elections under it. . . .

[The Supreme Court construed the District Court's order as dismissing the action due to a lack of subject matter jurisdiction as well as the absence of a justiciable issue because of the political question doctrine. The Court concluded that the case presented a federal question within the subject matter jurisdiction of the District Court. The Supreme Court also concluded that the parties had standing to present the claim.]

IV

Justiciability

In holding that the subject matter of this suit was not justiciable, the District Court relied on *Colegrove v. Green,* 328 U.S. 549 (1946), and subsequent *per curiam* cases. The court stated: "From a review of these decisions there can be no doubt that the federal rule . . . is that the federal courts . . . will not intervene in cases of this type to compel legislative reapportionment." We understand the District Court to have read the cited cases as compelling the conclusion that since the appellants sought to have a legislative apportionment held unconstitutional, their suit presented a "political question" and was therefore nonjusticiable. We hold that this challenge to an apportionment presents no nonjusticiable "political question." The cited cases do not hold the contrary.

Of course the mere fact that the suit seeks protection of a political right does not mean it presents a political question. Such an objection "is little more than a play upon words." *Nixon v. Herndon,* 273 U.S. 536, 540 (1927). Rather, it is argued that apportionment cases, whatever the actual wording of the complaint, can involve no federal constitutional right except one resting on the guaranty of a republican form of government,[30] and that complaints based on that clause have been held to present political questions which are nonjusticiable.

We hold that the claim pleaded here neither rests upon nor implicates the Guaranty Clause and that its justiciability is therefore not foreclosed by our decisions of cases involving that clause. The District Court misinterpreted *Colegrove v. Green* and other decisions of this Court on which it relied. Appellants' claim that they are being denied equal protection is justiciable, and if "discrimination is sufficiently shown, the right to relief under the equal protection clause is not diminished by the fact that the discrimination relates to political rights." *Snowden v. Hughes,* 321 U.S. 1, 11 (1944). To show why we reject the argument based on the Guaranty Clause, we must examine the authorities under it. But because there appears to be some uncertainty as to why those cases did present political questions, and specifically as to whether this apportionment case is like those cases, we deem it necessary first to consider the contours of the "political question" doctrine.

. . . [I]n the Guaranty Clause cases and in the other "political question" cases, it is the relationship between the judiciary and the coordinate branches of the Federal Government, and not the federal judiciary's relationship to the States, which gives rise to the "political question."

We have said that "In determining whether a question falls within [the political question] category, the appropriateness under our system of government of attributing finality to the action of the political departments and also the lack of satisfactory criteria for a judicial determination are dominant considerations." *Coleman v. Miller,* 307 U.S. 433, 454–55 (1939). The nonjusticiability of a political question is primarily a function of the separation of powers. Much confusion results from the capacity of the "political question" label to obscure the need for case-by-case inquiry. Deciding whether a matter has in any measure been committed by

---

[30] "The United States shall guarantee to every State in this Union a Republican Form of Government, and shall protect each of them against Invasion; and on Application of the Legislature, or of the Executive (when the Legislature cannot be convened) against domestic Violence." U.S. Const., Art. IV, § 4.

the Constitution to another branch of government, or whether the action of that branch exceeds whatever authority has been committed, is itself a delicate exercise in constitutional interpretation, and is a responsibility of this Court as ultimate interpreter of the Constitution. To demonstrate this requires no less than to analyze representative cases and to infer from them the analytical threads that make up the political question doctrine. We shall then show that none of those threads catches this case.

Foreign relations: There are sweeping statements to the effect that all questions touching foreign relations are political questions. Not only does resolution of such issues frequently turn on standards that defy judicial application, or involve the exercise of a discretion demonstrably committed to the executive or legislature; but many such questions uniquely demand single-voiced statement of the Government's views. Yet it is with error to suppose that every case or controversy which touches foreign relations lies beyond judicial cognizance. Our cases in this field seem invariably to show a discriminating analysis of the particular question posed, in terms of the history of its management by the political branches, of its susceptibility to judicial handling in the light of its nature and posture in the specific case, and of the possible consequences of judicial action. For example, though a court will not ordinarily inquire whether a treaty has been terminated, since on that question "governmental action . . . must be regarded as of controlling importance," if there has been no conclusive "government action" then a court can construe a treaty and may find it provides the answer. Though a court will not undertake to construe a treaty in a manner inconsistent with a subsequent federal statute, no similar hesitancy obtains if the asserted clash is with state law.

While recognition of foreign governments so strongly defies judicial treatment that without executive recognition a foreign state has been called "a republic of whose existence we know nothing," and the judiciary ordinarily follows the executive as to which nation has sovereignty over disputed territory, once sovereignty over an area is politically determined and declared, courts may examine the resulting status and decide independently whether a statute applies to that area. Similarly, recognition of belligerency abroad is an executive responsibility, but if the executive proclamations fall short of an explicit answer, a court may construe them seeking, for example, to determine whether the situation is such that statutes designed to assure American neutrality have become operative. *The Three Friends*, 166 U.S. 1, 63, 66 (1897). Still again, though it is the executive that determines a person's status as representative of a foreign government, *Ex parte Hitz*, 111 U.S. 766 (1884), the executive's statements will be construed where necessary to determine the court's jurisdiction, *In re Baiz*, 135 U.S. 403 (1890). Similar judicial action in the absence of a recognizably authoritative executive declaration occurs in cases involving the immunity from seizure of vessels owned by friendly foreign governments.

Dates of duration of hostilities: Though it has been stated broadly that "the power which declared the necessity is the power to declare its cessation, and what the cessation requires," *Commercial Trust Co. v. Miller*, 262 U.S. 51, 57 (1923), here too analysis reveals isolable reasons for the presence of political questions, underlying this Court's refusal to review the political departments' determination of when or whether a war has ended. Dominant is the need for finality in the political determination, for emergency's nature demands "A prompt and unhesitating obedience." *Martin v. Mott*, 25 U.S. 19, 30 (1827) (calling up of militia). Moreover, "the cessation of hostilities does not necessarily end the war power. It was stated in *Hamilton v. Kentucky Distilleries & W. Co.*, 251 U.S. 146,

161 (1919), that the war power includes the power 'to remedy the evils which have arisen from its rise and progress' and continues during that emergency. *Stewart v. Kahn*, 78 U.S. 493, 507 (1871)." *Fleming v. Mohawk Wrecking Co.*, 331 U.S. 111, 116 (1947). But deference rests on reason, not habit. The question in a particular case may not seriously implicate considerations of finality — *e.g.*, a public program of importance (rent control) yet not central to the emergency effort. Further, clearly definable criteria for decision may be available. In such case the political question barrier falls away: "[A] Court is not at liberty to shut its eyes to an obvious mistake, when the validity of the law depends on the truth of what is declared. . . . [It can] inquire whether the exigency still existed upon which the continued operation of the law depended." *Chastleton Corp. v. Sinclair*, 264 U.S. 543, 547–48 (1924). On the other hand, even in private litigation which directly implicates no feature of separation of powers, lack of judicially discoverable standards and the drive for even-handed application may impel reference to the political departments' determination of dates of hostilities' beginning and ending. *The Protector*, 79 U.S. 700 (1871).

Validity of enactments: In *Coleman v. Miller*, this Court held that the question of how long a proposed amendment to the Federal Constitution remained open to ratification, and what effect a prior rejection had on a subsequent ratification, were committed to congressional resolution and involved criteria of decision that necessarily escaped the judicial grasp. Similar considerations apply to the enacting process: "The respect due to coequal and independent departments," and the need for finality and certainty about the status of a statute contribute to judicial reluctance to inquire whether, as passed, it complied with all requisite formalities. *Field v. Clark*, 143 U.S. 649, 672, 676–77 (1892). But it is not true that courts will never delve into a legislature's records upon such a quest: If the enrolled statute lacks an effective date, a court will not hesitate to seek it in the legislative journals in order to preserve the enactment. *Gardner v. Collector of Customs*, 73 U.S. 499 (1867). The political question doctrine, a tool for maintenance of governmental order, will not be so applied as to promote only disorder.

The status of Indian Tribes: This Court's deference to the political departments in determining whether Indians are recognized as a tribe, while it reflects familiar attributes of political questions, *United States v. Holliday*, 70 U.S. 407, 419 (1865), also has a unique element in that "the relation of the Indians to the United States is marked by peculiar and cardinal distinctions which exist no where else. . . . [The Indians are] domestic dependent nations . . . in a state of pupilage. Their relation to the United States resembles that of a ward to his guardian." *The Cherokee Nation v. Georgia*, 30 U.S. 1, 16, 17 (1831). Yet, here too, there is no blanket rule. While " 'It is for [Congress] . . ., and not for the courts, to determine when the true interests of the Indian require his release from [the] condition of tutelage' . . ., it is not meant by this that Congress may bring a community or body of people within the range of this power by arbitrarily calling them an Indian tribe . . . ." *United States v. Sandoval*, 231 U.S. 28, 46 (1913). Able to discern what is "distinctly Indian," *id.*, the courts will strike down any heedless extension of that label. They will not stand impotent before an obvious instance of a manifestly unauthorized exercise of power.

It is apparent that several formulations which vary slightly according to the settings in which the questions arise may describe a political question, although each has one or more elements which identify it as essentially a function of the separation of powers. Prominent on the surface of any case held to involve a political question is found a textually demonstrable constitutional commitment of the issue to a coordinate political department; or a lack of judicially discoverable and manageable standards for resolving it; or the impossibility of deciding without an initial policy determination of a kind clearly for nonjudicial discretion; or the impossibility of a court's undertaking independent resolution without expressing lack of respect due coordinate branches of government; or an unusual need for unquestioning adherence to a political decision already made; or the potentiality of embarrassment from multifarious pronouncements by various departments on one question.

Unless one of these formulations is inextricable from the case at bar, there should be no dismissal for nonjusticiability on the ground of a political question's presence. The doctrine of which we treat is one of "political questions," not one of "political cases." The courts cannot reject as "no law suit" a bona fide controversy as to whether some action denominated "political" exceeds constitutional authority. The cases we have reviewed show the necessity for discriminating inquiry into the precise facts and posture of the particular case, and the impossibility of resolution by any semantic cataloguing.

But it is argued that this case shares the characteristics of decisions that constitute a category not yet considered, cases concerning the Constitution's guaranty, in Art. IV, § 4, of a republican form of government. A conclusion as to whether the case at bar does present a political question cannot be confidently reached until we have considered those cases with special care. We shall discover that Guaranty Clause claims involve those elements which define a "political question," and for that reason and no other, they are nonjusticiable. In particular, we shall discover that the nonjusticiability of such claims has nothing to do with their touching upon matters of state governmental organization.

Republican form of government: Luther v. Borden, 48 U.S. 1 (1849), though in form simply an action for damages for trespass was, as Daniel Webster said in opening the argument for the defense, "an unusual case." The defendants, admitting it an otherwise tortious breaking and entering, sought to justify their action on the ground that they were agents of the established lawful government of Rhode Island, which State was then under martial law to defend itself from active insurrection; that the plaintiff was engaged in that insurrection; and that they entered under orders to arrest the plaintiff. The case arose "out of the unfortunate political differences which agitated the people of Rhode Island in 1841 and 1842," *id.* at 34, and which had resulted in a situation wherein two groups laid competing claims to recognition as the lawful government. The plaintiff's right to recover depended upon which of the two groups was entitled to such recognition . . . .

Chief Justice Taney's opinion for the Court reasoned as follows: (1) If a court were to hold the defendants' acts unjustified because the charter government had no legal existence during the period in question, it would follow that all of that government's actions — laws enacted, taxes collected, salaries paid, accounts settled, sentences passed — were of no effect; and that "the officers who carried their decisions into operation [were] answerable as trespassers, if not in some cases as criminals." *Id.* at 39. There was, of course, no room for application of any doctrine of *de facto* status to uphold prior acts of an officer not authorized *de jure,* for such would have defeated the plaintiff's very action. A decision for the plaintiff would inevitably have produced some significant measure of chaos, a consequence to be avoided if it could be done without abnegation of the judicial duty to uphold the Constitution.

(2) No state court had recognized as a judicial responsibility settlement of the issue of the locus of state governmental authority. Indeed, the courts of Rhode Island had in several cases held that "it rested with the political power to decide

whether the charter government had been displaced or not," and that that department had acknowledged no change.

(3) Since "[t]he question relates, altogether, to the constitution and laws of [the] . . . State," the courts of the United States had to follow the state courts' decisions unless there was a federal constitutional ground for overturning them. *Id.* at 39, 40.

(4) No provision of the Constitution could be or had been invoked for this purpose except Art. IV, § 4, the Guaranty Clause. Having already noted the absence of standards whereby the choice between governments could be made by a court acting independently, Chief Justice Taney now found further textual and practical reasons for concluding that, if any department of the United States was empowered by the Guaranty Clause to resolve the issue it was not the judiciary:

> Under this article of the Constitution it rests with Congress to decide what government is the established one in a State. For as the United States guarantee to each State a republican government, Congress must necessarily decide what government is established in the State before it can determine whether it is republican or not. And when the senators and representatives of a State are admitted into the councils of the Union, the authority of the government under which they are appointed, as well as its republican character, is recognized by the proper constitutional authority. And its decision is binding on every other department of the government, and could not be questioned in a judicial tribunal. It is true that the contest in this case did not last long enough to bring the matter to this issue; and . . . Congress was not called upon to decide the controversy. Yet the right to decide is placed here and not in the courts.
>
> So, too, as relates to the clause in the above-mentioned article of the Constitution, providing for cases of domestic violence. It rested with Congress, too, to determine upon the means proper to be adopted to fulfill this guarantee. . . . [B]y the act of February 28, 1795, [Congress] provided, that, "in case of an insurrection in any State against the government thereof, it shall be lawful for the President of the United States, on application of the legislature of such State or of the executive (when the legislature cannot be convened), to call forth such number of the militia of any other State or States, as may be applied for, as he may judge sufficient to suppress such insurrection."
>
> By this act, the power of deciding whether the exigency had arisen upon which the government of the United States is bound to interfere, is given to the President. . . .
>
> After the President has acted and called out the militia, is a Circuit Court of the United States authorized to inquire whether his decision was right? . . . If the judicial power extends so far, the guarantee contained in the Constitution of the United States is a guarantee of anarchy, and not of order. . . .
>
> It is true that in this case the militia were not called out by the President. But upon application of the governor under the charter government, the President recognized him as the executive power of the State, and took measures to call out the militia to support his authority if it should be found necessary for the general government to interfere . . . . [C]ertainly no court of the United States, with a knowledge of this decision, would have been justified in recognizing the opposing party as the lawful government . . . . In the case of foreign nations, the government acknowledged by the President is always recognized in the courts of justice. . . .

48 U.S. at 42–44.

Clearly, several factors were thought by the Court in *Luther* to make the question there "political": the commitment to the other branches of the decision as to which is the lawful state government; the unambiguous action by the President, in recognizing the charter government as the lawful authority; the need for finality in the executive's decision; and the lack of criteria by which a court could determine which form of government was republican.

But the only significance that *Luther* could have for our immediate purposes is in its holding that the Guaranty Clause is not a repository of judicially manageable standards which a court could utilize independently in order to identify a State's lawful government. The Court has since refused to resort to the Guaranty Clause — which alone had been invoked for the purpose — as the source of a constitutional standard for invalidating state action. . . .

Just as the Court has consistently held that a challenge to state action based on the Guaranty Clause presents no justiciable question so has it held, and for the same reasons, that challenges to congressional action on the ground of inconsistency with that clause present no justiciable question. . . .

. . . .

We come, finally, to the ultimate inquiry whether our precedents as to what constitutes a nonjusticiable "political question" bring the case before us under the umbrella of that doctrine. A natural beginning is to note whether any of the common characteristics which we have been able to identify and label descriptively are present. We find none: The question here is the consistency of state action with the Federal Constitution. We have no question decided, or to be decided, by a political branch of government coequal with this Court. Nor do we risk embarrassment of our government abroad, or grave disturbance at home if we take issue with Tennessee as to the constitutionality of her action here challenged. Nor need the appellants, in order to succeed in this action, ask the Court to enter upon policy determinations for which judicially manageable standards are lacking. Judicial standards under the Equal Protection Clause are well developed and familiar, and it has been open to courts since the enactment of the Fourteenth Amendment to determine, if on the particular facts they must, that a discrimination reflects *no* policy, but simply arbitrary and capricious action.

This case does, in one sense, involve the allocation of political power within a State, and the appellants might conceivably have added a claim under the Guaranty Clause. Of course, as we have seen, any reliance on that clause would be futile. But because any reliance on the Guaranty Clause could not have succeeded it does not follow that appellants may not be heard on the equal protection claim which in fact they tender. True, it must be clear that the Fourteenth Amendment claim is not so enmeshed with those political question elements which render Guaranty Clause claims nonjusticiable as actually to present a political question itself. But we have found that not to be the case here.

. . . .

We conclude then that the nonjusticiablity of claims resting on the Guaranty Clause which arises from their embodiment of questions that were thought "political," can have no bearing upon the justiciability of the equal protection claim presented in this case. Finally, we emphasize that it is the involvement in Guaranty Clause claims of the elements thought to define "political questions," and no other feature, which could render them nonjusticiable. . . .

. . . .

. . . [A]s has been established, the equal protection claim tendered in this case does not require decision of any political question, and . . . the presence of a matter affecting state government does not render the case nonjusticiable . . . .

. . . .

The judgment of the District Court is reversed and the cause is remanded for further proceedings consistent with this opinion

JUSTICE WHITTAKER did not participate in the decision of this case.

JUSTICE DOUGLAS, concurring.

While I join the opinion of the Court and, like the court, do not reach the merits, a word of explanation is necessary. I put to one side the problems of "political" questions involving the distribution of power between this Court, the Congress, and the Chief Executive. We have here a phase of the recurring problem of the relation of the federal courts to state agencies. More particularly, the question is the extent to which a State may weight one person's vote more heavily than it does another's.

So far as voting rights are concerned, there are large gaps in the Constitution. Yet the right to vote is inherent in the republican form of government envisaged by Article IV, Section 4 of the Constitution. . . .

. . . .

The traditional test under the Equal Protection Clause has been whether a State has made "an invidious discrimination," as it does when it selects "a particular race or nationality for oppressive treatment." *See Skinner v. Oklahoma*, 316 U.S. 535, 541 (1942). Universal equality is not the test; there is room for weighting. . . .

. . . We are told that a single vote in Moore County, Tennessee, is worth 19 votes in Hamilton County, that one vote in Stewart or in Chester County is worth nearly eight times a single vote in Shelby or Knox County. The opportunity to prove that an "invidious discrimination" exists should therefore be given the appellants.

. . . .

With the exceptions of *Colegrove v. Green*, 328 U.S. 549 (1946); *MacDougall v. Green*, 335 U.S. 281 (1948); *South v. Peters*, 339 U.S. 276 (1950), and the decisions they spawned, the Court has never thought that the protection of voting rights was beyond judicial cognizance. Today's treatment of those cases removes the only impediment to judicial cognizance of the claims presented in the present complaint.

The justiciability of the present claims being established, any relief accorded can be fashioned in light of well-known principles of equity.

JUSTICE CLARK, concurring.

. . . The Court holds that the appellants have alleged a cause of action. However, it refuses to award relief here — although the facts are undisputed — and fails to give the District Court any guidance whatever. . . . I believe it can be shown that this case is distinguishable from earlier cases dealing with the distribution of political power by a State, that a patent violation of the Equal Protection Clause of the United States Constitution has been shown, and that an appropriate remedy may be formulated.

. . . .

Although I find the Tennessee apportionment statute offends the Equal Protection Clause, I would not consider intervention by this Court into so delicate a field if there were any other relief available to the people of Tennessee. . . . It is said that there is recourse in Congress and perhaps that may be, but from a practical standpoint this is without substance. To date Congress has never undertaken such a task in any State. We therefore must conclude that the people of Tennessee are stymied and without judicial intervention will be saddled with the present discrimination in the affairs of their state government.

. . . .

As John Rutledge (later Chief Justice) said 175 years ago in the course of the Constitutional Convention, a chief function of the Court is to secure the national rights. Its decision today supports the proposition for which our forebears [sic] fought and many died, namely, that to be fully conformable to the principle of right, the form of government must be representative. That is the keystone upon which our government was founded and lacking which no republic can survive. . . .

JUSTICE STEWART, concurring.

[Omitted.]

JUSTICE FRANKFURTER, whom JUSTICE HARLAN joins, dissenting.

The Court today reverses a uniform course of decision established by a dozen cases, including one by which the very claim now sustained was unanimously rejected only five years ago. The impressive body of rulings thus cast aside reflected the equally uniform course of our political history regarding the relationship between population and legislative representation — a wholly different matter from denial of the franchise to individuals because of race, color, religion or sex. Such a massive repudiation of the experience of our whole past in asserting destructively novel judicial power demands a detailed analysis of the role of this Court in our constitutional scheme. . . . The Court's authority — possessed of neither the purse nor the sword — ultimately rests on sustained public confidence in its moral sanction. Such feeling must be nourished by the Court's complete detachment, in fact and appearance, from political entanglements and by abstention from injecting itself into the clash of political forces in political settlements.

A hypothetical claim resting on abstract assumptions is now for the first time made the basis for affording illusory relief for a particular evil even though it foreshadows deeper and more pervasive difficulties in consequence. The claim is hypothetical and the assumptions are abstract because the Court does not vouchsafe the lower courts — state and federal — guidelines for formulating specific, definite, wholly unprecedented remedies for the inevitable litigations that today's umbrageous disposition is bound to stimulate in connection with politically motivated reapportionments in so many States. . . . One of the Court's supporting opinions, as elucidated by commentary, unwittingly affords a disheartening preview of the mathematical quagmire (apart from the divers judicially inappropriate and elusive determinants) into which this Court today catapults the lower courts of the country without so much as adumbrating the basis for a legal calculus as a means of extrication. Even assuming the indispensable intellectual disinterestedness on the part of judges in such matters, they do not have accepted legal standards or criteria or even reliable analogies to draw upon for making judicial judgments. . . .

. . . Considering the gross inequality among legislative electoral units within almost every State, the Court naturally shrinks from asserting that in districting at least substantial equality is a constitutional requirement enforceable by courts. Room continues to be allowed for weighting. This of course implies that geography, economics, urban-rural conflict, and all the other non-legal factors which have throughout our history entered into political districting are to some extent not to be ruled out in the undefined vista now opened up by review in the federal courts of state reapportionments. . . .

. . . In this situation, as in others of like nature, appeal for relief does not belong here. Appeal must be to an informed, civically militant electorate. In a democratic society like ours, relief must come through an aroused popular conscience that sears the conscience of the people's representatives. . . .

. . . .

I

In sustaining appellants' claim, based on the Fourteenth Amendment, that the District Court may entertain this suit, this Court's uniform course of decision over the years is overruled or disregarded. Explicitly it begins with *Colgrove v. Green*, decided in 1946, but its roots run deep in the Court's historic adjudicatory process.

Colegrove held that a federal court should not entertain an action for declaratory and injunctive relief to adjudicate the constitutionality, under the Equal Protection Clause and other federal constitutional and statutory provisions, of a state statute establishing the respective districts for the State's election of Representatives to the Congress. Two opinions were written by the four Justices who composed the majority of the seven sitting members of the Court. Both opinions joining in the result in *Colegrove v. Green* agreed that considerations were controlling which dictated denial of jurisdiction though not in the strict sense of want of power. While the two opinions show a divergence of view regarding some of these considerations, there are important points of concurrence. Both opinions demonstrate a predominant concern, first, with avoiding federal judicial involvement in matters traditionally left to legislative policy making; second, with respect to the difficulty — in view of the nature of the problems of apportionment and its history in this country — of drawing on or devising judicial standards for judgment, as opposed to legislative determinations . . .; and, third, with problems of finding appropriate modes of relief — particularly, the problem of resolving the essentially political issue of the relative merits of at-large elections and elections held in districts of unequal population.

The broad applicability of these considerations — summarized in the loose shorthand phrase, "political question" — in cases involving a State's apportionment of voting power among its numerous localities has led the Court, since 1946, to recognize their controlling effect in a variety of situations. (In all these cases decision was by a full Court.) . . . In *Colegrove v. Barrett*, 330 U.S. 804 (1947), litigants brought suit in a Federal District Court challenging as offensive to the Equal Protection Clause Illinois' state legislative-apportionment laws. They pointed to state constitutional provisions requiring decennial reapportionment and allocation of seats in proportion to population, alleged a failure to reapportion for more than forty-five years — during which time extensive population shifts had rendered the legislative districts grossly unequal — and sought declaratory and injunctive relief with respect to all elections to be held thereafter. After the complaint was dismissed by the District Court, this Court dismissed an appeal for want of a substantial federal question. A similar District Court decision was affirmed here in *Radford v. Gary*, 352 U.S. 991 (1957). *And cf. Remmey v. Smith*, 342 U.S. 916 (1952). In *Tedesco v. Board of Supervisors*, 339 U.S. 940 (1950), the Court declined to hear, for want of a substantial federal question, the claim that the division of a municipality into voting districts of unequal populations for the selection for councilmen fell afoul of the Fourteenth Amendment, and in *Cox v. Peters*, 342 U.S. 936, *reh'g denied*, 343 U.S. 921 (1952), it found no substantial federal question raised by a state court's dismissal of a claim for damages for "devaluation" of plaintiff's vote by application of Georgia's county-unit system in a primary election . . . . And in *South v. Peters*, 339 U.S. 276 (1950), another suit attacking Georgia's county-unit law, it affirmed a District Court dismissal, saying

Federal courts consistently refuse to exercise their equity powers in cases posing political issues arising from a state's geographical distribution of electoral strength among its political subdivisions.

Id. at 277.

. . . [Counsel's suggestion of bases to distinguish certain precedents fall short.] Suffice it that they do not serve to distinguish *Colegrove v. Barrett* which is on all fours with the present case, or to distinguish *Kidd v. McCanless*, 352 U.S. 920 (1956), in which the full Court without dissent, only five years ago, dismissed on authority of *Colegrove v. Green* and *Anderson v. Jordan*, 343 U.S. 912 (1952), an appeal from the Supreme Court of Tennessee in which a precisely similar attack was made upon the very statute now challenged. . . .

II

The *Colegrove* doctrine, in the form in which repeated decisions have settled it, was not an innovation. It represents long judicial thought and experience. From its earliest opinions this Court has consistently recognized a class of controversies which do not lend themselves to judicial standards and judicial remedies. To classify the various instances as "political questions" is rather a form of stating this conclusion than revealing of analysis. Some of the cases so labeled have no relevance here. But from others emerge unifying considerations that are compelling.

1. The cases concerning war or foreign affairs, for example, are usually explained by the necessity of the country's speaking with one voice in such matters. While this concern alone undoubtedly accounts for many of the decisions, others do not fit the pattern. It would hardly embarrass the conduct of war were this Court to determine, in connection with private transactions between litigants, the date upon which war is to be deemed terminated. But the Court has refused to do so. . . . And even for the purpose of determining the extent of congressional regulatory power over the tribes and dependent communities of Indians, it is ordinarily for Congress, not the Court, to determine whether or not a particular Indian group retains the characteristics constitutionally requisite to confer the power. A controlling factor in such cases is that, decision respecting these kinds of complex matters of policy being traditionally committed not to courts but to the political agencies of government for determination by criteria of political expediency, there exists no standard ascertainable by settled judicial experience or process by reference to which a political decision affecting the question at issue between the parties can be judged. Where the question arises in the course of a litigation involving primarily the adjudication of other issues between the litigants, the Court accepts as a basis for adjudication the political departments' decision of it. But where its determination is the sole function to be served by the exercise of the judicial power, the Court will not entertain the action. The dominant consideration is "the lack of satisfactory criteria for a judicial determination. . . ." *Coleman v. Miller*, 307 U.S. 433, 454–55 (1939).

. . . .

2. The Court has been particularly unwilling to intervene in matters concerning the structure and organization of the political institutions of the States. The abstention from judicial entry into such areas has been greater even than that which marks the Court's ordinary approach to issues of state power challenged under broad federal guarantees. . . .

Where, however, state law has made particular federal questions determinative of relations within the structure of state government, not in challenge to it, the Court has resolved such narrow, legally defined questions in proper proceedings. In such instances there is no conflict between state policy and the exercise of federal judicial power. . . .

3. The cases involving Negro disfranchisement are no exception to the principle of avoiding federal judicial intervention into matters of state government in the absence of an explicit and clear constitutional imperative. For here the controlling command of Supreme Law is plain and unequivocal. An end of discrimination against the Negro was the compelling motive of the Civil War Amendments. The Fifteenth expresses this in terms, and it is no less true of the Equal Protection Clause of the Fourteenth. Thus the Court, in cases involving discrimination against the Negro's right to vote, has recognized not only the action at law for damages, but, in appropriate circumstances, the extraordinary remedy of declaratory or injunctive relief. *Schnell v. Davis,* 336 U.S. 933 (1949); *Terry v. Adams,* 345 U.S. 461 (1953). . . .

4. The Court has refused to exercise its jurisdiction to pass on "abstract questions of political power, of sovereignty, of government." *Massachusetts v. Mellon,* 262 U.S. 447, 485 (1923). The "political question" doctrine, in this aspect, reflects the policies underlying the requirement of "standing": that the litigant who would challenge official action must claim infringement of an interest particular and personal to himself, as distinguished from a cause of dissatisfaction with the general frame and functioning of government — a complaint that the political institutions are awry. . . . The crux of the matter is that courts are not fit instruments of decision where what is essentially at stake is the composition of those large contests of policy traditionally fought out in non-judicial forums, by which governments and the actions of governments are made and unmade. . . .

5. The influence of these converging considerations — the caution not to undertake decision where standards meet for judicial judgment are lacking, the reluctance to interfere with matters of state government in the absence of an unquestionable and effectively enforceable mandate, the unwillingness to make courts arbitrators of the broad issues of political organization historically committed to other institutions and for whose adjustment the judicial process is ill-adapted — has been decisive of the settled line of cases, reaching back more than a century, which holds that Art. IV, § 4, of the Constitution, guaranteeing to the States "a Republican Form of Government," is not enforceable through the courts.

. . . .

III

The present case involves all of the elements that have made the Guarantee Clause cases non-justiciable. It is, in effect, a Guarantee Clause claim masquerading under a different label. But it cannot make the case more fit for judicial action that appellants invoke the Fourteenth Amendment rather than Art. IV, § 4, where, in fact, the gist of their complaint is the same — unless it can be found that the Fourteenth Amendment speaks with greater particularity to their situation. . . . When what was essentially a Guarantee Clause claim was sought to be laid, as well, under the Equal Protection Clause in *Pacific States Telephone & Telegraph Co. v. Oregon,* 223 U.S. 118 (1912), the Court had no difficulty in "dispelling any mere confusion resulting from forms of expression and considering the substance of things . . . ." *Id.* at 140.

Here appellants attack "the State as a State," precisely as it was perceived to be attacked in the *Pacific States* case, *id.* at 150. Their complaint is that the basis of representation of the Tennessee Legislature hurts them. They assert that "a minority now rules in Tennessee," that the apportionment statute results in a "distortion of the constitutional system," that the General Assembly is no longer "a body representative of the people of the State of Tennessee," all "contrary to the basic principle of representative government. . . ." Accepting appellants' own formulation of the issue, one can know this handsaw from a hawk. Such a claim would be non-justiciable not merely under Art. IV, § 4, but under any clause of the Constitution, by virtue of the very fact that a federal court is not a forum for political debate. *Massachusetts v. Mellon,* 262 U.S. 447 (1923).

But appellants, of course, do not rest on this claim *simpliciter.* In invoking the Equal Protection Clause, they assert that the distortion of representative government complained of is produced by systematic discrimination against them, by way of "a debasement of their votes . . . ." Does this characterization, with due regard for the facts from which it is derived, add anything to appellants' case?

At first blush, this charge of discrimination based on legislative underrepresentation is given the appearance of a more private, less impersonal claim, than the assertion that the frame of government is askew. Appellants appear as representatives of a class that is prejudiced as a class, in contradistinction to the polity in its entirety. However, the discrimination relied on is the deprivation of what appellants conceive to be their proportionate share of political influence. This, of course, is the practical effect of any allocation of power within the institutions of government. Hardly any distribution of political authority that could be assailed as rendering government nonrepublican would fail similarly to operate to the prejudice of some groups, and to the advantage of others, within the body politic. It would be ingenuous not to see, or consciously blind to deny, that the real battle over the initiative and referendum, or over a delegation of power to local rather than state-wide authority, is the battle between forces whose influence is disparate among the various organs of government to whom power may be given. No shift of power but works a corresponding shift in political influence among the groups composing a society.

What, then, is the question of legislative apportionment? Appellants invoke the right to vote and to have their votes counted. But they are permitted to vote and their votes are counted. They go to the polls, they cast their ballots, they send their representatives to the state councils. Their complaint is simply that the representatives are not sufficiently numerous or powerful — in short, that Tennessee has adopted a basis of representation with which they are dissatisfied. Talk of "debasement" or "dilution" is circular talk. One cannot speak of "debasement" or "dilution" of the value of a vote until there is first defined a standard of reference as to what a vote should be worth. What is actually asked of the Court in this case is to choose among competing bases of representation — ultimately, really, among competing theories of political philosophy — in order to establish an appropriate frame of government for the State of Tennessee and thereby for all the States of the Union.

In such a matter, abstract analogies which ignore the facts of history deal in unrealities; they betray reason. This is not a case in which a State has, through a device however oblique and sophisticated, denied Negroes or Jews or redheaded persons a vote, or given them only a third or a sixth of a vote. That was *Gomillion v. Lightfoot,* 364 U.S. 339 (1960). What Tennessee illustrates is an old and still widespread method of representation — representation by local geographical division, only in part respective of population . . . .

. . . .

The notion that representation proportioned to the geographic spread of population is so universally accepted as a necessary element of equality between man and man that it must be taken to be the standard of a political equality preserved by the Fourteenth Amendment — that it is, in appellants' words "the basic principle of representative government" — is, to put it bluntly, not true. However generally desirable and however desired by some among the great political thinkers and framers of our government, it has never been generally practiced, today or in the past. It was not the English system, it was not the colonial system, it was not the system chosen for the national government by the Constitution, it was not the system exclusively or even predominantly practiced by the States at the time of adoption of the Fourteenth Amendment, it is not predominantly practiced by the States today. . . .

. . . .

. . . Today, only a dozen state constitutions provide for periodic legislative reapportionment of both houses by a substantially unqualified application of the population standard, and only about a dozen more prescribe such reapportionment for even a single chamber. "Specific provision for county representation in at least one house of the state legislature has been increasingly adopted since the end of the 19th century . . . ."

. . . .

. . . A survey made in 1955, in sum, reveals that less than thirty percent of the population inhabit districts sufficient to elect a House majority in thirteen States and a Senate majority in nineteen States. These figures show more than individual variations from a generally accepted standard of electoral equality. They show that there is not — as there has never been — a standard by which the place of equality as a factor in apportionment can be measured.

. . . The practical significance of apportionment is that the next election results may differ because of it. Apportionment battles are overwhelmingly party or intra-party contests. It will add a virulent source of friction and tension in federal-state relations to embroil the federal judiciary in them.

. . . .

JUSTICE HARLAN, whom MR. JUSTICE FRANKFURTER joins, dissenting.

The dissenting opinion of Justice Frankfurter, in which I join, demonstrates the abrupt departure the majority makes from judicial history by putting the federal courts into an area of state concerns — an area which, in this instance, the Tennessee state courts themselves have refused to enter.

It does not detract from his opinion to say that the panorama of judicial history it unfolds, though evincing a steadfast underlying principle of keeping the federal courts out of these domains, has a tendency, because of variants in expression, to becloud analysis in a given case. With due respect to the majority, I think that has happened here.

Once one cuts through the thicket of discussion devoted to "jurisdiction," "standing," "justiciability," and "political question," there emerges a straightforward issue which, in my view, is determinative of this case. . . . [I]n my opinion, appellants' allegations, accepting all of them as true, do not, parsed down or as a whole, show an infringement by Tennessee of any rights assured by the Fourteenth Amendment. Accordingly, I believe the complaint should have been dismissed for "failure to state a claim upon which relief can be granted." . . .

. . . The issue here relates not to a method of state electoral apportionment by which seats in the *federal* House of Representatives are allocated, but solely to the right of a State to fix the basis of representation in its *own* legislature. Until it is first decided to what extent that right is limited by the Federal Constitution . . . we need not reach the [other] issues . . . .

Exercise 18:

Consider the following questions in connection with *Baker v. Carr:*

(1) How, if at all, does the "political question" doctrine articulated in this case differ from the concerns addressed in *Marbury v. Madison?*

(2) How, if at all, is the "political question" doctrine (either as formulated in this case or as in *Marbury*) consistent with the view that the judiciary has an obligation to address any matter within its jurisdiction, as stated in *Cohens v. Virginia?*

(3) Identify seven examples of matters that the Supreme Court has held are "political questions."

(4) Identify the six factors that distinguish "political questions" from matters appropriate for judicial resolution.

(5) As a result of *Baker v. Carr* and its progeny, every ten years every State must re-draw districts not only for members of the U.S. House of Representatives but also for members of each house of the state legislature, as well as many districts for town or city council, and many other offices. The new districts must be drawn with a high degree of mathematical precision in terms of equal numbers of people. Because such decisions have a tendency to benefit one political party at the expense of others, the drawing of districts is frequently challenged in court. There are now numerous such cases filed every ten years.

(a) Are these decisions appropriate for the judiciary?

(b) If the *Baker v. Carr* majority could have foreseen the volume of litigation regarding reapportionment, would it have resolved the case differently?

(c) Is there any alternative basis on which the Supreme Court could have required Tennessee to reapportion its legislature without opening the door to potentially having to approve every state and local district drawn every ten years?

(d) Assuming that Tennessee would not voluntarily reapportion its legislature to reflect changes in population, does the Constitution (as of 1962) provide a basis for one of the other branches of the federal government other than the judiciary to require Tennessee to do so? If so, does that indicate that the matter was constitutionally committed to another branch of government?

(6) In 1901, Tennessee determined the number of state legislators that would be allocated to each of its different counties. Although the relative population of the counties changed by 1960, the State declined to change the apportionment of legislators. Does the federal Constitution provide any textual support for the position of the State? Does a historical analysis of the federal Constitution provide any support for the position of the State?

(7) What are the two reasons articulated by the dissent in support of avoiding consideration of the merits in *Baker v. Carr?*

(8) Does the Court in *Baker v. Carr* approach its precedents consistently with the views expressed in *Casey?* Even if the Court did not explicitly overrule any cases in *Baker v. Carr,* does the subsequent development of routine judicial involvement in reapportionment disputes suggest that there are more than the two examples of departure from prior precedent identified in *Casey?* If so, how does that change the weight that should be accorded to *stare decisis?*

ADJUDICATION BY NON-ARTICLE III TRIBUNALS

In *Northern Pipeline Construction Co. v. Marathon Pipe Line Co.*, 458 U.S. 50 (1982), the Court held that "Congress may not vest in a non-Article III court the power to adjudicate, render final judgment, and issue binding orders in a traditional contract action arising under state law, without consent of the litigants, and subject only to ordinary appellate review." *Thomas v. Union Carbide Agricultural Products Co.*, 473 U.S. 568, 584 (1985). The consequence of that ruling was to invalidate the federal bankruptcy courts as structured at that time.

In *Thomas*, however, the Court ruled that an arbitration scheme established under the Federal Insecticide, Fungicide, and Rodenticide Act did "not contravene Article III and, more generally, held that 'Congress, acting for a valid legislative purpose pursuant to its constitutional powers under Article I, may create a seemingly "private" right that is so closely integrated into a public regulatory scheme as to be a matter appropriate for agency resolution with limited involvement by the Article III judiciary.'" *Id.* at 593.

The Court confronted the tension between the two cases in *CFTC v. Schor*, 478 U.S. 833 (1986). That case arose after Congress authorized the Commodity Futures Trading Commission (CFTC) to adjudicate complaints by customers of professional commodity brokers for the broker's violation of the CFTC's enabling statute or CFTC regulations. The CFTC promulgated a regulation in which it permitted adjudication of counterclaims, including counterclaims grounded on state law. The question was whether Article III required that state law claims be adjudicated before an Article III court rather than a federal agency. After acknowledging that the Court's "precedents in this area do not admit of easy synthesis," 478 U.S. at 847, the Court asserted that although a litigant's right to adjudication before an Article III judge could be waived, *id.* at 848–49, Article III, § 1 also served to maintain "the constitutional system of checks and balances" by "barring congressional attempts 'to transfer jurisdiction [to non-Article III tribunals] for the purpose of emasculating' constitutional courts." *Id.* at 850 (citations omitted). With respect to those structural limitations, the Court "declined to adopt formalistic and unbending rules," *id.* at 851, and instead identified a non-exclusive list of factors considered in earlier cases.

> Among the factors upon which we have focused are [1] the extent to which the "essential attributes of judicial power" are reserved to Article III courts, and, conversely, the extent to which the non-Article III forum exercises the range of jurisdiction and powers normally vested only in Article III courts, [2] the origins and importance of the right to be adjudicated, and [3] the concerns that drive Congress to depart from the requirements of Article III. *See, e.g., Thomas.* 473 U.S. at 587, 589–93; *Northern Pipeline*, 458 U.S. at 84–86.

Schor, 478 U.S. at 851. Considering those factors, the Court concluded that the CFTC adjudication comported with Article III.

With respect to the first factor, the Court observed as a preliminary matter that the CFTC scheme departed from the "traditional agency model" of adjudication only with respect to its jurisdiction over common law counterclaims. Then the Court noted four respects in which the CFTC adjudication was more like the traditional model of federal agency adjudication (that is, more in line with *Thomas* and its predecessors) than like the jurisdiction of the bankruptcy courts addressed in *Northern Pipeline*. First, the Court explained that the CFTC, like the traditional agency authorized to adjudicate matters, "deals only with a 'particularized area of law,' *Northern Pipeline*, 458 U.S. at 85, whereas the jurisdiction of the bankruptcy courts found unconstitutional in *Northern Pipeline* extended to broadly 'all civil proceedings arising under title 11 or arising in or *related to* cases under title 11.' " *Schor*, 478 U.S. at 852–53. Second, the CFTC orders were enforceable only by order of a district court, again adhering to the traditional agency model, and again distinguishing the situation from the bankruptcy courts at issue in *Northern Pipeline*. *Id.* at 853. Third, the CFTC orders would be subject to judicial review under a standard previously upheld for agency adjudications, "rather than the more deferential standard found" to be inadequate in *Northern Pipeline*. *Id.* Fourth, "the CFTC, unlike bankruptcy courts under the 1978 Act, d[id] not exercise 'all ordinary powers of district courts,' and thus [could] not, for instance, preside over jury trials or issue writs of habeas corpus." *Id.* This factor thus favored upholding the CFTC adjudication.

With respect to the second factor, the Court acknowledged that the "counter-claim asserted in this litigation is a 'private' right for which state law provides the rule of decision" so that it was "a claim of the kind assumed to be at the 'core' of matters normally reserved to Article III courts." *Id.* The Court explained that quasi-judicial resolution of "public" rights posed less danger of encroaching on the judicial power but that "where private, common law rights are at stake, [the Court's] examination of the congressional attempt to control the manner in which those rights are adjudicated has been searching." *Id.* at 854. This factor seemed to militate against the CFTC adjudication, but only very weakly, as the Court again emphasized both the "narrow class of common law claims" at issue and the fact that the CFTC had non-exclusive jurisdiction. *Id.* at 854–55.

With respect to the third factor, the Court observed that "Congress intended to create an inexpensive and expeditious alternative forum" within the context of "a specific and limited regulatory regime" as to which the agency possessed expertise in applying the statute and its regulations. *Id.* at 855–56. The Court rejected any notion that Congress was primarily interested in "allocating jurisdiction among federal tribunals" and noted "the perception that the CFTC was relatively immune from political pressures." *Id.* at 855. Because the CFTC counterclaim jurisdiction was "incidental to, and completely dependent upon, adjudication of reparations claims created by federal law" and "limited to claims arising out of the same transaction or occurrence as the reparations claim," the Court found "any intrusion on the Judicial Branch can only be termed *de minimis*." *Id.* at 856. In contrast, without permissive counterclaim jurisdiction, the CFTC remedy would be ineffec-tive in practice and the congressional purpose would be frustrated. Consequently, the third factor also favored upholding the CFTC adjudication.

Justice Brennan, joined by Justice Marshall, dissented in *Schor*. Starting with a textual argument, he observed: "On its face, Article III, § 1, seems to prohibit the vesting of *any* judicial functions in either the Legislative or the Executive Branch." *Id.* at 859 (Brennan, J., dissenting). Justice Brennan then drew upon judicial precedent that previously departed from such a bright-line approach.

> The Court has, however, recognized three narrow exceptions to the otherwise absolute mandate of Article III: [1] territorial courts, *see, e.g., American Ins. Co. v. Canter*, 26 U.S. 511 (1828); [2] courts-martial, *see, e.g., Dynes v. Hoover*, 61 U.S. 65 (1857); and [3] courts that adjudicate certain disputes concerning public rights, *see, e.g., Murray's Lessee v. Hoboken Land & Improvement Co.*, 59 U.S. 272 (1856); *Crowell v. Benson*, 285 U.S. 22 (1932); *Thomas v. Union Carbide Agricultural Products Co.*, 473 U.S. 568 (1985).

Schor, 478 U.S. at 859 (Brennan, J., dissenting). On the basis of *stare decisis*, Justice Brennan accepted those "few, long-established exceptions" but opposed any further expansion of legislative power to transfer adjudications from Article III courts. *Id.* Justice Brennan supported his position with structural arguments based upon separation of powers concerns. He also asserted: "Because the individual and structural interests served by Article III are coextensive, I do not believe that a litigant may ever waive his right to an Article III tribunal where one is constitutionally required." *Id.* at 867.

As this brief summary illustrates, the Supreme Court has upheld adjudication of certain matters by federal tribunals other than courts within the meaning of Article III of the Constitution. The boundaries of such authorization, however, remain controversial.

TABLE OF CASES

[References are to pages]

[References are to pages]

[References are to pages]

FEDERAL CONSTITUTIONAL LAW

[References are to pages.]

[References are to pages.]

[References are to pages.]

[References are to pages.]

[References are to pages.]